CONTENTS

MISSOURI LEGENDS

History and Politics

Business, Science, and Technology

Arts and Entertainment

JOHN W. BROWN

MEDIA AND BROADCASTING

Sports Heroes

The Show Me Honor Roll

Bibliography

JOHN W. BROWN

ACKNOWLEDGMENTS

As with any book of this size, it is always more than a one-person project. It started out as a nice little hobby of looking up famous names and places and turned into an exhaustive search over the course of four years. I had the unique opportunity to speak with a number of amazing people over the past few years while researching this book. As expected, when I called these "famous" individuals, they all said something along the lines of, "Why are you including me with those people?!" It is this sort of humility that describes a large number of the people in this book. I want to thank so many of them for opening up their amazing lives to me so I could capture their legacy on paper.

I also want to thank the large number of people from the Show Me State who tipped me off about celebrities from their hometowns. I think many people in Missouri have no idea how much greatness surrounds them. We hear of newsmakers from other parts of the country but never take the time to realize how many Missourians have had a huge impact on our world. Missourians often have an "inferiority" complex when it comes to our state, which is certainly not grounded in the facts. One of the reasons for this book is to motivate people to believe that something great can come from both big and small towns across this state. There is excellence in every nook and cranny of Missouri, but we often fail to realize it.

I also need to thank those closest to me during this time of writing. I often felt like a recluse in my upstairs office typing away until all hours of the night, tracking down a famous person's phone number or trying to make sense of so much information. My wife, Teresa, has been more than patient. She often took on the role of single parent for months at a time so I could meet the deadlines. My daughter, Lauren, was also very patient, watching reruns of *Dora the Explorer* while I typed next to her. And my baby, Sophie, spent part of her infancy on my shoulder as I tried to type with one hand. I also want to thank my extended families at Fox 2, the *Daily Buzz*, and *Springfield 33*. I know you all got tired of hearing about the book, but thanks for letting me talk my way through the process. I also need to thank my family for moving us around the state so much! If we hadn't moved so many times, I never would have had the experience I needed to put this book together.

I met some helpful people all over the state, including many of the historical societies and state organizations who helped fill in some gaps and correct historical information. The people I met were a wealth of knowledge, and they all shared their expertise with a smile on their face. I also need to thank the people close to the stars who helped proofread the biographies for the following people:

Jesse Barnes—Julie Barnes McClure
Thomas Hart Benton—Steve Sitton
Sen. Bill Bradley—Beth Montgomery and Mr. Bradley
Joe Buck—Mark Hulsey
Harry Caray—Martin Cohn
Dale Carnegie—Michael Crom
George Washington Carver—Scott Bentley
Samuel Clemens—Megan Rapp and Henry Sweets of the Mark Twain Museums
Walter Cronkite—Mr. Cronkite and his assistant
Robert Heinlein—David Silver
Mary Engelbreit—Beth Lauver
Ella Ewing—Kathy Jenkins
Eugene Field—Kristin Little of the Eugene Field House
Shandi Finnessey
Jane Froman—Ilene Stone and Barbara Sueling
Scott Joplin—Vicky Love at the Scott Joplin House
Ewing Marion Kauffman—Matt Pozel with the Kauffman Foundation
Kathleen Madigan—Kate Madigan
Steve McQueen—Chris Lambos
Missouri Sports Hall of Fame, Todd Yearack
The O'Reilly Family—Tricia Headley and the O'Reilly Family
Marlin Perkins—Jill Gordon, Angela Gore and Janet Powell at the St. Louis Zoo
Stone Phillips—Stone and Patricia Sullivan
Brad Pitt—Doug Pitt
Jon Sundvold
Harry S Truman—Carol Dage of the National Parks Service
Dennis Weaver—Alice Billings
Jason Whittle—Jason and Lolly Whittle
Laura Ingalls Wilder—Daryls Wynn of the Laura Ingalls Wilder Museum
Grant Wistrom—Diane Brendel of the Grant Wistrom Foundation

And lastly, thanks to you, the reader! No matter where I travel across the country, I always call Missouri my home. When I'm away I seem to miss it more and more. We truly have a wonderful gem, from the Ozark Mountains, to the beautiful cities of St. Louis and Kansas City. My fondest memories are from road trips through Missouri wine country and through the cotton fields in the bootheel. The smell of spring in Northern Missouri and the beauty of fall at the Lake of the Ozarks are like no other. We live in the middle of one of God's most beautiful creations. I hope this book helps us all realize how special it is to be from the Show Me State!

INTRODUCTION

My years as a radio show personality, reporter, and news anchor in the state of Missouri and on a national TV show have shown me one thing: no matter what happens in the world, there is usually somebody from the Show Me State involved. When this project first started, I was simply looking to see how many famous people called Missouri their home. What I found as this endeavor evolved was that everybody knew somebody who was famous for something.

So what makes me an expert on all these famous faces from Missouri places? If travels bring experience, then I have a unique understanding of the Show Me State. From the time I was born, I have lived in or attended schools in St. Joseph, Wentzville, Pendleton, Troy, Warrenton, Wright City, Iberia, Belle, Alton, Bolivar, Fayette, St. Louis, Maplewood, St. Elizabeth, Springfield, Nevada, Union, and St. Clair. I attended colleges in Columbia, Union, Fayette, Bolivar, Webster Groves, and St. Louis as well. All of these places have given me a thorough understanding of this great state.

Sure, there are great people in every community, but this book focuses on the people who have risen to *National Prominence*. I have met some of these people, interviewed many of them, and known many people who have had direct contact with them. The sheer number of people who could be considered "famous" is staggering, so I had to come up with criteria. We found a writer for the hit ABC show *Desperate Housewives*, the first woman governor of a state, President Richard Nixon's favorite baseball player, the "Father of Physical Fitness," the inventors of the car radio and the digital clock, and the only person to be named *People Magazine*'s Sexiest Man Alive twice! I also found out that famous people like the rapper Eminem, makeup guru Max Factor, country singer Chely Wright, and author Maya Angelou were born in Missouri but moved soon after they were born. So I decided to only include people who were raised here, or spent their formative years in the Show Me State, not the people who only passed through. With these criteria in place, I had to leave out people like Stan Musial and Bob Costas because they came to the Show Me State later in life, sometimes after they already reached stardom. Granted, many people see them as Missourians, but the fact remains that they did not "grow up" here, so we had to leave them out. Many politicians were also left out, unless they made an impact on national issues. Senator Christopher Bond is known nationally but elected locally, so he was not included. Attorney General John Ashcroft qualifies because he held a national office.

Also left out were many athletes. It's difficult to fit all the stars in one book because there are simply so many sports and too many people who participated. Again, the demarcation line of national prominence was taken into account. I tended to focus on contemporary stars in this book because there have been numerous listings and books about the elder athletes. The Honor Roll is devoted to people who moved to the state later in life, who are not yet a bona fide star, spent a small but significant portion of their lives here, or simply did not receive a separate entry due to space contraints. I understand people will be left out, and I apologize for any omissions. I will try my best to include them in Volume 2! I hope this list will not only inform and entertain but also be a valuable resource for schools and libraries across the state.

It is impossible to track down every single famous person who spent time here, so we are doing our best to list them, through personal knowledge, via the Internet, or from Missouri historical records. I hope this book will help instill pride in all people who call this state home, and I hope it will cause the next generation to dream big dreams and understand that anything is possible, especially with roots in the place known as the Show Me State. So here we go, it's time to walk the red carpet of our famous past and present.

MISSOURI LEGENDS

John Ashcroft

Politician, Lawyer

John Ashcroft is "a man of great integrity, a man of great judgment and a man who knows the law."
—*President George W. Bush*

John Ashcroft is a true Missouri success story. He was raised in the Ozarks, elected governor and U.S. Senator, and then appointed attorney general of the United States. He will go down in history not only as one of the most famous Missourians of all time, but also one of the most polarizing figures during his reign in office. His term as attorney general will be remembered for the period during and after the terrorist attacks of September 11, 2001, when his office was given tremendous powers under the Patriot Act.

The Early Years

John Ashcroft was born in Chicago on May 9, 1942. He and his family moved to Springfield soon after, primarily to be closer to the headquarters of the Assemblies of God. The deeply religious and goal-driven young man graduated from Hillcrest High School with honors and set off for Yale University. After graduating from the Ivy League, he went on to receive his law degree from the University of Chicago in 1967.

Rise To Fame

Ashcroft moved back to the Show Me State after completing law school to teach business law at Southwest Missouri State University, but his sights were set on making laws, not teaching them. So in 1973 he set off for the realm of public service and a job in the State Auditor's Office.

His next step was big, as he landed the position of Missouri's assistant attorney general. He was the assistant only one year before being elected Missouri attorney general in 1976. He went on to win reelection and ultimately became president of the National Association of attorneys general.

Missouri Attorney General John Ashcroft became Governor John Ashcroft in 1984, a position he held until 1993. His time in office is highlighted by his efforts to crack down on crime and increase support of law enforcement. He focused his efforts on gun laws and stiffening penalties for law breakers. His reputation as a tough but productive politician catapulted him into the U.S. Senate one year after leaving the Governor's Mansion.

He lost the Senate seat after a controversial election in 2000, which may have been a blessing in disguise. His reelection bid was against then-Governor Mel Carnahan who died in an airplane crash two weeks before the election. Carnahan's name could not be removed from the ballot, so his wife, Jean Carnahan, announced that she would serve in her husband's place if he won, which he did. One month after losing the election to a dead man, president-elect George W. Bush named Ashcroft as the nominee for U.S. attorney general. He won the confirmation from the Senate with a vote of 58–42.

Show Me Success

John Ashcroft took over the position of attorney general during one of the most difficult periods in our nation's history. Not long after assuming the post, the country was attacked by terrorists on September 11. His primary role became prosecuting the people behind the attacks on the World Trade Center and the Pentagon. He pushed for the passage of the USA Patriot Act, which expanded the government's power to detain non-citizens, conduct surveillance, and investigate persons suspected of involvement in criminal activity. This act became the official law enforcement tool used to arrest these suspects, including more than 1,200 people jailed after the attacks. After a turbulent time presiding over the office of attorney general, he announced his resignation on November 9, 2004. His term officially ended on February 3, 2005.

After stepping down from the Justice Department, Ashcroft formed a consulting company specializing in homeland security and other business and legal issues. Despite his high-profile positions in Washington, D.C., he always made time to "get back home" to his farm near Willard. His job put him on the front lines of history, but his life continued to revolve around a small town in the Ozark hills.

Extra, Extra!

*John Ashcroft sang with a group of politicians known as "The Singing Senators."

*Fortune Magazine *named him one of the Top 10 Education Governors in the country.*

Authored Lessons from a Father to His Son.

JOSEPHINE BAKER

ENTERTAINER, HUMAN RIGHTS PIONEER

"Since I personified the savage on the stage, I tried to be as civilized as possible in daily life."
—Josephine Baker

"I wasn't really naked. I simply didn't have any clothes on."
—Josephine Baker

Known as "The Black Venus," Josephine Baker became one of the biggest international stars of the early and mid-1900s. Her fame in Europe exceeded her notoriety in the United States, likely because of racial inequality in her home country. Her fight for human rights was as much a part of her identity as her entertainment career.

THE EARLY YEARS

Freda Josephine McDonald was born in St. Louis on June 3, 1906, to former vaudeville performers Carrie McDonald and Eddie Carson. Her father was absent for much of her childhood, and her family struggled financially. She grew up in the slums of inner-city St. Louis, and she quit school around the age of ten and began working to help put food on the table and even then dreamed of making it big around the world.

RISE TO FAME

Baker began her quest for stardom on the vaudeville stage when she was just sixteen. She toured with a dancing and singing troupe from Philadelphia where she performed the musical comedy *Shuffle Along*. Her travels eventually took her to New York City during the Harlem Renaissance, where she made a name for herself performing at the Plantation Club.

Tragically, her rising fame was overshadowed by racial turmoil in the era approaching the 1920s. Racial discrimination was working against her, and it became apparent that bigger and better opportunities could be found in Europe. So the St. Louis girl packed her bags and headed overseas.

SHOW ME SUCCESS

The early 1900s were a wild time in Europe, so it was easy for her to get exposure, both in song and in body. In 1925, she began her rise to prominence primarily through dance performances that made her a national star in France.

Her act was taken to the next level when she orchestrated a semi-nude dance routine, complete with a G-string that was decorated with bananas. This unique act made her a huge sensation with thousands of adoring fans flocking to see her on stage. She knew she still needed a career in film to eventually reach the masses so she began singing professionally in 1930. This additional exposure opened the doors for movie roles four years later. She appeared in only a few films before World War II brought her performing career to a halt. During the war she worked tirelessly as a courier for the French underground and used her home as a base of operations. Years later, Baker received the Legion of Honor medal, France's highest military honor.

As she got older, one of her missions was to open doors for minorities to perform in more places. She refused to perform in clubs unless they followed nondiscriminatory seating practices, which led to the integration of nightclubs in Europe, and to some extent, in America. As her life on stage wound down, she began focusing primarily on civil rights. She took part in the 1963 March on Washington for Jobs and Freedom, where she gave a speech alongside Dr. Martin Luther King, Jr.

Baker died in Europe on April 12, 1975, fifty years after first performing in Paris. Nearly twenty thousand people filled the streets of Paris to pay their respects.

EXTRA, EXTRA!

Baker was married six times.

In the 1950s, she adopted twelve children of different nationalities, which became known as the Rainbow Family.

Thomas Hart Benton

Artist

"(Thomas Hart Benton is) the best damn painter in America."
—Harry S Truman

Thomas Hart Benton captured the attention of Missouri and the art world with his paintings depicting life in America. He was on the forefront of what is now known as the American Regionalism Movement in the late 1920s and 1930s, focusing his art on "real life" paintings of Americana. These magnificent panoramas of Missouri history still adorn the Missouri State Capitol. His paintings were more than just a symbol of life in the Midwest and South; they were also a rallying cry for the positive aspects of "America First" or Isolationism, which would steer the course of American history for years to come.

The Early Years

Benton was born on April 15, 1889, in Neosho, Missouri, which lies in the Ozark Hills south of Joplin. His great-great uncle and namesake—Senator Thomas Hart Benton—served thirty years in the U.S. Senate. His father was a four-term congressman and U.S. district attorney. The family spent time in Washington, D.C., when his father was in office but returned to Neosho after he was defeated for reelection. Early on, the young Benton showed great promise as an artist, but his father pushed for a career in law. But the young Benton's fate was about to change after a local newspaper came calling.

Rise to Fame

Thomas was working as a surveyor in 1906 when a random encounter in a barroom led to a job at the *Joplin American* newspaper. His job was to draw humorous portraits of city leaders and local citizens, which paid him about fourteen dollars a week. Even though the pay was low, the job was a perfect fit for the blossoming young artist.

During his late teens and twenties, he continued to pressure his father into sending him to art school, but his plan backfired when his father shipped him off to military school in Alton, Illinois. One year in military school was enough for Benton, as he finally convinced his father to send him to the Art Institute of Chicago.

SHOW ME SUCCESS

His years at art schools in Chicago and Paris refined his abilities, but he truly came into his own as an artist during his travels in the early 1920s. He ventured into remote areas near his home in the Midwest and also in the South, where he captured images of everyday people on canvas. It was a style he hadn't studied much in art school, but he quickly mastered the techniques of painting landscapes and images he saw.

By the late 1920s he was already one of the top American Regionalist painters on the art scene. He used vivid colors that jumped off the canvas and painted almost cartoon-like images of people. Those characteristics defined his famous style.

Many of his famous works are still on display throughout the country. His panorama mural of Missouri history still graces the walls of the lounge for the House of Representatives in Jefferson City, where thousands of people pack the chambers every year to get a look. His depictions of Western migration are also on display at the Truman Presidential Library in Independence. His 1947 mural, *Achelous & Hercules,* which was painted for Harzfeld's Department Store in downtown Kansas City, has since been moved to the Smithsonian Institution.

Not only did Benton become popular with "common" folks of his day, but he also led a charge within the art world to rebel against the French dominance of artwork in the United States. Many contemporary artists are still feeling his influence, and his leadership in the Regionalist Movement helped pave the way and open doors for other artists of his style to follow.

EXTRA, EXTRA!

Benton taught at the Art Student League in New York where his most famous student was Jackson Pollock.

His nude painting, "Persephone," often called Kansas City's Mona Lisa, helped cost him his job at the Kansas City Art Institute.

He lived in Kansas City from 1935 until his death in 1975. His home and art studio at 3616 Belleview is now a museum open to the public.

YOGI BERRA

BASEBALL PLAYER AND MANAGER

"It ain't over 'til it's over."
—*Yogi Berra*

Yogi Berra may go down in history as one of the greatest baseball players of all time and one of the most colorful characters to ever play the game. He was born and raised in St. Louis, where he might have become a St. Louis Cardinal had it not been for his childhood friend. Berra set numerous records for catchers during his time in the big leagues, while also making quite an amusing persona for himself along the way. Not only was he a great player, coach, and manager, but the *Economist Magazine* also named him the "Wisest Fool over the Past 50 Years" for his famous Yogi-isms.

THE EARLY YEARS

Lawrence Peter "Yogi" Berra was born on May 12, 1925, in St. Louis. He spent his early years in the Italian section of the city known as the Hill. He was originally nicknamed Lawdie (short for Lawrence), but the name Yogi stuck after a friend said he looked like a Hindu holyman that they had seen in a movie.

Baseball was an important part of the culture on the Hill when Berra was growing up. He first played organized baseball with a YMCA team and later played American Legion baseball alongside his close friend, Joe Garigiola. They were both outstanding young players, and it was only a matter of time before the Major Leagues came calling for both.

RISE TO FAME

Berra's early dream was to play catcher for his hometown heroes, the St. Louis Cardinals. He was offered a contract by the Cardinals, but since they appeared to be more interested in Garigiola, he signed a contract with the New York Yankees in 1942 instead.

He spent only one year in the minors before heading to the U.S. Navy for service during World War II. He returned in 1946, where he was able to move up to the big leagues by the end of the season. He even hit a home run in his first big league game! His catching was inconsistent during his early years, which forced managers to send him to the outfield for the next three seasons. Those years in the grass transformed him into what would ultimately earn him the reputation as one of the best players in the history of the game.

Show Me Success

Berra's play in the field, and at the plate, steadily improved until Yankees Manager Casey Stengel (also a famous Missourian) moved him back behind the plate. His fantastic play as catcher earned him the honor of the American League Most Valuable Player in three different seasons, making him one of only four players to achieve that status.

His greatest accomplishment is the fourteen World Series Championships he played in with the Yankees, which helped set a record for catching in more series games than any player in history. His status as one of the all-time greats was further solidified when he hit a home run in his first World Series appearance. He ended his career with a grand total of twelve home runs in World Series play.

After his stellar playing career was over, Berra took over the reins of the Yankees as manager. He led the team to the World Series in his first season, where he managed against his hometown team, the St. Louis Cardinals. His first managerial tenure with the Yankees only lasted one year after losing the series to the Cardinals.

He didn't have to travel far for his next job, as the New York Mets immediately snatched him up to be their new skipper. He made history once again when the Mets won the pennant in 1973, becoming only the third manager in history to win pennants in both the American and National Leagues. He went on to manage again in the 1980s for the Yankees and Houston Astros, ending his time in the majors as one of the greatest of all time, both on the field and in the dugout.

Yogi continued to remain in the public eye long after his baseball career was over. He became a commercial spokesman for products like AFLAC insurance, wrote books, and continued to be a great ambassador for America's game. His induction into the Baseball Hall of Fame in 1972 solidified his place among the greats and immortalizing this Missourian for all time in Cooperstown.

Extra, Extra!

The Hanna-Barbera cartoon character Yogi Bear was named after Berra.

Famous Yogi-isms:

"It's like déjà vu all over again."

"When you get to a fork in the road, take it."

"Nobody goes there anymore. It's too crowded."

"Ninety percent of this game is half mental."

CHUCK BERRY

MUSICIAN

"If you tried to give rock and roll another name, you might call it 'Chuck Berry'."

—John Lennon

Chuck Berry is one of the most influential and popular singer/songwriter/ guitarists of our generation. Numerous artists have copied his on-stage flair over the years, from Elvis Presley to the Rolling Stones, and even the Beatles. Despite the worldwide fame and the riches that came along with it, Berry continued to make Missouri his home. It just goes to show that you can take the star out of the Show Me State, but you can't take the Show Me State out of the star.

THE EARLY YEARS

Charles Edward Anderson Berry was born on October 18, 1926, on Goode Avenue in North St. Louis. His family lived in the section of the city known as the Ville, which was a growing African American community and one of the few areas where black families could buy property. This distinction of owning their own property made them and their neighbors a part of the growing black prosperity movement.

Berry attended Sumner High School in St. Louis, but his carefree school years were cut short after he was arrested during a joy ride to Kansas City. At eighteen, he had a rap sheet that included armed robbery, which sent him to prison at the Algoa Correctional Center in Jefferson City.

RISE TO FAME

He spent his time wisely behind bars by being a model prisoner and joining a gospel-singing group. His ten-year sentence was cut short after only a few years and was released on his twenty-first birthday in 1947. Even though he had become a talented singer, he had to put performing on hold while he looked for steady work after getting out of jail. The music career was pushed further back after he got married one year later. The newlywed migrated between jobs as auto assembly plant worker, photographer, and even went through training to be a hairdresser.

His musical career finally got back on track on New Year's Eve in 1952 when he joined the Sir John's Trio. Soon after that first gig, Chuck hooked up with music producer Leonard Chess, who produced the song that became known as "Maybellene." That record landed on the desk of world-famous disc jockey Alan Freed, who put the song into heavy rotation and put Berry on the road to stardom. Freed played the song for two straight hours during his show in New York City, which sent the album to No. 1 on Billboard's R&B chart and No. 5 on the Hot 100.

SHOW ME SUCCESS

Berry's next few songs didn't bring the type of success he had achieved with "Maybellene," which frustrated the performer. "Roll Over Beethoven" did reach the Top 30 on Billboard's Hot 100 chart, but his other singles failed to garner any attention. That was until the release of "School Days" in 1957.

Like "Roll Over Beethoven," "School Days" drew on a universal adolescent theme and climbed all the way to No. 5 on the Hot 100. With only one exception, Berry enjoyed an unbroken string of ten chart hits for the next two-and-a-half years. His musical success translated into movie appearances, including *Rock, Rock, Rock*; *Mr. Rock and Roll*; and *Go, Johnny, Go*.

His legal problems cropped up once again in 1959 when he brought a fourteen-year-old waitress he met in Mexico back to the United States to work as a hatcheck girl at his nightclub in St. Louis. Berry and the young girl were both arrested on prostitution charges, which sent him back to prison for five years. He was released in 1963, but his best years in the music business were now behind him.

Despite all the legal trouble, he remains a true American and Missouri musical legend. He was the first person inducted into the Rock and Roll Hall of Fame and is a member of the Songwriters Hall of Fame. He recorded more than thirty Top 10 hits, putting him in the history books as one of the most successful entertainers in history.

EXTRA, EXTRA!

Other Sumner High School alumni include Tina Turner, Arthur Ashe, Robert Guillaume, Robert McFerrin, and Dick Gregory.

"Johnny B. Goode" is on a copper record that was launched on the Voyager Space Probe to let the universe know about the best of our culture.

His first group consisted of superstar Johnnie Johnson, the namesake for the hit "Johnny B. Goode."

BILL BRADLEY

ATHLETE, SENATOR

Bill Bradley achieved more success at an early age than most people hope to accomplish in a lifetime. He was a brilliant student who earned a Rhodes Scholarship, a star basketball player in the Ivy League and the NBA, a senator on the front lines of American history, and even a candidate for president of the United States. These impressive accomplishments are just a part of the amazing legacy of a man from a small Missouri town along the banks of the Mighty Mississippi.

THE EARLY YEARS

Bill Bradley was born on July 28, 1943, and grew up in the small town of Crystal City, about thirty-five miles south of St. Louis. He began playing basketball at the age of nine and through his high school years became one of the best players ever to come from the Show Me State. His abilities extended into the world of academics as well. His talents in the classroom and on the court led to scholarship offers from more than seventy universities, including schools in the prestigious Ivy League.

RISE TO FAME

Bradley chose Princeton University to continue his studies where his performance on the court had pro scouts knocking on his door long before he graduated. He dominated the game from the moment he stepped onto the court at the college level, where he set a number of records during his tenure. He averaged more than thirty points per game during his three seasons, which helped Princeton win the Ivy League championship, while also earning All-American honors himself. He also played on the U.S. national team that won the gold medal at the 1964 Olympic Games in Tokyo.

For most people, a jump to the NBA right after college would be a dream come true, but Bradley wasn't ready to put his studies aside. Instead, he accepted a Rhodes Scholarship at Oxford University in Europe to pursue his master's degree.

Show Me Success

Bradley's next step was back to the court as he joined the NBA and the New York Knicks. He impressed coaches by taking a scientific approach to professional basketball, studying the intricacies of the game. Using his intelligence to improve his value on the basketball court, he led the Knicks to the 1970 and 1973 NBA championships. He retired from basketball in 1977 and was inducted into the Basketball Hall of Fame in 1982. In 1984, the Knicks retired his No. 24 jersey.

It didn't take Bradley long to launch the next phase of his career, this time as a politician. He used his name recognition to propel himself to the U.S. Senate in 1978. Over the course of nearly two decades in the Senate, he became known as an expert in international finance and also in domestic issues, especially health care.

Riding the success he had in the Senate, he next turned his attention to the country's highest office. He ran a very successful primary campaign in 2000, going head to head against eventual winner, Vice President Al Gore. After that race, he decided it was time for yet another career change, this time in the private sector. He turned his attention to banking, writing books, hosting radio shows, and continuing to work in Democratic politics, only now on the sidelines. Bradley is a supremely gifted and intelligent man who continues to prove that in whatever endeavor he chooses to pursue, he will succeed.

Extra, Extra!

*Bill Bradley is an Olympic gold medalist and has two NBA championship rings.

*His nickname on the court was "Dollar Bill."

*He was the first basketball player to win the Amateur Athletic Union's Sullivan Award for the amateur athlete of the year.

*Senator Bradley is the author of five books, two of which, Time Present, Time Past and Values of the Game, were on the New York Times Best Seller's List.

DALE CARNEGIE

AUTHOR, MOTIVATIONAL SPEAKER

"If you want to be enthusiastic, act enthusiastic."
—*Dale Carnegie*

Dale Carnegie was born into poverty, but he made a millionaire of himself, along with scores of devotees through his writings, speaking engagements, and personal development classes. His start in life was that of a humble country boy, but his achievements would last far beyond his lifetime. Today, many of the world's top business and political leaders, along with practically every salesperson who has ever lived, have all adopted his teachings to become more successful.

THE EARLY YEARS

Dale Carnegie was born on November 24, 1888, and grew up in the small town of Maryville in the northwest corner of the state known for large farms and wide-open spaces. In fact, his family farm was so remote that he never even saw a train until he was almost a teenager.

The farm life was lonely, but it taught him a lesson about hard work that he never forgot: Sometimes you have to work long hours to get the job done. Even as a child, he was required to get up at 3:30 a.m. to start his chores. Life on a desolate farm wasn't easy, but it provided him the finances to attend college in Warrensburg.

RISE TO FAME

After attending the State Teacher's College, now known as Central Missouri State University, he set off to become a salesman. His first job was selling correspondence classes to farmers who were unable to attend school, whether because of financial limitations or because they lived too far from a town where educational classes were offered. He moved on quickly to take the role of salesman for Armour and Company, selling household items like soap, bacon, and lard. He had such a knack for selling that he was soon the national leader in sales for the company.

Carnegie, however, didn't stop with being just a top salesman. He went off

JOHN W. BROWN

to try to realize another dream: To become an actor. He traded in the job at Armour in order to move to New York City, where he did some acting and taught public speaking at a YMCA. His classes drew large crowds, so he began to look for ways to capitalize on his success. His first step was to publish a book with tips on effective public speaking. *Practical Course for Business Men* was published in 1926, setting the path for his next career move that would make his name and techniques known all over the world.

Show Me Success

His training in personality development and public speaking became very profitable. He expanded his reach by touring the country, and teaching ways to improve sales and be more effective at speaking in any social situation. He again put these ideas into book form in 1936 with the release of *How to Win Friends and Influence People*. The book was an instant hit and has proven itself timeless, selling more than fifty million copies in nearly forty languages.

Carnegie followed that book in 1948 with *How to Stop Worrying and Start Living*. His texts became standard reading material in many industries, and the founding of the Dale Carnegie Institute has insured that his techniques are still taught to business leaders today. Carnegie died in 1955, leaving behind a legacy both in the written word and in the institute classes that are now being taught by nearly three thousand instructors in more than sixty-five countries.

Extra, Extra!

Carnegie wrote a biography of Abraham Lincoln titled Lincoln the Unknown.

Famous Dale Carnegie quotes:

"Any fool can criticize, condemn, and complain—and most fools do."

"You can make more friends in two months by becoming interested in other people than you can in two years by trying to get other people interested in you."

"Do the hard jobs first. The easy jobs will take care of themselves."

George Washington Carver

Inventor, Chemist, Agronomist

"When you do the common things in life in an uncommon way, you will command the attention of the world."
—George Washington Carver

George Washington Carver was born a slave but rose to international fame as a scientist, inventor, botanist, and educator. He revolutionized agriculture in the South by inventing agricultural techniques that are still impacting our lives today. He also developed more than three hundred byproducts from the peanut and sweet potato. Through his success, Carver also spearheaded the battle for racial equality.

The Early Years

George Washington Carver was born around 1860 near Diamond, Missouri, to a slave woman named Mary, who was owned by Moses Carver. Much of his early life, including his date of birth and his father, is left up to speculation. Some accounts say that he was sent to Arkansas during the Civil War. Other historians claim that antislavery activists kidnapped him. And one other theory states that he was born in 1865, which if true, means that he was actually born a free man.

Another common story that is widely told is that George's father was a slave from a neighboring farm who was killed in an accident before George was born. According to the story, mother and son were abducted during the end of the Civil War and George was supposedly later found near the border of Missouri and Arkansas.

Regardless of the details of his early years, it is known that the Carver family informed George during his childhood that he was no longer a slave, yet he stayed at their home until he was nearly a teenager.

Rise to Fame

Carver spent his early teen years moving from place to place nurturing his fascination with nature and learning everything he could about plants and animals. He took odd jobs, including work as a cook, a farmhand, a homesteader, and even a laundryman. He also read everything he could get his hands on, which likely made him one of the most highly educated young people of his time. His application was accepted at Highland College in Highland, Kansas, but when he arrived for the first day of classes, he was rejected because he was black.

His nomadic travels continued until he landed in Winterset, Iowa, where a prominent family became impressed with his artistic skills and encouraged Carver to apply to Simpson College. Carver studied at Simpson for about one year, then transferred to Iowa State College of Agricultural and Mechanic Arts, which today is known as Iowa State University. He earned his bachelor's degree in 1894 and a master's degree in agriculture two years later, becoming the first African American to receive both degrees.

His next stop was a job as the head of a newly formed department of agriculture at Tuskegee Normal and Industrial Institute, which was run by none other than Booker T. Washington.

Show Me Success

Carver became the director of agricultural research soon after his arrival at Tuskegee, where he worked on research projects aimed at improving southern agriculture. He knew that many farmers in the South were facing hard times because cotton crops had overwhelmed and devastated the fields. His solution: Plant soybeans and peanuts on the land. This technique replenished the soil while also providing a source of protein for the residents of the South.

Despite all of the varied success he achieved during the course of his lifetime, his push to develop new ways to use the peanut remains the hallmark of his success. He ultimately developed three hundred byproducts from peanuts—including cheese, milk, coffee, flour, ink, dyes, plastics, wood stains, soap, linoleum, medicinal oils, and cosmetics, plus another 118 derivatives from sweet potatoes including flour, vinegar, molasses, rubber, ink, a synthetic rubber, and postage stamp glue.

Through his innovative research, he changed the economy of the South and helped spawn entire new industries all over the world. His fame spread throughout the world, even enticing the former Soviet Union to request his expertise.

In 1940, Carver donated his life savings to the establishment of the Carver Research Foundation at Tuskegee for continuing research in agriculture. He died in 1943 and is buried on the Tuskegee Institute campus near Booker T. Washington.

EXTRA, EXTRA!

Despite common misconceptions, peanut butter was not one of his contributions to American society.

Carver was the first African American appointed to the faculty at Iowa State.

He was elected to Britain's Society for the Encouragement of Arts, Manufactures, and Commerce (London) in 1916.

His friends included Henry Ford and Mahatma Gandhi.

SAMUEL CLEMENS
(MARK TWAIN)

AUTHOR

"I am a border ruffian from the State of Missouri. I am a Connecticut Yankee by adoption. In me you have Missouri morals, Connecticut culture; this, gentlemen, is the combination which makes the perfect man."
—Mark Twain

"Familiarity Breeds Contempt—and children."
—Mark Twain

"Hannibal has had a hard time of it ever since I can recollect, and I was 'raised' there. First, it had me for a citizen, but I was too young then to really hurt the place."
—Mark Twain

Mark Twain is one of the most famous literary names in American history and Samuel Clemens's pen-name is synonymous with river life in Missouri. He was one of the greatest thinkers, humorists, and writers this country has ever seen and was one of the biggest celebrities of his day. His stories of Tom Sawyer and Huckleberry Finn have stood the test of time and still entertain readers a century after his death.

THE EARLY YEARS

Samuel Langhorne Clemens was born in Florida, Missouri, on November 30, 1835. He was raised in the river town of Hannibal, where he developed a deep love and respect for the Mississippi River.

His father was a speculator, a profession that forced the family to deal with dramatic reversals in fortune on a constant basis. The worst of all came when John Clemens died when Samuel was only ten, leaving the family with a pile of debt. This forced the young Clemens prematurely into the workforce where he held jobs as an apprentice for a printer and as a newspaperman. Despite his ability and success as a young writer, he had to put that career on hold to follow his true love, the Mississippi River.

Rise to Fame

Clemens loved being on the river and quickly earned his riverboat pilot's license where he worked until the outbreak of the Civil War. Clemens then headed off to the Nevada Territory and landed a job as an editor at a local newspaper in Virginia City. It was there that he took the name of Mark Twain at age twenty-seven, setting the stage for literary stardom.

Show Me Success

After his early brush with success at the newspaper, Twain took more time to travel, moving around until he met and married Olivia Langdon in 1870. The couple moved to Buffalo, New York, and eventually to Connecticut where his newfound fame and wealth as a writer allowed him to build a lavish home where he and his family would spend the next twenty years. He continued working as a writer, while also winning over live audiences with his increasingly popular public speeches. He soon was spending a great deal of time traveling and lecturing both in America and in Europe. But between 1876 and 1885, he reached his highest level of success with the release of *The Adventures of Tom Sawyer, The Prince and the Pauper, Life on the Mississippi,* and *The Adventures of Huckleberry Finn.*

Soon after that career pinnacle, the mistakes of his father and other childhood tragedies began to surface in his own life. He lost much of his wealth in bad business deals and financial speculation, which forced the family to vacate the home that he loved and move to smaller dwellings in Europe. Soon thereafter came a threefold tragedy: His oldest daughter died while Twain was on a sixteen-month worldwide speaking tour, his youngest daughter was found to have an incurable illness, and his wife began to suffer health problems as well.

The stress of his lost fortune, along with the family tragedies were beginning to take a toll on him. Clemens moved back and forth between America and Europe during the ensuing years, vowing to pay back all of his debts. He continued writing and gaving speeches until his death in 1910. Despite his reversal in fortune later in life, Americans will forever remember him as one of our country's pride and joys, while Missourians will always remember him as one of our own.

Extra, Extra!

Mark Twain is river talk for "Two Fathoms Deep."

Clemens wrote under the name Thomas Jefferson Snodgrass at the Keokuk Post.

He received an honorary doctorate from Oxford University.

WALTER CRONKITE

JOURNALIST, NEWS ANCHOR

"And that's the way it is."
—*Walter Cronkite*

One of the most famous Missourians of all time, Walter Cronkite was known as the "Most Trusted Man in America" for more than five decades. The Missouri native traveled the world to show Americans what was happening in places they would never see in person. For three decades he practically wrote the book on being a news anchor as America turned to him to learn of the assassinations of Dr. Martin Luther King, Jr., and President John F. Kennedy. He was with the American people through practically every event of his tenure, from the Watergate scandal to the first American landing on the moon.

THE EARLY YEARS

Walter LeLand Cronkite, Jr., was born in St. Joseph on November 4, 1916. His family moved during his childhood first to Kansas City and then south to Houston, Texas, where he attended middle and high school. His interest in the news business blossomed when he took a job selling newspapers during his school years. After graduating from high school, he went on to get his formal journalism education at the University of Texas.

RISE TO FAME

Cronkite enrolled in the University of Texas in 1933 but stayed at the school only a couple of years. He had already worked part time at the *Houston Post* during high school and college and decided to pursue his news career full time instead of completing his degree. His duties at the paper put him back at the university, where he worked as the *Post*'s campus correspondent.

A visit to see his grandparents in Missouri the next year landed him a new career and ultimately a wife. He accepted a job as a "one-man band" news reporter and sports anchor with KCMO radio station in Kansas City. There he met an advertising writer named Betsy Maxwell, whom he later married. But his time in Missouri would once again be short lived. He joined the United Press in 1937 and covered World War II battles in North Africa and Europe. He also covered the Nuremburg trials after the close of the war and served as chief reporter in Moscow for two years.

SHOW ME SUCCESS

Cronkite next joined the upstart CBS News operation in 1950 as a Washington correspondent and anchor of political coverage. His big break came when he assumed the role as news anchor of the CBS Evening News on April 16, 1962. He became a national icon when CBS expanded the evening news from fifteen minutes to half an hour the year after he took over the helm. He launched the new extended format in front of millions of viewers with an interview with President John F. Kennedy. Two months later, millions more saw Cronkite become visibly upset on the anchor desk as he announced the news that President Kennedy had been shot and killed in Dallas, Texas.

During his years at CBS, he covered practically every major event of the day, from Vietnam to Watergate, coronations to assassinations, and perhaps his personal favorite, space travel. Cronkite's expertise on the space program gave him unique insight into the *Apollo XI* landing on the moon, as well as his later coverage of John Glenn's second trip into space in 1998.

Even though his retirement was a national event in 1980, Cronkite continued to cover the news on a part-time basis. He also tried his hand at other roles including a syndicated newspaper columnist, the voice character of Benjamin Franklin on an animated children's TV show, a contributor to numerous news programs, and an outspoken advocate of liberal causes. His popularity waned very little after he left the anchor desk and was voted the "Most Trusted Man in Television News" in 1995, nearly fifteen years after his official retirement.

EXTRA, EXTRA!

*Cronkite appears at Walt Disney World in the attraction the Magic of Disney Animation.

*His nickname is "Old Iron Pants" because of his calmness under pressure.

*He was awarded a special George Foster Peabody Award for his contributions to broadcast journalism and has been inducted into the Academy of Television Arts and Sciences Hall of Fame.

*He was awarded the Medal of Freedom by Jimmy Carter, the nation's highest award to a civilian.

*He has authored books about sailing, and in 1996 he wrote his best-selling autobiography, A Reporter's Life.

SHERYL CROW

SINGER, MUSICIAN

"All I wanna do is have some fun. I have a feeling, I'm not the only one."
—*Sheryl Crow lyrics*

You might say that every day of Sheryl Crow's rise to fame has been a long and winding road. She started her professional career as a school music teacher near St. Louis, but her dreams of fame pushed her toward a performing career and eventually landed her on the top of the music charts. The risk she took to become an American icon paid off, as she became one of the biggest selling artists of all time.

THE EARLY YEARS

Sheryl Suzanne Crow was born on February 11, 1962, and grew up in the bootheel town of Kennett. Her father was an attorney and her mother was a piano teacher who exposed her to jazz, blues, and swing music at an early age. These early influences allowed her to develop an appreciation of varying genres of music that she would eventually blend into her own songs.

By the age of six, Sheryl was already playing songs on the piano that she had just heard on the radio. She even wrote her first song by the time she was thirteen. She graduated from Kennett High in 1980 and then headed off to the University of Missouri–Columbia, where she majored in music and played in the band Cashmere.

RISE TO FAME

After Crow graduated from Mizzou, she moved to the St. Louis area to teach music in the Rockwood School District. The teaching job lasted only a few years, because her dream to be a music star drew her to Los Angeles. In 1986, at the age of twenty-three, she headed west where she landed backup singing gigs for music legends like Eric Clapton, Sting, Sinead O'Connor, and Rod Stewart. Her first big break came when she was hired as a singer for Michael Jackson's international "Bad" concert tour.

The tour lasted about a year, and she again found herself out of work and depressed. The down time allowed her to write more songs, sing backup for more major artists, and look for a record company to sign her. Finally, A&M Records came calling.

SHOW ME SUCCESS

Crow became a worldwide success in 1993 with the release of the album, *The Tuesday Night Music Club*. "Leaving Las Vegas" was her first song from the album to generate radio play, but when "All I Wanna Do" was put into rotation, she suddenly became the music industry's newest "It" girl. The song was one of the biggest summer singles of 1994, falling just one position short of number one and the album sold around seven million copies. The former schoolteacher now graced the covers of practically every entertainment magazine, her songs were on the radio constantly, and she was a staple of MTV's top video playlist.

Her second album was also full of hits, making her a proven music star. She went on to headline concert tours like Lilith Fair, produce hits for movies including the James Bond film *Tomorrow Never Dies*, and even try her hand at acting.

Crow has won Grammys for Best New Artist, Best Pop Vocal Performance—Female, Best Rock Vocal Performance—Female, Best Rock Album, and Record of the Year. She has racked up record sales of more than 20 million. But even when she is busy dominating the entertainment industry, she still finds time to help out with charitable causes in her home state, proving that one of the biggest-selling female acts in history still knows where she came from.

EXTRA, EXTRA!

One of her early singing jobs in California was a commercial jingle for McDonald's.

"If It Makes You Happy" was originally written as a country song.

* Crow opened for the Rolling Stones on several occasions.*

Sheryl rides motocross and is a fan of NASCAR.

Gibson makes a Sheryl Crow Signature Edition Guitar.

She was briefly engaged to Tour de France champion Lance Armstrong.

WALT DISNEY

MOTION PICTURE PIONEER, AMUSEMENT PARK DEVELOPER

"I only hope that we don't lose sight of one thing—that it was all started by a mouse."
—Walt Disney

Walt Disney was first and foremost a fantastic storyteller, but his ability to entertain and stretch our imaginations allowed him to build a multimedia empire that would change the way the world watches TV and movies. In fact, some historians point out that he developed an entire industry off of the idea of a talking mouse. Tens of millions of people watch his movies every year, and millions more make the trek to visit his theme parks, making the name Disney synonymous with entertainment.

THE EARLY YEARS

Walter Elias Disney was born in Chicago, Illinois, on December 5, 1901. He was named after his father, Elias, and his father's good friend and minister Walter Parr. He became a Missourian when the family moved to the small town of Marceline, in north-central Missouri, when he was very young.

Disney was just nine years old when his father sold the family farm and moved the family to Kansas City. He attended the Benton Grammar School where he showed an early aptitude in the arts. He also took classes at an art school in Kansas City before the family moved back to Chicago where he graduated from high school. Disney returned to the Show Me State shortly after graduation and developed the basis of his animation.

RISE TO FAME

After serving in the Red Cross during World War I, Disney moved back to Kansas City where he worked as an advertising cartoonist. He had hoped to work at the local paper but was only able to find work at a commercial art studio. He bounced between jobs before he landed a job at the Kansas City Slide Company making animated commercials.

Animated art was still in its infancy, and Disney was intrigued by the opportunity to make an impact on such a new industry. At the age of nineteen, he helped develop the basis for animated films by combining live action and animation together on the screen. Disney left the Midwest for Hollywood in 1923, where he joined his brother Roy and borrowed money to construct a camera stand in their uncle's garage so they could try and make a new type of movie.

Show Me Success

Walt and his brother now had the expertise, the tools, and the drive to make the Disney name famous around the world with this new form of entertainment. The first step on that quest was the release of an animated movie character called *Oswald the Lucky Rabbit*, which generated enough money for them to continue their movie-making enterprise. His quest hit a slight bump when Universal Pictures informed Walt that they owned the rights to Oswald. So Disney knew he had to come up with something new to keep his empire growing, and that's when a mouse named Mickey was born.

Mickey Mouse made his screen debut in *Steamboat Willie*, which was the world's first fully synchronized sound cartoon. The film premiered at the Colony Theatre in New York on November 18, 1928. By 1932, Mickey Mouse was the most popular cartoon character in the world and helped Walt win his first Academy Award. Disney used the success of Mickey Mouse to make bigger and better animations. The next step was producing films in the new Technicolor process, which made possible the first commercial films presented in true color.

His place in history as a filmmaker was already set in stone, but Disney dreamed of turning his creations into a different type of empire. In the late 1940s he began drawing up plans for an amusement park for his employees where staff members could relax with their children. That idea eventually expanded into the concept that became Disneyland in California. The theme park opened in 1955 and has been one of the top tourist attractions in the world since its grand opening. The second Disney park, Walt Disney World in Orlando, Florida, was his crowning achievement, although he never saw it to completion. Disney died in 1966, five years before it opened in 1971.

Walt Disney continues to win over new generations of fans even today. He also continues to rack up awards for his work, including a record forty-eight Academy Awards and seven Emmys during his lifetime, in addition to many posthumous awards. His legend is cemented with the chain of Disney theme parks, movies, and cartoon characters that are famous the world over.

EXTRA, EXTRA!

Disney produced the first feature-length animated movie, Snow White and the Seven Dwarfs, in 1937.

Disney was once called "the most significant figure in graphic arts since Leonardo DaVinci."

Many historians claim that Marceline, Missouri, is the model city for his theme parks.

Disney was the voice for Mickey Mouse until 1947.

T. S. ELIOT

AUTHOR, PLAYWRIGHT, POET

"This is the way the world ends . . . Not with a bang but a whimper."
—*The Hollow Men by T.S. Eliot*

T. S. Eliot is one of the greatest-known poets and playwrights in our country's history. His words have become part of the American lexicon, though many times we don't even realize we are reciting his writings. He is the only Missouri-born citizen to win a Nobel Prize, and he continues to be a major force in literature after his death.

THE EARLY YEARS

Thomas Stearns Eliot was born on September 26, 1888, in St. Louis. His grandfather, William Greenleaf Eliot, was the founder of the prestigious Washington University in St. Louis, the Smith Academy preparatory school for boys, Mary Institute prepatory school for girls, and the city's first Unitarian congregation. His aristocratic family spent summers in Massachusetts and the school year at various private learning establishments. Eliot graduated from Smith Academy before heading off to Milton Academy and ultimately Harvard University.

RISE TO FAME

Eliot quickly established a reputation as a gifted thinker and academic at Harvard. He completed his bachelor's degree in only three years but remained at the campus to work on graduate studies before heading to Europe to travel and study at Oxford. His educational pedigree and well-established family connections allowed him to rub elbows with some of the best and brightest minds of his time. This not only expanded his thinking but also put him in contact with others who would help him on the path to literary fame.

The start of World War I ended his travels in Europe, so he settled at Merton College at Oxford. He now considered England his home, and he became a British citizen and was received into the Church of England. The fact that he did the majority of his writing in England continues to spark debates about whether he was actually an American or British author.

SHOW ME SUCCESS

Eliot was a leader of what is known as the Modernist Movement in poetry. His titles such as *The Waste Land* and *The Four Quartets* put him at the forefront of the modern literary evolution and his writings were a dominant influence on both American and English cultures for several decades. The publication of *The Four Quartets* even led to his recognition as the greatest living English poet. In 1948, he was awarded both the Order of Merit and the Nobel Prize for Literature for his writings. Eliot's *The Waste Land* is recognized as the most famous English poem of the twentieth century.

Interestingly, he also wrote a children's book that would become one of the most famous Broadway plays in history. The *Old Possum's Book of Practical Cats* was turned into the long-running Broadway musical known as *Cats*, though he didn't live to see it become a success on the stage.

His literary acclaim did not equate to personal happiness though. Eliot met Vivien Haigh-Wood only a few months before they were married, and acquaintances say that the marriage was doomed from the start. Vivien had a number of health problems, both physical and mental, that led to difficult times for the couple. The couple split in 1935, and Vivien spent the last few decades of her life in various mental institutions. Eliot married again in the 1950s to Valerie Fletcher, who was a receptionist at the firm of Faber and Faber where he worked. This marriage was also full of problems. He refused to sleep in the same bed with her, and she eventually had an affair.

Eliot spent much of his adult life in England, but a decade before he died he came back to Missouri to speak about how the Show Me State impacted his writings and his life. During a speech at Washington University, he said, "St. Louis affected me more deeply than any other environment"—quite a lofty compliment, considering the incredible life the author lived.

EXTRA, EXTRA!

*The annual meeting of the T. S. Eliot Society takes place in St. Louis on his birthday.

*The Eliot family is noted on the list of Distinguished Families of America.

*He won the Nobel Prize for Literature in 1948.

Edwin Hubble

Edwin Hubble grew up in a small town in southwest Missouri, but his sights were always set on the stars, literally. There's a saying that the country allows you the best view of the stars, and the early days of Hubble's life planted the seeds that would change the way all of us view space. At the peak of his career, he was considered the foremost expert on extragalactic astronomy, and he even provided the first evidence that the universe is constantly expanding.

The Early Years

Edwin Powell Hubble was born on November 20, 1898, and spent his early years in Marshfield. Hubble was a good student as well as an outstanding athlete. His father was a well-to-do insurance executive, and it wasn't long before his family packed their bags and moved to Illinois.

In high school, Edwin won numerous athletic awards and even set the state record for high jump. His next stop was the University of Chicago, where his athletic abilities continued to shine while his intellectual prowess began to blossom, leading him to a Rhodes Scholarship at Oxford University. He often pointed out that his interest in science was generated while reading scientific books during his quiet days in rural Missouri.

Rise to Fame

Despite talents in a vast array of subjects, Hubble struggled with choosing a career path. At Oxford University he shifted from the study of astronomy to law. He switched again after graduation, returning to the United States to take a job as a high school basketball coach. He eventually decided to return to law, passed the bar exam, and set up a law practice in Kentucky. But again, he gave up a promising legal career to pursue his passion for astronomy at the Yerkes Observatory and the University of Chicago.

Upon completion of his graduate studies in 1917 and his service in World War I, he moved to California and accepted a position at the Carnegie Institution's Mount Wilson Observatory near Pasadena, California, where he settled down and spent much of the rest of his career.

SHOW ME SUCCESS

His first major study at Mount Wilson helped scientists to understand galaxies, their composition, and how they originated. It was generally believed that the fuzzy clouds of light that are visible at night were comprised of stars, but very little else was known. His viewings in 1924 gave us all a better understanding of what we were seeing. He measured the distance to the Andromeda Nebula, proving that it was one hundred thousand times further away than our nearest stars. His conclusion was that it must be a separate galaxy at least the same size as our Milky Way, only millions of miles away.

His observations of other distant galaxies also led to the breakthrough discovery in 1929 that the universe is expanding, and that our own galaxy is likely moving through space at amazing speeds. He showed that a star's apparent brightness is a rough measure of its distance from Earth, and that galaxies are moving away from us with a speed proportional to their distance.

Hubble's findings were probably a combination of solid science and a bit of luck. Numerous studies since then, combined with improved techniques and equipment, have proven that much of his original research was sound. His findings, and Albert Einstein's theories of gravity and relativity, are the key pieces that still lead many scientists to believe the universe originated with a Big Bang millions of years ago.

EXTRA, EXTRA!

The orbiting Hubble Space Telescope, which has significantly advanced the study of the universe, is named in his honor.

Shortly before his death, Palomar's 200-inch Hale Telescope was completed and Hubble was the first to use it.

In 1946, he was awarded the Medal of Merit for exceptional conduct in providing outstanding services to citizens.

The asteroid known as 2069 Hubble and the Hubble crater on the Moon are also named in his honor.

JOHN W. BROWN

JESSE WOODSON JAMES

OUTLAW

"Ain't gonna hang no picture, ain't gonna hang no picture frame. Well, I might look like Robert Ford, but I feel just like a Jesse James."

—Bob Dylan

The legend of Jesse James is famous around the world. His life has been captured in movies, books, songs, and TV shows, including the Brady Bunch! His early years, however, were exactly opposite of the life he would assume as a killer and outlaw. His family had deep roots in the Baptist Church, even taking part in the founding of one of the most prestigious private universities in the Midwest. He is known as a brutal killer, but the start of his life of crime started with noble intentions, fighting for a cause he believed in.

THE EARLY YEARS

Jesse Woodson James was born on September 5, 1887, near the town of Kearney, not far from Kansas City. His father was a Baptist minister and very active in the community. Jesse had a strict religious upbringing in the church, and religion was a major part of his daily life. His family was so ingrained in the Baptist Church that his father even helped found William Jewell College in Liberty.

He and his older brother, Frank, spent their early years on the family farm where they learned to live off the land. When the Civil War broke out, the family joined up with Confederate soldiers, a decision that laid the foundation that would impact the rest of their lives.

RISE TO FAME

The Civil War pitted family against family and brother against brother. But in the case of the James clan, both brothers believed in the Southern cause and joined up with like-minded fighters. Frank James took off to fight with Cole Younger and his Confederate guerillas, while seventeen-year-old Jesse James joined up with Bloody Bill Anderson's band of fighters.

Legend has it that Jesse was shot and injured by Federal soldiers while he was trying to surrender near the end of the war. That action stirred up plenty of resentment in the young man and is likely one of the key incidents that led him to become an outlaw. The hatred ran even deeper as he began to feel that his family was under constant attack for standing up for the cause they believed in.

SHOW ME "INFAMY"

Jesse and Frank were reunited after their gangs dissolved at the conclusion of the war. Missouri was right in the middle of the conflict, with the state divided between the North and the South. The South's surrender led to tensions among citizens in all parts of the state, where many Confederate sympathizers say they were persecuted long after the war was over. This led the James brothers to take drastic steps that made an impact on American history like few others.

The outlaw career for Jesse officially began in 1866 when he and Frank joined with eight other men to rob a bank in Liberty (not far from where his father founded the Baptist college). That robbery was just the beginning. Soon, their string of violent hold-ups spanned from Iowa to Alabama, and Missouri to Texas. The group became more brazen and more famous with every robbery as they turned their attention to robbing stores, stagecoaches, and even people on the street.

The gang's wild times began to wind down after they were decimated during a botched robbery in Minnesota. Jesse and his brother were the only two of the gang who escaped the First National Bank, where the rest were captured or killed. The brothers regrouped with a new gang, only to have Missouri Governor Thomas Crittenden offer a large reward for their capture.

Jesse's wild life came to a violent but unceremonious end when one of his new henchmen shot him in the back of the head as he hung a picture on the wall of his home in St. Joseph for a $10,000 reward. His brother was captured a short time later and tried in numerous states on a number of charges. Each time, Frank

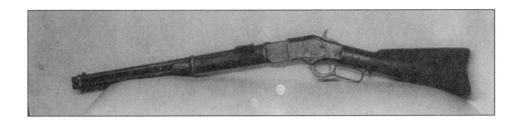

was found not guilty. He spent the rest of his life in solitude on the family's farm and died in the same room in which he was born.

Even though Jesse James was wanted for murders and robberies throughout much of his adult life, many people in Missouri saw him as a heroic figure. There were large groups of people who even said his actions were justified because of their allegiance to his causes and the Southern resistance.

Extra, Extra!

*James's epitaph, selected by his mother, read:

"IN LOVING MEMORY OF MY BELOVED SON, MURDERED BY A TRAITOR AND COWARD WHOSE NAME IS NOT WORTHY TO APPEAR HERE."

*The body buried in Missouri as Jesse James was exhumed in 1995 and DNA analysis gave a 99.7 percent match to Jesse James, which largely put an end to the legend that his death was staged.

*Actors who have portrayed James include fellow Missourian Brad Pitt, Roy Rogers, George Reeves, Lawrence Tierney, Clayton Moore, Audie Murphy, Macdonald Carey, Lawrence Tierney, Robert Wagner, Christopher Lloyd, Kris Kristofferson, and Rob Lowe.

Scott Joplin

Musician, Composer

When people think of ragtime music, one name comes to mind: the "King of Ragtime" Scott Joplin. As with many musicians of the time, Joplin bounced around from city to city, and venue to venue, trying to make a living. Although he traveled much of his life, he still considered Missouri his home. He enjoyed a fair amount of success during his lifetime, but true fame came after his death.

The Early Years

Joplin is one of the most famous musicians of all time, yet little is known about his birth. It is still unknown where or when he was born, although historians believe he may have been born sometime around 1868. Joplin showed a tremendous amount of musical aptitude early in life after taking lessons on European musical art forms, including opera. This influence is often credited for his ability to blend musical styles, including classical and rhythmic.

He moved to Sedalia in his teenage years where some historians believe he attended Lincoln High School and later the George R. Smith College for Negroes. What is known for sure is that a music teacher named Julius Weiss taught him the basics of music while growing up. His time in west-central Missouri made a lasting impact with him, as he called Sedalia his home for the rest of his life.

Rise to Fame

Joplin moved throughout the Midwest in his late teens and early twenties, where he played at local saloons, community events, and restaurants. He made a few stops in St. Louis in the 1890s, which was becoming the home of ragtime and blues. He officially moved to St. Louis in 1901 and stayed until 1907, and it was there that he perfected the musical style that made him famous.

He used his background in classical music and combined it with the African American harmonies and rhythms that were popular in taverns of his day. He gained a loyal following of fans at his performances but was still waiting for that first big hit that would make him a household name in the American music scene.

Show Me Success

When he wasn't in St. Louis or traveling, Joplin worked in Sedalia as a pianist. He set up shop at the town's two social clubs for black men, the Maple Leaf and Black 400. He had already sold six musical pieces for the piano by 1898, which received modest attention, but produced little money and less acclaim. But in 1899, Joplin published the "Maple Leaf Rag," which became his most famous piece of music. This hit was followed a few years later by "The Entertainer," which was written and published in St. Louis in 1902.

The "Maple Leaf Rag" sold relatively well but didn't make him wealthy. He signed a music deal with John Stark and Son that paid him a royalty of one cent for each copy sold, which earned him approximately $360 per year over the rest of his life. That would be less than $6,000 a year today.

He spent his latter years in New York teaching, composing, and trying to get his opera *Treemonisha* to the stage, which never happened during his lifetime. He achieved a minor degree of fame while he was alive, but he received greater critical acclaim decades after his death. In fact, in 1973, nearly sixty years after he died, his music appeared in the movie *The Sting*, which won an Academy Award for film score. In 1976, Joplin's opera *Treemonisha* won the coveted Pulitzer Prize for contribution to American music. Joplin is buried in New York, but his home and old stomping grounds in Missouri still draw thousands of admirers every year.

Extra, Extra!

Joplin's legacy is still celebrated in Sedalia during the annual Scott Joplin Festival.

His home near downtown St. Louis is now a State Historic Site.

The Maple Leaf Club in Sedalia provided the title for his best-known composition, the "Maple Leaf Rag."

WILLIAM POWELL LEAR

INVENTOR, AVIATOR

"There are two kinds of inventors. There is the inventor who just likes to be clever and come up with a new idea. And there is the inventor who realizes there is a need and tries to fill it. I have spent my whole life discovering needs and then finding ways to fulfill them."

—Bill Lear

Bill Lear is best known for designing and building the small jet airplane that carries his name, the Learjet, but he also has a number of inventions that don't bear his name. This amazing man had only an eighth grade formal education, but he invented the 8-track tape player, the car radio, the navigational radio, and the autopilot technology for aircraft. Many businessmen and inventors who worked with him say he was a man of incredible intellect and exceptional personal determination. His foes, who were also numerous, viewed him as a dictator who did anything to get his way. But "his way" was successful, as he landed nearly 160 patents, many of which changed the way we live.

THE EARLY YEARS

Bill Lear was born on June 26, 1902, in Hannibal. He was an extremely intelligent youngster who showed a great deal of determination and hard-headedness, which likely came from his efforts to please his parents in their on-again off-again relationship.

When he was only twelve years old, he told his friends that he planned to become rich by inventing things that people wanted. In fact, he was so agitated with the slow pace of formal schooling that he started looking for ways to join the workforce before he was even a teenager. He moved to Chicago when he was still young, then dropped out of school in the eighth grade when he ran away from home to pursue his dreams.

Rise to Fame

Lear spent little time in school, which didn't stop his quest for knowledge. He became a self-taught electrical engineer, a mechanic, and even lied about his age to join the military when he was only sixteen. The Navy turned out to be a great place for him to continue his education because he was able to study radio design and electronics in a practical setting while getting paid for his training in the process.

Not long after he left the Armed Services, he put his new skills to work by designing the first car radio. He was unable to find a company to financially back his plan, so he ultimately sold his plans to the Motorola Corporation. That sale was the first step towards putting him on the path to fame as a successful and well-known inventor.

Show Me Success

Lear's next invention gave him large financial rewards and the reputation of a man who could get things done. He designed a universal radio amplifier, where he once again sold the plans to a major corporation.

The money he made from that invention gave him the financial support he needed to expand his blossoming empire. He founded the Avia Corporation in 1934 to produce radio and navigational devices for aircraft. Over the next five years, he dominated the industry by producing more than half of all aircraft radio and navigational equipment sold.

Despite the success he was having with instrumentation, his real dream was to design and manufacture aircraft. He started Lear, Incorporated in 1939, building stereo systems and communication satellites, and reaching sales of $90 million between 1950 and 1962. The business was rapidly expanding, but Lear's plans to build the world's first inexpensive, mass-produced business jet put him in disfavor with the board of directors of his company. When he failed to convince them of his plan, he sold his interest in the company and formed Lear Jet, Inc.

The first compact jet from Lear Jet was produced in 1963 and quickly became the most popular private jet in the world. In the company's infancy the planes had several problems, which caused a number of crashes and pushed aviation experts to question the design. Bad press reports and sagging sales caused Lear to lose interest in aviation for a while. Gates Rubber Company stepped in and bought the company, which freed him to pursue his next endeavor, the steam-powered car.

Lear Motors Corporation was designed to take automotive transportation to the next level, but he never made much progress towards the next generation of automotive engines. The process of getting people interested in an automobile that ran on something other than gasoline proved to be an uphill climb. Just like in previous endeavors, he lost interest in the project and returned to aviation.

Lear's final venture into aircraft manufacturing led him on a quest to develop a faster and more efficient type of business jet, known as the Learfan. Not long after his second venture in aircraft design he discovered that he had leukemia and didn't have much time to live. This medical revelation sent him into overdrive to complete his designs for the turboprop jet. His time ran out on May 14, 1978, and he died without finishing his final project. Despite his failure to leave one final mark on aviation, he left behind a legacy of success in a number of industries and a name still known around the world today.

EXTRA, EXTRA!

Lear won the Frank M. Hawks Award for designing the Learmatic Navigator in 1940.

He was the first pilot to fly a plane to the Soviet Union.

President Harry S Truman gave Lear the Collier Trophy for developing the autopilot.

The city of Paris presented Lear with its Great Silver Medal for his aid in developing the autopilot for the Caravelle jetliner in 1962.

Rush Limbaugh

Radio Personality

"Broadcasting with talent on loan from God."
—*Rush Limbaugh*

Rush Limbaugh is heard by millions of people throughout the world on a daily basis. In fact, many radio historians credit him with being the most popular radio personality in history. Missouri is known for producing famous broadcasters, but Limbaugh took it to a whole new level. He not only changed the course of radio history, but he also changed the course of elections with the power of the spoken word and a Golden Microphone.

The Early Years

Rush Hudson Limbaugh, III, was born in Cape Girardeau on January 12, 1951. He was the eldest of two sons born to Mildred and Rush Limbaugh, Jr. His father was a successful attorney in the bootheel, imbuing a conservative ideology into his kids from an early age.

Rush's love for radio began when he took his first job in broadcasting at a Top 40 radio station when he was just a teenager. He graduated from Central High School in Cape Girardeau and then headed off for Southeast Missouri State at the urging of his father. Rush was a voracious reader and a highly intelligent student, but college wasn't in the cards for him as he stayed at the university only a year and a half. His passion simply didn't include sitting in classrooms and taking tests, but rather working his way to the top as a radio personality.

Rise to Fame

Limbaugh left the bootheel in 1971 to pursue a radio career in bigger cities, including Pittsburgh and Kansas City. His outspokenness while reading the news cut short his early career because he was fired in both cities. He was now frustrated and looking for something a little more stable, so he took a job with the Kansas City Royals in 1978 as an account executive selling ticket packages for the games. The job lasted five years, but his love for radio and conservative politics led him back to the microphone as a news commentator.

At the age of thirty-three, he took a job in Sacramento where the radio station KFBK was looking for someone to replace controversial talk show host Morton Downey, Jr. His style was exactly what they were looking for: wild, opinionated, offensive, and most importantly, charismatic. Within a year, Limbaugh had the top-rated radio show in one of the biggest cities in the nation. It was just a matter of time before people across the country would come to love, or loathe, the name of Rush Limbaugh.

SHOW ME SUCCESS

In 1988, he took his show to a national audience. Limbaugh was signed to a two-year contract at WABC in New York City, where he debuted his nationwide program. Rush's show became an instant success as stations across the country began signing up for rights to broadcast his show. A mere five years later, his syndicated program, "The Rush Limbaugh Show," was the most popular radio talk show in the country, reaching an estimated 20 million listeners a day. Some restaurants even opened what they called "Rush Rooms," where people would gather over lunch and listen to his program.

He was truly a media powerhouse, which led to book deals, a television show, and even changing the course of elections across the United States. The Rush Limbaugh television show debuted in 1992 and quickly climbed the ratings, but it faded away a few years later as Limbaugh complained that it was airing too late at night in many cities. He also dominated book sales during that time, with *The Way Things Ought to Be* spending over a year on the bestseller list. His next book, *See, I Told You So* received the largest ever first printing of any book in U.S. history. Limbaugh's impact is also credited with Republicans winning numerous elections in the 1990s and the shift in power in the House, Senate, and even the White House.

Rush Limbaugh still dominates the airwaves nearly twenty years after the nationwide syndication of his talk show. He has been called to greatest broadcaster in history, the most controversial person on the airwaves, and one of the most famous Missourians of all time. His lasting impact on the radio industry was set in stone when he was inducted into the Radio Hall of Fame in 1993.

EXTRA, EXTRA!

Limbaugh underwent cochlear implant surgery, which restored a measure of hearing in one ear.
Limbaugh has won the Marconi Radio Award for Syndicated Radio Personality of the Year numerous times.
His first radio name in Pittsburgh was Jeff Christie.
Limbaugh's first television exposure came with a 1990 guest host stint on Pat Sajak's late-night program on CBS.

STEVE McQUEEN

ACTOR

"I live for myself and I answer to nobody."
—Steve McQueen

"The King of Cool," "The Bandito," and "The Rebel Legend" are all terms used to describe the man known for his great films, crazy life, and wild antics. Steve McQueen was the quintessential Hollywood bad boy, driving fast cars, riding motorcycles, performing his own stunts, fighting with other actors, and playing the rough and tumble drifter in numerous movies. He was one of the movie industry's biggest draws during the 1960s and '70s, all thanks to a rugged persona cultivated right here in Missouri.

THE EARLY YEARS

Terrence Steven McQueen was born on March 24, 1930, in Beech Grove, Indiana. His father deserted the family when Steve was just a few months old, sending him and his mother packing to the small town of Slater in west-central Missouri. He lived with his uncle on a farm outside of town, where his love for racing apparently began. But trouble seemed to follow McQueen wherever he went, both at school (when he attended) and all over town.

When his mother remarried, she moved Steven back to Indianapolis. He didn't like the new city and ultimately joined street gangs. His mother moved the family to California a few years later with her abusive husband, where Steve once again found trouble. After eighteen months in a reform school, he joined the military, then landed on his feet in New York City after a dishonorable discharge from the U.S. Marine Corps.

RISE TO FAME

McQueen moved to Greenwich Village in 1950 at the age of twenty. The Village was the center of counterculture, and he seemed to find a group that he could identify with. He met a woman who stimulated his interest in acting and urged him to take classes. Those classes helped him land several small roles before he finally got a shot on Broadway in *A Hatful of Rain*.

His explosive temperament and rough childhood experience finally paid off, as critics hailed his wide range of emotions portrayed on-stage. He was very successful on Broadway, but Hollywood and the world of motion pictures were calling McQueen to bigger and better things.

Show Me Success

In the early 1960s, the "King of Cool" attained nationwide stardom, appearing in *The Magnificent Seven* and *The Great Escape*. Both movies were huge hits, landing him on Hollywood's A-list. He became the highest paid actor in Hollywood with roles in films like *The Thomas Crown Affair*, which turned out to be one of his most famous performances.

The 1970s were equally as good for the rugged and popular actor. He starred in *The Getaway*, *Papillon*, and *The Towering Inferno*. He also became a producer during that time with the film *An Enemy of the People*.

McQueen's health began to deteriorate in the late 1970s. His final film was in 1980, where McQueen played a bounty hunter in *The Hunter*. He became a born-again Christian shortly before he died due to the influence of his wife, Barbara. He died of a heart attack at the age of fifty, but his lifetime of work continues to be enjoyed by moviegoers today.

Extra, Extra!

*McQueen was ranked No. 30 in Empire Magazine's "The Top 100 Movie Stars of All Time" list.

*He was expelled from the Carnegie Institute of Technology (now Carnegie Mellon University) for riding his motorcycle through the College of Fine Arts Building.

*He had mesothelioma at the time of his death, which he may have contracted from the asbestos suits he wore while racing cars.

*His body was cremated and his ashes scattered into the Pacific Ocean.

*He was a pallbearer at the funeral of actor Bruce Lee.

J. C. PENNEY

ENTREPRENEUR

"Every business is built on friendship."
—*James Cash Penney*

The department store J.C. Penney is known all over the world, yet few people realize that the namesake for the store, James Cash Penney, grew up in a small town in Missouri. The "man with a thousand partners" relied on an unshakable belief in God, self-reliance, discipline, and the morals of the Golden Rule. His high ethical standards, combined with hard work and sound economic practices, turned his small store into one of the biggest retail empires in history.

THE EARLY YEARS

James Cash Penney was born on September 16, 1875, and grew up on a farm near Hamilton. He was the seventh of twelve children to Fannie and James Cash, who was a Baptist preacher and farmer in rural Caldwell County.

James grew up with a strong work ethic stemming from his strict parents. In fact, his knack for sales was stimulated after his father made him start buying his own clothes. Penney sold whatever he could, including pigs, to raise enough money for a pair of shoes. Those early lessons about the value of a dollar were a driving force behind his success and in the way he treated employees and customers.

He planned to become a lawyer after graduating from Hamilton High School, but a two-year layoff from studies, and the death of his father, forced him to become a clerk at a small retail store in order to provide money for his large family.

RISE TO FAME

Medical problems were the motivating force behind Penney's decision to leave Missouri to live in the clean air of Colorado when he was about twenty-two years old. He took up a clerking job at a dry-goods store called the "Golden Rule Stores," which was run by Guy Johnson and T. M. Callahan. Because of his work ethic, Penney became a one-third partner a few years later. He eventually bought his partners' shares of the business to begin what would become known as the J.C. Penney Company. Many people told James that his business would fail because of his moral opposition to credit, but his customer service skills and the outstanding quality of his stores proved the critics wrong.

Penney's rise to business success, however, came with personal tragedy. His first wife died of pneumonia, leaving him with two small children to raise. His second wife died suddenly in 1924, leaving him with another son. But his third and final marriage lasted forty-five years until his death, which also gave him two more daughters.

Show Me Success

Penney expanded his business by stocking the highest quality merchandise, offering fair prices, and hiring the best employees he could find. The number of his stores grew at an amazing rate and covered numerous states in the West only five years after he took ownership of the company. His goal was to have a chain of retail stores that covered the entire country. That dream came true a few years later when J.C. Penney stores opened in every state. Before his death in 1971 at the age of ninety-five, Penney saw his company grow from a frontier town dry-goods store to the second largest non-food merchandiser in the country, trailing only Sears, Roebuck and Co.

He was known as a retail genius, world traveler, philanthropist, farmer, author, lecturer, and the founder of one of the most successful chain of stores in the world. But the key to his success was rooted in his Missouri values and always following the Golden Rule.

Extra, Extra!

The Rev. Norman Vincent Peale spoke at Penney's funeral.

After his success in the retail industry, he began buying farms around Hamilton until he owned the original farm of his parents and the house where he was born.

John W. Brown

General John J. Pershing

Military Leader

"We came American. We shall remain American and go into battle with Old Glory over our heads. I will not parcel out American boys."
—Gen. John J. Pershing

General John J. Pershing rose from humble beginnings to be one of the most effective leaders in U.S. military history. He attained the highest rank ever held in the military, equivalent only to the posthumous rank of George Washington: "General of the Armies." His tough decisions were the key to leading America out of World War I, which made him so popular that he almost became the first U.S. president from the Show Me State, long before Harry S Truman.

The Early Years

John Joseph Pershing was born on September 13, 1860, and grew up in north-central Missouri near the town of Laclede. His mother and father held numerous jobs to support nine children after they moved from Pennsylvania to Missouri, including work as farmers, store clerks, and even running a hotel. The frontier family was relatively wealthy for the time period but lost most of their wealth when land prices collapsed.

John also worked the farm as a young man but made plans to attend college when he could save enough money. He worked as a teacher at a pair of schools, including an all-black school near his home. His teaching salary provided him enough money to finally leave home for the Kirksville Normal School where he earned his college degree by the time he was twenty.

Rise to Fame

Pershing's next move was to the U.S. Military Academy at West Point where he graduated in 1886 and became a military instructor at the school. He longed to see the world while also protecting his country, so he signed for duty as soon as he had the chance.

His first tour of duty involved a battle with the Sioux and Apache. He showed a great deal of skill in battle and earned accolades from superiors during the Indian Wars, so he was shipped off to fight in the Spanish-American War in 1898. He followed with tours as a commander during a raid on Pancho Villa during the Mexican revolution. His next appointment put him on the forefront of a war that changed the course of history: World War I.

Show Me Success

Pershing was appointed commander in chief of the American Expeditionary Force (AEF) where he led troops into battle during the height of World War I in Europe. He saw death and destruction all around him during those early days of fighting, but the news from the home front may have hit him the hardest. During the fighting, he was told that his wife and three daughters died in a fire, with his son the only person to survive. Pershing only took a few days off from the war for the funeral and burial and returned to the battlefield a short time later.

Upon his return, he commanded the entire American land force in Europe, making his mark as one of the greatest military leaders in our country's history. One of Pershing's moves was to request more soldiers, which raised troop levels from very few to several million in a relatively short period of time. His request for more soldiers was a shock to President Woodrow Wilson, who had not planned on supplying so many soldiers that quickly. Pershing got his way and assembled one of the largest armies ever to fight the battles raging in Europe. Pershing's forces took part in the Meuse-Argonne offensive in France, destroying the German resistance and ultimately leading to the Armistice Day one month later.

Pershing returned home a hero, which led many people to urge him to run for president. He was often quoted as saying he didn't want the job, but he wouldn't decline to serve if elected. Instead, the Republican Party nomination went to Warren G. Harding, and Pershing settled in as the chief of staff of the U.S. military. He died on July 15, 1948, and was buried in Arlington National Cemetery near the gravesites of the soldiers he commanded in Europe.

Extra, Extra!

His memoirs, My Experiences in the World War, were awarded the 1932 Pulitzer Prize for history.

The Pershing Missile and Pershing Tank were named after him.

Missouri has a state park and more than a dozen roads named in his honor.

Pershing County, Nevada, is named in honor of Pershing.

BRAD PITT

ACTOR

"I'm one of those people you hate because of genetics."
"Heartthrobs are a dime a dozen."
—Brad Pitt

Brad Pitt is, by some estimates, one of the most popular and highest paid entertainers in history. But just like many actors, he had to pay his dues before fame and fortune finally came his way. He was twice named *People Magazine*'s Sexiest Man Alive, and his status as one of the most powerful men in Hollywood continues to rise. He is not only a great actor, but he also spends considerable time volunteering his time and money for charitable causes around the world. He is an American icon, and a true Missouri legend.

THE EARLY YEARS

William Bradley Pitt was born in Shawnee, Oklahoma, on December 18, 1963. His family moved to Springfield soon after his birth, where he spent the remainder of his childhood. He grew up in a middle-class family, graduating from Kickapoo High School in 1984. In school, he was involved in sports, school musicals, and student government. After graduation, he headed off to the University of Missouri–Columbia but dropped out two credits shy of attaining his journalism degree to try his hand at acting in Hollywood.

RISE TO FAME

As most actors discover, the road to success in Hollywood is difficult. Pitt endured the tough years by working odd jobs like transporting exotic dancers in limos, moving refrigerators, and modeling. He started getting small TV and movie roles in shows such as *Dallas, thirtysomething, 21 Jump Street, Growing Pains,* and *Head of the Class.* In 1988, he landed his first starring role in *The Dark Side of the Sun.* But while the film was being produced, civil war broke out in Yugoslavia where the film was being made. Much of the country was damaged or destroyed, including the foot-

JOHN W. BROWN

age. The video reels remained lost until 1996, when the film was finally released.

SHOW ME SUCCESS

Pitt's big break came in 1991, when he turned a small movie role into the most talked about part of the year. In *Thelma & Louise*, Pitt played the role of J. D., a drifter who coached Thelma (Geena Davis) on how to rob a store. His shirtless dance in the hotel room made him an overnight sensation and an actor in high demand. That role paved the way for even bigger parts in movies like *A River Runs Through It* and *Se7en*.

Pitt was now one of the biggest stars in Hollywood history, and also one of the highest paid actors ever, commanding more than $20 million per movie. As Pitt continued to rack up movie roles and enormous amounts of money for the studios, he began winning numerous awards as well. He was honored with awards for Best Male Performance and Most Desirable Male for *Interview With a Vampire* in 1995 in the MTV Movie Awards. He followed those awards up the very next year, again winning Most Desirable Male for *Se7en*. Also in 1996, he won his first Golden Globe Award for Best Performance by a Supporting Actor for *Twelve Monkeys*, followed by a Best Actor Award in the Rembrandt Audience Awards for *Seven Years in Tibet*.

Brad turned his acting career in a new direction by creating a production company called Plan B Productions. He combined his acting skills and his producing interest in 2005 to make a film based on fellow Missourian Jesse James.

His private life has also been of epic proportions, with his every move splashed across the front of newspapers and magazines around the world. His marriage and divorce to actress Jennifer Aniston played out like a real-life soap opera for everyone to see, as well as his relationship with actress Angelina Jolie. Pitt's adoption of Jolie's two children and the birth of his first biological child made front-page news across the world. Between his movie roles and personal life, Pitt continues to prove that he is truly one of the biggest stars in history. Much to the joy of many Missourians, the foundation for his success was built right here in the Show Me State.

EXTRA, EXTRA!

In 1995, he was chosen by Empire Magazine as one of the 25 Sexiest Stars in Film History.

Brad was a tennis star and basketball player at Kickapoo High School.

He posed for the Men of Mizzou calendar.

JOHN ELROY SANFORD
(REDD FOXX)

ACTOR

"Ohhh . . . this is the big one. You hear that Elizabeth? I'm comin' to join you honey!"
—Redd Foxx as Fred Sanford

Redd Foxx is one of the best-known comedians and actors of the late twentieth century. He was often vulgar, raunchy, and politically incorrect, but to millions of Americans, he was also the funniest person on television. His standup routines were huge hits, influencing scores of comedians to follow. His crass performances drew the ire of critics long before the likes of Eddie Murphy and Chris Rock, but the role that made his a household name was that of Fred Sanford on the show *Sanford and Son*. The classic television show was an instant hit during a time when there were very few African American stars on network television.

THE EARLY YEARS

John Elroy Sanford was born on December 9, 1922, and grew up in St. Louis. His comedic talent was showcased early in life as he worked the nightclubs around St. Louis as a teenager. He left home at sixteen and got into trouble with the law on numerous occasions, especially after he joined a New York street gang. It was during this time that he befriended another up-and-coming black man who would later become known as Malcolm X.

RISE TO FAME

Sanford worked every nightclub he could as he developed his style during the early 1940s. Part of the reputation he developed in the clubs was that of a foul mouth, which was a big draw for some crowds but limited his appeal to larger audiences.

He worked the so-called "chitlin' circuit," where black clubs became the training grounds for larger venues that he would later sell out. He came up with a new stage name in the clubs, combining his nickname "Red" with the last name of the baseball star Jimmie Foxx.

During the 1950s and 1960s, Sanford drew larger audiences to his shows and sold a large number of comedy albums. His audience was still largely African American men, but times were changing and his comedy was beginning to reach people from all walks of life. He landed a movie role in the film *Cotton Comes to Harlem* in 1970, which was the springboard he needed to finally become a household name.

SHOW ME SUCCESS

Soon after his first movie role, television producer Norman Lear approached Sanford about starring in his own show. The show was based on a popular British comedy, but in America it took the name of *Sanford and Son*. The show was set in the Watts neighborhood of Los Angeles and gave many white Americans their first real look inside the lives of black families. He played Fred Sanford, the lovable junk dealer who was always bickering with his son. The show was an instant hit across racial lines, lasting five years and leading to more roles and more stardom for the St. Louis–born actor.

Sanford went on to star in a number of other TV shows, including the *The Redd Foxx Comedy Hour* and *The Redd Foxx Show*. He used his immense popularity to garner even more movie roles for himself. In the late 1980s, he starred with Eddie Murphy in the critically acclaimed *Harlem Nights,* and worked the Las Vegas comedy circuit. His life came to a sudden end doing what he loved to do. He was shooting a new sitcom, *The Royal Family,* when he died from a heart attack in 1991.

Sanford's body of work continues to entertain a new generation of fans even today while continuing to rack up accolades. During his life, he became one of the small number of performers to have the lead role in a television show on each of the big three networks, *Sanford and Son* on NBC, *The Royal Family* on CBS, and *The Redd Foxx Comedy Hour* on ABC. His character, Fred Sanford on *Sanford and Son,* was ranked No. 42 in *TV Guide*'s list of the "50 Greatest TV Dads of All Time."

EXTRA, EXTRA!

Sanford was the only artist invited to Elvis Presley's wedding at the Aladdin Hotel in Las Vegas in 1967.

Eddie Murphy footed the bill for Foxx's funeral, because of Foxx's troubles with the IRS.

PAYNE STEWART

PRO GOLFER

"I'm going to a special place when I die, but I want to make sure my life is special while I'm here.."
—*Payne Stewart*

Payne Stewart will forever be known for his flawless golf swing on the PGA Tour, flamboyant outfits, and a life cut short by a tragic accident. He was a winner at every level of play, including the Missouri Amateur Championship, the Southwest Conference Championship in college, and the PGA Championship. He was poised to win many more honors before a fateful flight claimed his life when he was only forty-two years old.

THE EARLY YEARS

William Payne Stewart was born on January 30, 1957, and grew up in Springfield. His father was a champion golfer, so it didn't take much for the youngster to develop an interest in the game. His father, Bill Stewart, was actually his first golf coach who taught him the finer points of the game that translated into the graceful style that he displayed on the professional tour.

RISE TO FAME

Stewart accepted a scholarship to play golf at Southern Methodist University, where he quickly adapted to the higher level of play. He was a standout at SMU where he won the Southwest Conference Championship in 1979 and became an All American in the process. He came back to Missouri during summer breaks where he picked up the title of Missouri Amateur Champion. His next step was the Asian Tour where he picked up a few more titles, and also a wife. He met Tracey Ferguson during a tournament, and they married a few years later.

Life on the minor tours was difficult, but the hard times paid off in 1982 when Payne finally got the chance to play on the PGA Tour and won his first event at the Quad Cities Open. He quickly became a fan favorite with stylish clothes and dramatic flair, but he later became a target of sports writers who claimed that

Payne could never win the big one, which changed during a tournament in his own backyard in Orlando, Florida.

Show Me Success

The first big win for Stewart was at the Bay Hill Classic on Arnold Palmer's home course. Over the next few years, the press was relentless on him for failing to win a major tournament championship. Then came the 1989 PGA Championship, in what many sports enthusiasts call the best championship in history. Payne was still reeling from a disappointing loss the previous year, so he focused his sights on finally winning the major. The outcome of the tournament came down to a fifteen-foot putt on the very last hole, which Stewart made, giving him a coveted major championship win and a spot in golf's history books.

He went on to win the U.S. Open in 1991 and 1999, represented the United States on five Ryder Cup teams and three World Cup teams. He ended his pro golfing career with eleven Tour wins, more than $11 million in earnings, and a place in the hearts of golf fans around the world.

One month after his team rallied to win the Ryder Cup in 1999, the forty-two-year-old golfer and five other people died while flying in a private jet. Investigators say the aircraft lost cabin pressure, which killed everybody on board. Television viewers around the world were glued to pictures of the plane flying on autopilot across the country until it finally crashed in South Dakota. The nation mourned the passing of a legend, as he left behind a wife, two young children, and millions of devoted fans. In 2001, just two years after his death, Stewart was inducted into the World Golf Hall of Fame.

Extra, Extra!

*A golf course in Springfield is named after Payne and his father, Bill.

*Michael Jackson was one of the prospective buyers for Payne Stewart's mansion in Orlando.

*He was ranked eighth in the world at the time of his death

Harry S Truman

Thirty-third President of the United States of America

"I never did give them hell. I just told the truth, and they thought it was hell."

—*Harry S Truman*

President Harry S Truman is perhaps the best known and most famous of all Missourians. He rose to political power in his home state and then climbed the ladder to worldwide prominence as the leader of the free world. He was the first and so far the only Missourian to call the White House his home, as he served as the thirty-third president of the United States of America. But no matter how far his travels took him, Truman still considered the Show Me State his home.

The Early Years

He was one of the most revered presidents in our nation's history, and his story began in the small town of Lamar. Harry S Truman was born on May 8, 1884, to John Anderson Truman and Martha Ellen (Young) Truman. He was the first child, later joined by a brother, Vivian, and sister, Mary Jane.

The family moved several times during Truman's childhood, including to a farm near Grandview in 1887 when he was three, then again when he was around six years old to Independence. That's where Harry attended public schools and graduated from high school in 1901.

Rise to Fame

After high school, Truman worked briefly as a timekeeper for a railroad construction contractor. The position wasn't exactly a dream job for a restless youngster, so he quit to take a job as a clerk in a pair of Kansas City banks. After a taste of the big city, he returned to Grandview in 1906 at the age of twenty-two to help his father run the family farm where he worked for the next eleven years.

During his time on the farm, he also served in the Missouri National Guard. His leadership skills and strong work ethic allowed him to take part in organizing the 2nd Regiment of Missouri Field Artillery as the United States entered World War I. His artillery group was mobilized into action in France, where the thirty-three year old was promoted to captain and given command of the regiment's Battery D. After his World War I duty was over, he joined the reserves and rose to the rank of colonel. He tried to return to active duty when World War II started, but he was declined.

Harry returned home after WWII and married his childhood sweetheart, Bess Wallace. His postwar job was running a men's clothing store in Kansas City, but times were hard and the business went belly-up in the postwar recession. Truman avoided bankruptcy, but the lessons learned from this difficult time made a lasting impact on his character and how he treated others. His next stop: elective office.

Truman was elected one of three judges of the Jackson County Court in 1922. Judge Truman's duties were more administrative than judicial, and he built a reputation for honesty and efficiency in the management of county affairs. He was defeated for reelection in 1924 but won his next election to become the presiding judge in the Jackson County Court in 1926.

SHOW ME SUCCESS

In 1934, Truman was elected to the U.S. Senate. He had significant roles in the passage of the Civil Aeronautics Act of 1938 and the Transportation Act of 1940. After being reelected in 1940, Truman gained national prominence as chairman of the Senate Special Committee to Investigate the National Defense Program, which became known as the Truman Committee. The job of the agency was to make sure that defense contractors made quality goods for the armed services while charging the government fair prices. A large number of critics, however, contend that the agency didn't exactly fulfill its mission.

In July 1944, Truman was nominated to run for vice president with President Franklin D. Roosevelt. The pair won the election, and on January 20, 1945, he took the vice presidential oath of office. President Roosevelt's unexpected death eighty-two days later ushered Truman into the oval office as he was sworn in as the nation's thirty-third president.

He took the helm of the presidency during a tumultuous time in United States and world history. He presided over the country during the waning stages of World War II, where he made the decision to drop the atomic bomb on Japan. He also led the country through the Korean Conflict and became the namesake for the Truman Doctrine, which was a foreign policy initiative designed to curtail the spread of communism.

Truman won reelection in 1948, despite predictions of defeat. Newspapers even jumped the gun, proclaiming the demise of the Truman presidency, made famous by Truman holding up the newspaper proclaiming, "Dewey Defeats Truman." Much of his second term is defined by the continuing struggle to keep the Soviet Union and the spread of communism in check.

Truman retuned to Independence in January 1953, where he spent the rest of his life. For the next twenty years, he worked at what he called being "Mr. Citizen." He spent his days reading, writing, lecturing, taking long walks, and founding his presidential library. Truman died in 1972, his wife passed away in 1982, and they are buried side by side in Independence in the library's courtyard. President Truman's popularity continues to remain high even to this day, as thousands of people visit his hometown every year to pay their respects to our nation's thirty-third president.

EXTRA, EXTRA!

Harry S Truman's middle name is "S." He ended up with the single-letter name because of a feud between his parents about which grandfather to name him after!

When Truman was growing up, Independence was one of the last civilizations of the West before travelers entered the wilderness.

Sam Walton

Entrepreneur

"The key to success is to get out into the store and listen to what the associates have to say. It's terribly important for everyone to get involved. Our best ideas come from clerks and stockboys."
—Sam Walton

Sam Walton was a man who took a simple idea of offering customers low prices and excellent service and built one of the biggest businesses in the history of the United States. In the process, he became the wealthiest person of his time and made millionaires out of scores of other people. Some business experts say that his basic ideas have changed the way Americans shop, more so than any other person in our country's history. He started with practically nothing, except a will to succeed, yet proved that hard work and a good idea are still the keys to wealth in America.

The Early Years

Samuel Moore Walton was born on March 29, 1918, in Oklahoma, but he spent the majority of his formative years in the Show Me State. Farming in Oklahoma wasn't paying off for the Walton clan, so when Sam was five, they packed up and moved to Missouri. The family bounced around to several small towns as Thomas Walton pursued numerous jobs in the post–World War I economy. They ultimately settled in the northeast Missouri town of Shelbina. Sam attended eighth grade in the small community where he made a name for himself as the youngest Eagle Scout in Missouri history.

The family moved again as Sam entered high school so his father could find work in mid-Missouri. Sam attended school at Hickman High School in Columbia and was active in a number of extracurricular activities, including being the starting quarterback on the state champion football team in 1935. He also played on the basketball team and served as president of the student body his senior year. Sam had plenty of success in high school, while developing his business abilities. The early lessons from his father about hard work and treating people fair helped kick-start a career that would eclipse levels greater than the world had ever seen.

Rise to Fame

Sam grew up during tough economic times for most Americans. Thus, it was expected that most children would hold down jobs while attending school. Sam helped the family by tending to farm chores, delivering milk to customers, and delivering newspapers. Instead of heading off to the workforce after graduation like many people of his time, Sam worked part time so he could attend classes at the University of Missouri–Columbia.

For most people, majoring in economics at a rigorous university would keep them busy enough, but Walton was a master at multitasking. He took a full course load while delivering newspapers, working as a lifeguard, waiting tables, acting as an officer in his fraternity, working as an ROTC officer, and serving as president of his university class. He still managed to graduate soon after his twenty-second birthday. Upon graduation, Sam entered the world of retail sales by taking a job with the J.C. Penney Company in Des Moines, which just happened to be founded by fellow Missourian James Cash Penney. His first salary as a management trainee: seventy-five dollars a month!

Walton's business career was sidetracked for a while as America entered World War II. He worked in a munitions plant in Oklahoma, where he met his soon-to-be wife, Helen Robson, in 1943 and married one year later. One year after that, they had their first son, Samuel, followed by John in 1946, James in 1948, and Alice in 1949.

When Sam got out of the military, he decided it was time to open his own retail store. He used the five thousand dollars he saved from military service and twenty thousand dollars borrowed from his father-in-law to purchase a Ben Franklin store in Newport, Arkansas. He relocated to the growing town on Bentonville, Arkansas, a few years later.

Over the next fifteen years, Sam and his brother, James, built some of the most profitable stores in the Ben Franklin franchise. They wanted to expand their influence, so they approached the company's owners about opening a chain of retail stores in small towns. Sam figured he knew that niche of the business particularly well because of all the small towns he lived in as a child. The company rejected the idea, so the brothers decided that it was time to branch out on their own.

Show Me Success

The first Wal-Mart Discount City opened in Rogers, Arkansas, in 1962. It was a far cry from the stores we see today, but the concept was the same: a wide variety of household goods at discount prices. His idea of discount stores in small towns went against conventional wisdom, which said that stores had to be situated in major cities because customer traffic must remain high to be profitable. He dotted the countryside with the blue and white Wal-Mart signs because he believed that people in rural communities needed the low-priced items. He also believed they would drive a short distance to make their purchases. He was right, and the Wal-Mart empire grew more rapidly than anyone ever imagined.

The chain experienced tremendous growth in the first fifteen years, growing from one store in northern Arkansas to 190 stores by 1977, and 800 stores by 1985. In 1972, the company was big enough to be listed on the New York Stock Exchange. The listing made instant millionaires of many of his top executives and managers who took advantage of the profit-sharing plan he set up in the early years of the company. Walton's empire continued to branch out as he opened a warehouse outlet chain called Sam's Wholesale Club in 1983. The company expanded in 1988 to include Supercenters (which included grocery stores) and became one of the largest real estate holders in the world.

Sam died in 1992 and left a legacy as being one of the most successful business leaders in the history of our country. *Forbes Magazine* named Sam Walton the richest man in the world from 1985 to 1988. His fortune would still be the largest in the world today, but it has been split among his numerous family members who still have enough money to remain on the *Forbes* list of wealthiest Americans.

Sam Walton not only changed the way Americans shop, but he also changed the way businesses are built and managed. He came from humble beginnings, but his life and work ethic transformed the world.

EXTRA, EXTRA!

*He was voted the "Most Versatile Boy" in his graduating class.

*Walton joined the Beta Theta Pi fraternity. Upon graduation, he was voted "Permanent President" of the class.

*Walton introduced the concept of checkout counters at one location in the store. Registers throughout the store were then moved to one location near the exits.

*It's estimated that if Sam were alive in 2005, his fortune would be twice that of Bill Gates.

*The first Wal-Mart Supercenter opened in Washington, Mo.

Laura Ingalls Wilder

Author

"I am beginning to learn that it is the sweet, simple things of life which are the real ones after all."
—Laura Ingalls Wilder

Laura Ingalls Wilder was a world famous author, but today she is better known for the television series that originated from her *Little House* books. In fact, many city dwellers in America got their first glimpse of small town America thanks to the books and stories by Wilder. Her family sporadically lived in Missouri during her childhood, so she could never really call anyplace home for an extended period (which allows Missouri to claim her). But the countryside of the Show Me State and a railroad advertisement touting Missouri as "The Land of the Big Red Apple" made enough of an impression on her that she ultimately chose to make her adult home in the Missouri Ozarks. Her best-selling books about westward expansion still make her a household name today.

The Early Years

Laura Elizabeth Ingalls was born on February 7, 1867, in Wisconsin. She spent time during her childhood in a number of states, including early years in north-central Missouri. Her family moved by covered wagon to Minnesota, Iowa, Kansas, the Indian and Dakota Territories, and Chariton County, Missouri, which meant that she could not call one place home for an extended period of time. She did return to the Show Me State as an adult after a series of tragedies, including the death of an infant son.

Rise to Fame

Laura Ingalls met her husband Almanzo Wilder while living in Dakota Territory where she worked as a teacher. When she was twenty-seven, the family moved to southwest Missouri and the small town of Mansfield. Laura yearned to write, so she began putting together articles for a number of publications, including *McCall's Magazine*, *Country Gentleman*, the *St. Louis Star*, and the *Missouri Ruralist*.

The couple had a daughter named Rose who urged her mother to tell the stories of life on the prairie. So Laura put those stories on paper and called the book *Pioneer Girl.* The success of those books pushed Wilder to write a series of adventures surrounding two girls named Laura and Mary, which became known as the *Little House* books.

Show Me Success

After writing *Little House in the Big Woods* in 1932, she went on to write a story about her husband's childhood adventures called *Farmer Boy.* Her next book—*Little House on the Prairie*—was written in 1935 and was her claim to fame. It was loosely based on her time in Indian country after the Homestead Act of 1862, which offered 160 acres of land to families that settled in the West. She once remarked, "I had no idea I was writing history" when she penned the books. The novels were popular with critics and were bought up quickly by her fans. The stories remained popular and grew to even greater fame more than two decades after her death when the television series *Little House on the Prairie* debuted.

Ingalls Wilder continued writing books in the Little House series, including *On the Banks of Plum Creek, By the Shores of Silver Lake, The Long Winter, Little Town on the Prairie,* and *These Happy Golden Years* in the following years. She died at the Rocky Ridge Farm in 1957, three days after her ninetieth birthday. The town of Mansfield has developed an entire industry surrounding the popularity of the *Little House* books, where an average of 45,000 visitors annually make a trek to Laura's farm at Rocky Ridge.

Extra, Extra!

Laura and her husband briefly moved to Florida, but the women did not accept her because she was a "Yankee."

Laura met the snobby and cruel girl she called Nellie Owens at a church in Minnesota.

Ingalls Wilder's farmhouse carries a National Historic Landmark designation.

TENNESSEE WILLIAMS

PLAYWRIGHT, AUTHOR

"Stella! Stella!"
—*A Streetcar Named Desire*

Tennessee Williams is one of the most successful playwrights of the twentieth century, with a body of work that includes *The Glass Menagerie, The Night of the Iguana, A Streetcar Named Desire,* and *Cat On a Hot Tin Roof.* He won major awards, including the Pulitzer Prize and the New York Drama Critics Circle Award. His writings often had an underlying conflict with sex and violence, possibly because of the frustration he faced as a homosexual living in a time when his lifestyle was not accepted, and possibly because of the violence he witnessed as a child. He is an American literary legend, and a Missourian through and through.

THE EARLY YEARS

Thomas Lanier Williams was born on March 26, 1911, into a troubled family in Columbus, Mississippi. His father was a traveling salesman who moved the family to St. Louis when he was eight years old.

The young man had an amazing ability to write compelling stories when he was still just a child. His paper, *Can a Wife Be a Good Sport?,* even won an essay contest sponsored by *The Smart Set* magazine when he was a teenager. He attended Soldan and University City High Schools in the St. Louis area before setting off for the University of Missouri–Columbia to further his education. He spent a short time in Columbia where the university setting expanded his interest in writing, but his college years coincided with the Depression, which meant that money was tight. He returned to St. Louis to find a job until he could save enough money to pursue writing.

Rise to Fame

Williams took a job at the International Shoe Company after leaving college but continued writing in the evenings. The difficult times he endured not only helped build his character but also provided plenty of material for his future manuscripts. He took classes at Washington University near his home where theatre groups produced some of his works. This small amount of success encouraged him to study dramatic writing at the University of Iowa where he earned his degree in 1938.

Tennessee received his first real recognition as a writer the very next year when he won a Group Theatre Award for his one-act play titled *American Blues*. The short stories provided some notoriety but certainly not the money he needed to make a living. So Williams continued working side jobs over the next five years while perfecting his craft until his "glass" ceiling finally broke.

Show Me Success

The Glass Menagerie was completed in 1944 and became his first real hit. In the play, Williams portrayed a Southern family living in a tenement in St. Louis. The play was a work of fiction that included some very real themes from his life. The central character, Laura, was likely patterned after his sister, while the domineering mother was a reflection of his real mother.

His next major play won him a Pulitzer Prize and a place in American theatrical history. *A Streetcar Named Desire* was the story of the mental and moral ruin of Blanche Du Bois, who was once again based on his sister. More hits followed, including *Camino Real* (1953) and *Cat On a Hot Tin Roof* (1955). The latter play was a huge hit and once again won him a Pulitzer Prize and monetary success.

Williams' writing always had a conflicting underlying theme, but a pair of life events in the mid-1940s contributed to his dark style even more. His sister had often suffered from mental problems, but intensive therapy did little to help her condition. Her parents decided on a frontal lobotomy for her in 1944, which didn't go as planned and left her incapacitated for the rest of her life. She was one of Tennessee's primary influences, and he never forgave his parents for the procedure. His other main struggle was a homosexual relationship with his secretary, Frank Merlo. Same-sex couples in the 1940s were taboo, but the committed relationship allowed him to produce some of his best writings.

He had more success with *The Night of the Iguana, Suddenly, Last Summer,* and *Sweet Bird of Youth.* But his health was getting worse in the 1960s, and he struggled with depression following Merlo's death. He developed addictions to alcohol and sleeping pills, then had a severe mental and physical breakdown and never regained the popularity he previously attained. His next few works provided him little success and even poorer reviews, which was something quite new to him.

Tennessee's life came to an unceremonious end when he died from choking on a bottle cap at the age of seventy-one at his home in New York City. Some people believe he was murdered, but a police report indicates pills were found under his body, likely indicating that they believe drugs were involved in his death. He was buried in St. Louis, despite the fact that he asked to be buried at sea near where poet Hart Crane's body was placed.

Extra, Extra!

*His abusive father is given credit for being the motivation for many of Tennessee's dark stories.

*He adopted the pen name "Tennessee" from his father's upbringing in the Southern state.

HISTORY AND POLITICS

William "Bloody Bill" Anderson

Outlaw

"I have chosen guerilla warfare to revenge myself for the wrongs that I could not honorably avenge otherwise."
—*Bloody Bill*

"Bloody Bill" Anderson is one of the most notorious outlaws ever to come from the Show Me State. He earned the title of "Bloody Bill" for his violent crimes committed during the Civil War. He grew up in a region split between Confederate and Union sympathizers, which likely led to his distrust of practically everyone around him and the violence that came to encompass his life.

The Early Years

The early years of William Anderson's life are sketchy. It is speculated that he was born sometime between 1837 and 1840. Even his birthplace remains a mystery, with many historians believing that he was born in Jefferson or Randolph County. What is known from his childhood is that he grew up and went to school in Huntsville in mid-Missouri. That rural area was much like the rest of the country in the mid-1800s, with neighbors divided over states' rights and slavery. This tense time in American history likely led to a fertile ground for Anderson to develop his ferocious appetite for violence.

Rise to Fame

If the environment surrounding his childhood wasn't enough to push William to the brink of violence, the murder of his father probably was. His father had a reputation for shady dealings and was accused of stealing farm supplies, including horses. During a confrontation over the alleged robbery, his father was killed, filling William with rage and turning him toward revenge.

Anderson avenged his father's murder by searching out the men who shot him, one of which was a judge, earning him the nickname "Bloody." The violence was just beginning, though, as Bill set out to kill anyone whom he believed sympathized with the "Yankees."

Show Me Infamy

The Civil War was heating up when Bloody Bill was in his mid-twenties. He joined a group of rebels during a raid on Lawrence, Kansas, led by William Quantrill, where they vowed to kill all male inhabitants of the city. The violent confrontation ended with more than 150 men dead, and Bloody Bill's band of guerilla's claimed the most kills.

Oddly enough, many people say that Bill Anderson looked nothing like a violent killer. He was described as handsome, thin, and tall, with long dark hair and piercing eyes, but the emotions under the skin were always on the verge of exploding. His killing sprees spread around central Missouri, with trips into the counties of Carroll, Chariton, Boone, Shelby, and others. In Rocheport, he killed numerous Union soldiers and made sure the authorities knew who was behind the massacre by mutilating the bodies. Bloody Bill's men also massacred soldiers in Centralia, where they wiped out the 39th Missouri Infantry, and once again mutilated the dead.

Bill's violent life came to an equally violent end one month after the Centralia massacre. The Missouri militia found Anderson's camp near Albany and engaged Bloody Bill in one final battle. As he rallied his troops, militia soldiers shot his horse, causing Bill to fall. The twenty-four-year-old rebel was shot twice in the back of the head, and his body was taken back to Richmond and put on public display. Some historians believe that his death and public display of the corpse were a major setback for Confederate fighters in Missouri.

Extra, Extra!

*Some in the Southern United States still believe that William T. Anderson's ghost makes yearly appearances around Halloween.

*Bloody Bill and the guerilla conflict was the backdrop to the 1976 movie, The Outlaw Josie Wales.

Susan Blow

Founder of U.S. Kindergarten

"All I ever really needed to know I learned in kindergarten."
—*Robert Fulgham*

Susan Blow was an educator, intellectual, and founder of the kindergarten program in the United States. Her privileged upbringing gave her access to the brightest people of her day, which helped influence generations of children after she was gone. Not only did she expose St. Louis children to advanced teaching methods, but she also put the Show Me State on the intellectual front lines during the post–Civil War period in America.

The Early Years

Susan Elizabeth Blow was born in St. Louis on June 7, 1843. She grew up in the Carondelet area in an affluent family who put a great emphasis on education. Her father was a successful industrialist and a U.S. congressman. That pedigree allowed Susan to attend prep schools in New Orleans and New York City while partnering with a group of advanced thinkers in St. Louis to debate philosophical issues.

Rise to Fame

The philosophy group, the St. Louis Society, studied and discussed the important issues of the day, including law, music, idealism, and free thought. She was one of the early members who put St. Louis on the forefront of intellectual thought and culture in the late 1860s. During these debate sessions, she was first introduced to the thoughts of Frederick Froebel, a German intellectual who was pioneering a new way of teaching children in Europe in what was known as kindergarten.

Blow's father was appointed ambassador to Brazil following the conclusion of the Civil War, so she, then twenty-six years old, went along as his secretary to learn more about their culture. At the end of that appointment, the family toured Europe, where she learned firsthand the methods that Froebel incorporated into

John W. Brown

his teachings. She observed his techniques and prepared to bring this novel approach to education back to America.

SHOW ME SUCCESS

Blow returned to St. Louis and founded the first successful public kindergarten at Des Peres School in Carondelet in 1873. Her family's influence came in handy once again as she convinced city leaders to expand the program throughout the area.

Her techniques were simple, but effective. She taught children in the morning, where she allowed other teachers in the classroom to observe her methods. The teachers then took over teaching duties in the afternoon so Blow could continue in her administrative tasks. Over the next ten years, the program was expanded to every St. Louis public school, making the city an educational model for the entire country.

Once Blow had taught enough teachers in the St. Louis area on the Froebelian method, she wrote and traveled extensively, teaching others the kindergarten philosophy. Many teachers experimented with their own styles, which were often less rigid than Blow's methods. The frustration she endured, the stress of setting up the program, plus family issues took their toll on her health. She moved to New York to recover from Graves Disease while keeping up a busy schedule as a lecturer and author. She died on March 26, 1916, and was brought back to St. Louis and buried at Bellefontaine Cemetery.

EXTRA, EXTRA!

Her books include Symbolic Education, Kindergarten Education, Educational Issues in the Kindergarten, Letters to a Mother on the Philosophy of Froebel, *and a translation of* Froebel's Mutter- und Kose-Lieder (Mother Play).

Susan Blow worked primarily as an unpaid supervisor of the kindergarten system in St. Louis to ensure its longevity apart from financial constraints.

* *Dred Scott came to St. Louis as a slave of Susan's grandparents, who later sold him. Susan's father, Henry Taylor Blow, publicly sided with Scott during the trial.*

OMAR NELSON BRADLEY

GENERAL

"Bravery is the capacity to perform properly even when scared half to death."
—General Omar Bradley

General Omar Nelson Bradley rose from humble beginnings to become one of the most successful military leaders of all time. He graduated from a star-studded class at West Point, which included Dwight D. Eisenhower. Bradley rose through the ranks to become a five-star general, where he bravely led soldiers into battle during World War II. He was also one of President Harry Truman's confidants during the Korean War and one of the most decorated soldiers in America's history.

THE EARLY YEARS

Omar Nelson Bradley was born in a log cabin near the small town of Clark on February 12, 1893. His parents lived a hard life on the frontier, and Omar was their only child to survive childhood. His father passed away when Omar was only thirteen, but he instilled lessons about integrity and moral character that stuck with the youngster for life. Omar and his mother later moved to Moberly where he became a star athlete and scholar and was accepted into the West Point Military Academy.

RISE TO FAME

Bradley's time at West Point was spent more on the baseball field than in the classroom. He was a star player for the academy and also one of the most popular young men on campus. The relationships he developed in college turned out to be a great asset during his army career. He finished 44th in his class of 164, while picking up the values of discipline and teamwork that set him apart from many of the other students. In fact, his 1915 graduating class was called "the class that the stars fell on" because of the high caliber of students. More than thirty generals emerged from the class, including President Eisenhower.

His early military career was less than stellar as he saw very little action and was actually relegated to duty in Montana during much of World War I. After the war, he continued his studies in military disciplines and taught mathematics at West Point. Little did he know, another major conflict—World War II—was brewing, which would change the face of the world forever.

Show Me Success

When World War II broke out, Bradley was acting as commandant of the U.S. Army Infantry School at Fort Benning, Georgia. He continued to move up the military ladder when General George S. Patton put him in charge of the II Corps. Bradley led his troops to victory in Tunisia in 1943, including the surrender of 250,000 Axis troops. The next year, he was given command of the U.S. First Army, where he took part in the invasion of France, including the assault on the beaches of Normandy. He later took leadership of the largest force ever placed under an American group commander throughout the end of World War II.

After the war, General Bradley served his country as administrator of Veterans Affairs and then chief of staff of the Army. He was chosen in 1949 to be the first chairman of the joint chiefs of staff and was ultimately promoted to general of the army, making him the fifth and last person to hold that post in the twentieth century. He retired a few years later to private industry where he took time to write his memoirs of the war, titled *A Soldier's Story*. He spent his final few years at a military medical center where he passed away in 1981 as one of the most decorated generals in the history of our country.

Extra, Extra!

The U.S. Army's M2 Bradley infantry fighting vehicle and M3 Bradley cavalry fighting vehicle were named after General Bradley.

Bradley was supposed to leave for Europe early in his career, but the influenza pandemic and the armistice prevented him from leaving the United States.

Bradley lettered both in football and baseball at West Point.

Martha "Calamity Jane" Cannary

Frontierswoman

"...she soon gained a local reputation for daring horsemanship and skill as a rifle shot."
—*Buffalo Bill*

Calamity Jane is a household name across the country, although few people know much about the person they are referencing. Martha Jane Cannary was a hard-drinking, hard-living, vulgar, gun-toting frontierswoman who could dig up trouble with the dirtiest of all the men. The stories of her escapades in the Wild West are probably wildly exaggerated, but her connection to Wild Bill Hickok is well established. Her rugged life is the thing of which legends are made, and the legends only grew taller with a TV show called *Deadwood*.

The Early Years

Martha Jane Cannary was born sometime around 1850 in far north-central Missouri near Princeton. The young woman earned quite a reputation for wearing men's clothing, chewing tobacco, being a sharp shooter, and cursing. Legend has it that her family took off by wagon train to head west when she was in her early teens. Her mother died on the trail and her father passed away a short time later. She was left to fend for herself in the Wild West, and that's when the legend took on a life of its own.

Rise to Fame

Jane spent the next few years wandering around the West, picking up odd jobs to put food on the table. She worked as a cook, a dance hall girl, and a prospector. She landed in a town in South Dakota called Deadwood, which was a rough and tumble town that was a perfect match for her personality. She met a man in town who went by the name of Wild Bill Hickok, and they had some degree of a relationship. The two are linked forever in history, but they actually knew each other only a brief time because he was shot dead shortly after they met. Despite the short acquaintance, some historians contend that they were married and even had a child. She later married Clinton Burke after living with him for about six years, which of course was a big scandal at the time.

Calamity Jane got her nickname from the threats she would make to men who bothered her. She always assured them that a calamity would come their way. Her wild-living, unique personality and interesting stories captured the attention of Americans in other parts of the country. That's when she joined up with the Buffalo Bill Wild West Show where she showcased her abilities in horseback riding and shooting. Ironically, the reasons they signed her to do the show (crazy antics, fighting, and the ability to drink copious amount of liquor) were the same reasons they eventually had to fire her. She left the show and returned to Deadwood where she died from pneumonia in August of 1903. She was buried on a hill overlooking the city right next to Wild Bill Hickok.

Extra, Extra!

*Some historians say the TV series Deadwood was an accurate representation of her life.

*A musical called Calamity Jane, starring Doris Day, is the most famous interpretation of her life.

John Danforth

Senator, United Nations Ambassador

"Jack Danforth has been called attorney general, senator, special counsel, special envoy, and reverend. Today, I am very proud to name this good man and superb public servant America's next ambassador to the United Nations."
—President George W. Bush (July 1, 2004)

John C. "Jack" Danforth is one of the most respected politicians to ever come from the Show Me State. He is known as a man that is able to get along with anyone in any environment or political situation. His ability to bridge gaps between parties is one key to his rise in politics that eventually led to his appointment as the U.S. ambassador to the United Nations.

The Early Years

John Claggett Danforth was born on September 5, 1936, to a wealthy and influential family in St. Louis. His upbringing brought him into contact with many influential business and political leaders through his family's company, Ralston Purina. He was a fifth-generation Missourian that grew up in Clayton and attended Country Day School.

After completing his secondary education, he headed for the Ivy League. Danforth graduated from Princeton University then attended Yale's Law and Divinity Schools. He was admitted to the New York bar but decided it was time to head back to Missouri where a career in law and politics awaited him.

Rise to Fame

Danforth didn't waste time climbing the business and political ladder once he arrived back in the Show Me State. He set up office as an attorney, but soon after he served as Missouri Attorney General from 1969–1976. During his tenure, he ran unsuccessfully for the U.S. Senate in 1970, but eventually he won a term to the Senate six years later.

During his time in Washington, D.C., Danforth made a name for himself for his ability to find a consensus among party leaders. He took advantage of that talent by negotiating the confirmation of Clarence Thomas to the United States Supreme Court.

Show Me Success

For many people, a high-profile position in the U.S. Senate would be the top of the ladder. Danforth, however, continued to make his mark on national and world events, starting with an appointment to investigate how the FBI conducted a raid on the Branch Davidian religious compound near Waco, Texas. During that investigation, there was speculation that George W. Bush was going to pick Danforth to be his vice presidential running mate in the 2000 election. That speculation never came true, but a few years later, President Bush appointed him as special envoy to the famine and war-stricken country of Sudan. He once again rose to a high-profile position in 2004 by being appointed the U.S. ambassador to the United Nations.

His expert ability to negotiate and bring two sides together continues to win praise from people on all sides of the political spectrum. He has also used his high-profile career to bridge gaps between religious faiths. He continues to be one of the most influential political and religious leaders in the country while continuing to call Missouri his home.

Extra, Extra!

Danforth received honorary degrees from more than a dozen universities from across the country.

Danforth presided over the funeral of President Ronald Reagan.

He is an Episcopalian priest.

CHARLES STARK DRAPER

INVENTOR

One of the brightest scientists in the history of our country came from humble beginnings in west-central Missouri. The inventions of Charles Draper are beyond the scope of what many people can understand, but they changed the way many of us live our lives. He is best known as the "father of inertial navigation," which allows airplanes to travel around the world with incredible accuracy.

THE EARLY YEARS

Charles Stark Draper was born on October 2, 1901, and grew up in the small town of Windsor. He showed an amazing aptitude in sciences early in life, which allowed him to attend the University of Missouri for two years, and then Stanford University, where he attained a degree in psychology in 1922. Despite earning the life science degree, he turned his attention to engineering and technology at Massachusetts Institute of Technology. He earned an advanced degree in electrochemical engineering and a doctorate in physics in 1938.

RISE TO FAME

Dr. Draper's time at MIT was spent perfecting his scientific knowledge, while also showing his entrepreneurial side by founding the Instrumentation Laboratory (later known as the Charles Stark Draper Laboratory, Inc.). Even as a graduate student, he was recognized as a national expert on aeronautical and meteorological research instruments, eventually becoming the head of the department of aeronautics and astronautics. It became apparent that he was becoming an expert in navigational technology, so more and more of his time became wrapped up in developing these guidance systems.

SHOW ME SUCCESS

Draper rose to national prominence about the same time World War II was breaking out. Few people at the time knew who he was, but his inventions were leading to technological advances that transformed antiaircraft weapons. Airplanes were still relatively new, and much of the technology that we rely on today was not yet invented. His gyroscopic technology allowed the military to calculate an aircraft's future position, taking into account gravity, wind, and distance, both for defense purposes and for tracking our own aircraft. These technologies put the United States ahead of other countries in a period when aircraft were becoming vital for defense and transportation.

The technology he developed in the mid-1900s still impacts the way we travel. The same inventions he gave to the military were later used in civilian aircraft, space vehicles, and ships to sense changes in direction. This dramatically changed and accelerated the advent of mass transit and world travel. By the time Dr. Draper died in 1987, he had received more than seventy honors from all over the world, including the National Medal of Science from President Lyndon Johnson, the Langley Medal of the Smithsonian Institution, the Robert H. Goddard Trophy of the National Space Club, and the National Academy of Engineering's Founders Award.

EXTRA, EXTRA!

Draper's legacy is still honored today with the Draper Prize in Engineering.

His cousin was Missouri Governor Lloyd C. Stark.

His guidance system technology was used in the Apollo Space Program.

ELLA EWING

TALLEST WOMAN IN HISTORY

"See that apple at the top of the tree? Well, Ella can get it down for me."
—song lyrics about Ella Ewing

Most people don't know the name of Ella Ewing, but pictures of the "Missouri Giantess" have been seen around the world. She was born in a small town and became the tallest woman in history. The 8′ 4 ½″ woman lived a short life, much of which was spent touring the country with the Barnum and Bailey Circus. Her large frame made news while she was alive, but the question of what to do with her body in death also made for an interesting dilemma.

THE EARLY YEARS

Ella Ewing was born on March 9, 1872, in Lewis County and grew up near the town of Gorin. There was nothing abnormal about her early in life to signal a record body size. In fact, she was small and frail until about the age of nine when her growth spurt began. By the time she was a teenager, she was just a playful young girl, albeit living in a 6′ 9″ body. Word was beginning to spread about the giant who lived on the farm, so the family tried to keep her sheltered from curious onlookers who came to northeast Missouri looking to take pictures. The family was somewhat embarrassed by the attention, and it was just a matter of time before hordes of people wanted to see what a real-life "lady giant" looked like.

RISE TO FAME

Circuses were big entertainment and big business in the late 1800s. Ella's family was poor and needed financial help but refused offers from traveling shows to make her part of the act. They finally relented when the offers got high enough to ensure the family could travel together. She was a popular attraction at every stop, and the money was rolling in. Even greater fame and fortune was right around the corner as the most famous circus in the world got wind of the "giantess."

Show Me Success

The Barnum and Bailey Circus made an offer to Ella to make her the biggest act in their show. At first, her father was angry at the thought of his daughter becoming a sideshow act. When he realized the lucrative possibilities, he consented and the entire family went on tour with the show once again, which launched a seventeen-year career on the circus circuit.

The 8' 4 ½" woman, with size 24 shoes, was bringing in large crowds for Barnum and Bailey. Her pay increased as her fame spread throughout the United States and Canada. Even though many thought she was part of a freak show, the circus was where she found companies who also dealt with "unusual" physical issues. It was a business full of strange characters that likely didn't see her as unusual or different. She spent the rest of her life on tour, which proved to be rough on her large body. She got sick with pneumonia while on the road, dying soon afterward at forty years old.

Even in death her family had to deal with the effects of her fame. The family constantly had to worry about grave robbers stealing her body for medical purposes or exploitation. In fact, Ella wanted to be cremated so her body wouldn't be stolen, but her father went against her wishes and had a traditional burial.

After burial arrangements were made, a casket company worked around the clock to build a coffin that would hold her body. It was so long that the horse-drawn carriage had the seats removed so the back doors could close behind the casket.

Extra, Extra!

*Ella often appeared with a twenty-three-inch-tall Russian dwarf named "Peter the Small."

*Her shoes are on display at the Missouri Capitol and the Downing Museum in Memphis, Mo.

*In 1969, the Missouri Department of Conservation named a fifteen-acre lake near Gorin the Ella Ewing Lake.

Dick Gephardt

Congressman, Presidential Candidate

"Dick Gephardt, let me say this, is one of the finest leaders this nation has known. He's the hardest working . . . and frankly the most passionate Democrat in the House."

—Harold Ford

Dick Gephardt made his mark on politics in the 1990s and early 2000s as one of the most powerful Democrats on Capitol Hill. He served as one of the highest-ranking leaders of the party while being a frontrunner for the Democratic presidential nomination on numerous occasions. The key to his success was due in part to his ability to make personal connections to his working-class constituents while wielding significant political power in Washington, D.C.

The Early Years

Richard Andrew Gephardt was born on January 31, 1941, and grew up in south St. Louis, in the same neighborhood that he would one day represent in the U.S. House of Representatives. His father was a union truck driver and his mother a secretary. It was this working-class background that likely influenced many of his life choices, including his ultimate decision to enter politics later in life. He graduated from Southwest High School in 1958, then he was accepted at the prestigious Northwestern University in Chicago where he graduated with honors. He went on to earn his law degree from the University of Michigan in 1965.

Rise to Fame

After passing the bar exam in Missouri, Gephardt stayed busy by serving as a captain in the Missouri Air National Guard while getting his feet wet in politics. He first won an election as a committeeman in St. Louis and moved up the ranks three years later to become an alderman. His next step was a big one, all the way to Washington, D.C., where he stayed for the next twenty-six years as a congressman representing the state of Missouri.

SHOW ME SUCCESS

Gephardt quickly moved up the ranks in Congress, serving as House majority leader from 1989 to 1994, then as House minority leader through 2003. He also made unsuccessful bids for the Democratic nomination for president in 1988 and again in 2004. He dropped out of the latter race after a lackluster showing in the Iowa caucuses, only to be mentioned as a possible vice-presidential running mate for John Kerry.

Gephardt announced before his run for the presidency that he would not seek re-election for his congressional seat. So after dropping out of the 2004 race, Gephardt retired to private life after an amazing fourteen terms in office.

EXTRA, EXTRA!

*On the same day that John Kerry picked John Edwards to be his running mate in 2004, the New York Post published a headline stating that Gephardt had the pick.

*Gephardt was viewed as a social conservative when elected but moved progressively left during his terms in office.

MICHAEL HARRINGTON

SOCIALIST LEADER

"Had Harrington been born anywhere in Western Europe, he would have become a major social-democratic party leader."
—Maurice Isserman

When many people think of Missouri, they usually think of the core American principles of democracy and capitalism, but one of the most famous American socialist leaders in U.S. history also called the Show Me State his home. Michael Harrington rose to national prominence on the socialist platform with his look at "The Other America," which made a lasting impact on American culture.

THE EARLY YEARS

Edward Michael Harrington was born in St. Louis on February 24, 1928. His father was an attorney and his mother a teacher. His middle-class, conservative, Jesuit upbringing gave few hints into his later socialist writings and political activism. The gifted student attended St. Louis University High School before heading off to Holy Cross College, where he graduated when he was only nineteen years old. To keep his parents happy, he continued his studies at Yale University Law School, then by studying English at the University of Chicago.

RISE TO FAME

Harrington was poised to follow in his father's footsteps by becoming a lawyer, but he claimed that the study of law bored him so he began looking for something more fulfilling.

During a summer job in St. Louis, he had a so-called "conversion" to social activism after being exposed to the realities of the working poor. This experience in the slums changed the course of his life forever. He worked briefly for the Public Welfare Department in the public school system, where he came face to face with families in deplorable conditions. He knew instantly that he had to take action, so he moved to New York and joined the Catholic Worker Movement to help people living in poverty.

After a short time with the Catholic group, he again became disenchanted with their methods and began searching once again for an activist group to join. He hooked up with the Young Socialist League. He spent the next decade living in Greenwich Village socializing with well-known liberal writers, artists, and progressive socialist supporters. During this time, he gained a greater understanding of social policies while compiling information for a book.

SHOW ME SUCCESS

When his book *The Other America: Poverty in the United States* was published in 1962, it was an eye-opening look at how the poor lived in our country. The timing of the book (the "Happy Days" of the 1950s and early 1960s) was one of the key reasons it struck a chord with many people. For most Americans, times seemed to be good, but to a significant portion of society, it was something completely different. His book pointed out that the American government and society in general were not dealing with the problems of poverty that kept the poor trapped in a cycle of dependency. His book made such an impact that he was no longer just a fringe socialist but a major force in Washington, D.C., with a large number of politicians coming to him for answers.

His ideas are credited with helping pass the "War On Poverty" legislation by the Kennedy and Johnson administrations. He made an impact on social policies throughout the 1970s and much of the conservative 1980s. In fact, when the political tides were swinging right, he went in the opposite direction and moved even further left. He left the American Socialist Party because he believed they were getting too conservative, so he founded a new group which evolved into the Democratic Socialists of America. Under his leadership, the group became one of the largest socialist groups in the history of the United States. Harrington died in 1989 and was hailed by people on both sides of the political spectrum as a valiant fighter for the causes in which he believed.

EXTRA, EXTRA!

Harrington is often referred to as the most prominent socialist in the United States from the 1960s until his death in 1989.

He was an adviser to Martin Luther King, Jr.

BERNARR MACFADDEN

"FATHER OF PHYSICAL CULTURE"

"A practical working knowledge of how to keep well is the best form of life insurance one can possess."

—*Bernarr MacFadden*

Bernarr MacFadden was famous while alive, and although he is relatively unknown today his area of expertise is more popular than ever. He was known as the "Father of Physical Culture" and led the physical fitness movement. Many people of his day thought that his methods of getting in shape were a sure sign of insanity, but millions of others bought into his teachings as he inspired a generation of people to live healthier lives. He was often ignored by medical experts because of his unusual methods, but he would likely be a fitness icon if he were alive today.

THE EARLY YEARS

Bernard Adolphus MacFadden was born on August 16, 1868, in Mill Spring. He was a sickly child and was told that he wouldn't live to be very old. His father was abusive, his mother was constantly sick, and neither parent was alive by the time he was twelve years old. He almost died at age seven from the treatment he received by a doctor, making him forever distrustful of the medical field. He finally took his health into his own hands as a teen after a relative told him that just like his mother he would be dead soon.

RISE TO FAME

MacFadden gained an interest in physical labor while he was still a teenager after noticing that working in an office made him lose muscle mass. He also realized that exercising and eating right helped him perform better at work and heal more quickly. During this time, a flamboyant personality was developing alongside his body. He competed in wrestling competitions and was often the crowd favorite because of his physique and flair. Fans wanted to know his secret for vitality, which gave him the realization that his mission was to teach the world how to reclaim their health.

McFadden was about eighteen years old when he moved to the St. Louis area and opened an exercise studio, calling himself a kinestherapist, or "teacher of physical fitness." His slogan, "Weakness is a crime, don't be a criminal," got the attention of health enthusiasts, which made him a bigger celebrity than ever.

Show Me Success

MacFadden knew that in order to reach more people with his message on health he had to move to a bigger city. He opened an exercise studio in New York City and soon had a large and influential clientele. Around this time, he changed his name to Bernarr, from Bernard, because it sounded stronger and more distinctive.

He gained nationwide attention when *Time Magazine* called him "Body Love." Oddly enough, at the same time the medical establishment was calling him a "kook." His claims that a proper diet and healthy living helped him improve his eyesight and regrow hair raised plenty of eyebrows. He shunned the medical establishment, ate only natural foods, walked hundreds of miles at a time, campaigned against white bread, married four times, and was flamboyant to a fault. He even got arrested on obscenity charges for some of his physical displays and writings.

He ultimately published numerous books, newspapers, and magazines under his own publishing label, opened hotels and sanitariums in the name of natural health, and became a financial and business success. He even began his own body-building competition in 1903 to crown the most physically fit person in America. This competition was the springboard for more famous events, including the Mr. Universe contest and Mr. Olympia.

Bernarr MacFadden was now a bona fide star. He hung out with celebrities, the rich and famous, and even presidents. His books motivated millions to strive for better health, both physical and mental, which led the way for the fitness celebrities we know today. He developed entire communities devoted solely to physical health and even pioneered a form of solar energy in his healthy house. He lived to be eighty-seven years old and was healthy to the very end, physically outperforming many people half his age.

Extra, Extra!

Whole wheat bread likely stemmed from MacFadden's efforts against white bread.

He shocked people by urging them to wear loose clothing. He said that wearing tight-fitting garments was barbaric.

He always fasted when he was sick because he noticed that animals do not eat when they are ill.

Thomas J. Pendergast

Political Boss

"You can't coerce people into doing things for you, you can't make them vote for you. I never coerced anybody in my life."
—Tom Pendergast

Political machines were alive and well in the early 1900s, and Missouri had one of the most powerful bosses in the country. Some historians speculate that if there wasn't a Thomas Pendergast, there wouldn't have been a President Harry S Truman. His political opponents labeled him a corrupt leader and ruthless criminal, while his powerful allies allowed him to influence politicians across the country. It was this power, and the abuse of it, that eventually brought him down.

The Early Years

Thomas Joseph Pendergast was born in St. Joseph on July 22, 1872. He was a part of a large family, which included an ambitious older brother named James, who was a political dynamo in nearby Kansas City when Thomas was a child. Thomas was intrigued by the inner workings of politics, so he left St. Joseph when he was around eighteen years old to move with his brother in Kansas City to experience it firsthand.

James was a dynamic political leader and motivator that changed the course of Kansas City politics. He rallied blue-collar workers to his side and eventually passed those alliances along to Thomas's camp when the younger brother entered politics. The incredible political machine that James built was primed for bigger things. Thomas now had the experience, desire, and connections to make sure that the power and privilege expanded under his watch.

Rise to Fame

It only took about six years in Kansas City before Thomas started making a name for himself in local politics. His first position was the deputy marshal of Jackson County, followed by superintendent of streets, and then county marshal in 1902. He lost the marshal's post a few years later but remained active in Democratic politics.

Thomas moved up the political ladder by winning the aldermanic post that his brother had held for many years. Thomas understood how to work the system to gain an advantage, and a political move in 1922 may have proven to be one of the most beneficial in his career. Pendergast allied himself with Harry S Truman in Truman's bid for a judgeship. That alliance between the two men proved beneficial for both. In Tom's case, it allowed him to begin securing political dominance in Kansas City and the entire west-central Missouri area.

Show Me Success

Pendergast made it a habit of surrounding himself with powerful men, which helped keep many of his illegal activities suppressed. Truman, at this point, was still just a local politician, so Thomas knew he had to reach out to bigger leaders in order to expand his influence. His handpicked associate, Guy Bransfield Park, ascended to the governor's office in 1933, which allowed Pendergast to have state-wide power.

The Roosevelt Administration also recognized Pendergast's influence, so they too rewarded him with favors to keep the Democratic political machine churning. Truman was beginning to move up the political ladder as well, winning a seat in the U.S. Senate. This meant that Pendergast had his men in place in local, state, and federal offices, which gave him incredible influence in almost all aspects of government.

His next handpicked candidate proved to be the end of the machine. Lloyd Stark took Pendergast's endorsement all the way to the governor's office. Once there, Stark turned on his boss and helped prosecutors bring charges against him. Pendergast was charged with tax evasion for failing to disclose more than $1 million in income. A judge sentenced him to fifteen months in prison on the first charge and five years of probation on the second charge. The fall from power may have been too much for Pendergast to handle, as he died on January 26, 1945, before the probationary period expired.

Extra, Extra!

*Pendergast died just days after Truman's inauguration as vice president of the United States.

*It's estimated that Pendergast received over $30 million annually from gambling, prostitution, and narcotics in the 1930s.

Nellie Tayloe Ross

First Female Governor

"The Governor Lady."

—Good Housekeeping Magazine

Nellie Tayloe Ross was born in Missouri and rose to become the first female governor in our nation's history. Ross's rise to fame was truly amazing because of the time period in which it happened, and also because she never formally agreed to run for the office. Her time as first woman governor was followed by another prestigious honor, the first woman leader of the U.S. Mint.

The Early Years

Nellie Davis Tayloe was born in St. Joseph on November 29, 1876. Her family lived in the northwestern part of the state until she was about to enter school, when they moved to Omaha, Nebraska. Her family put a strong value on education, allowing Nellie to be educated at both public and private schools. Her original intent was to teach kindergarten in Nebraska, so she attended a two-year teaching program to pursue her original goal.

Rise to Fame

Nellie moved to Wyoming not long after she met William Bradford Ross during a visit to see her relatives. He was an attorney and aspiring politician, while she was content to play the role of mother and supporter of her husband's ambition. William was elected as the governor of Wyoming, but his time on the job was short-lived. One year after taking office, he died after an appendectomy operation.

The state had no lieutenant governor to take his spot, so the secretary of state filled the position until a special election could be held to elect his successor. Nellie was gaining support from many Democratic leaders, but she never officially claimed the nomination. She hinted that if she were elected, she would fulfill her husband's goals that he set forth during his short time in office. Wyoming voters also rallied around the fact that they were the first state to allow women to vote, so they too should have the first woman governor. Only one month after her husband passed away, Nellie won the 1924 election by only eight thousand votes, which made her the first woman governor in the history of the United States.

Show Me Success

Nellie was inaugurated as Wyoming's thirteenth governor on January 5, 1925, exactly fifteen days before the first woman governor of Texas was sworn into office. Historians agree that she did a capable job as the chief executive of the state, although few of her initiatives made it past the Republican-controlled legislature. She focused on core Democratic principles during her tenure, including tax relief for poor families and women's rights. Her time in office was also short, as Ross was defeated two years later by an opponent who received barely one thousand more votes than her.

The name recognition that came along with being the first woman in office brought some benefits. President Franklin D. Roosevelt made history once again for Ross, as he named her the first female director of the U.S. Mint. She held the post for twenty years, including the turbulent time during World War II where the amounts of copper, zinc, and nickel were reduced because of war rationing. Her job also allowed her to be the first woman to have her likeness stamped on a mint medal, and her name is engraved on the silver depository at West Point. Her long and historical life ended in 1977 at the age of 101.

Extra, Extra!

*Miriam Ferguson won the governorship of Texas on the same day as Ross but was inaugurated fifteen days after her.

*Ross believed that a woman's primary source of happiness should be inside the home with her children.

*She was appointed vice chairman of the Democratic National Committee in 1928 and directed the party's women's division.

BUSINESS, SCIENCE, AND TECHNOLOGY

HENRY BLOCH

ENTREPRENEUR

"I Should'a Come Here Last Year."
—H&R Block Commercial

Henry Bloch is a world-famous businessman, thanks in part to the company that bears his name and his down-home demeanor displayed on television commercials. He and his brother Richard started what became the largest tax services company in history: H&R Block. At one time, the company filed one out of every nine tax returns in the United States and served more than 20 million clients all over the globe.

THE EARLY YEARS

Henry Bloch was born in Kansas City on July 30, 1922. His father was a prominent lawyer, which likely stimulated his interest in business and legal issues. He attended Southwest High School and then attended the University of Missouri–Kansas City for a short time before transferring to the University of Michigan. He graduated in 1944 during the buildup to World War II and put his business dreams on hold to service in the U.S. military.

RISE TO FAME

Bloch entered the Army Air Corps shortly after graduation and served as a navigator on B-17 Bombers over Germany. He took part in thirty-one missions during the war, including three combat missions over Berlin. He was awarded the Air Medal and three Oak Leaf Clusters before the U.S. Air Force sent him to Harvard Business School to study statistical controls.

While studying at Harvard, a professor pointed out that large corporations had specialized departments to assist them in taxation and business issues, but small companies did not have the same resources. This is when Bloch cultivated the idea of offering bookkeeping services to assist small businesses.

Two years after graduating from Michigan, Henry and his brother Leon founded the United Business Company to offer bookkeeping and tax services to small businesses. Leon left the company to attend law school, but Henry and Richard persisted. Early in the company's development, they abandoned the tax preparation portion of the company because it wasn't proving to be a good source of revenue. A client urged them to run a small ad in the newspaper to see if there really was a demand for personal tax preparation. Much to their surprise, they were overwhelmed with the response from people who wanted their expertise and assistance.

At the same time they place the ad, the Kansas City IRS office discontinued offering free tax assistance. The time was right to capitalize on a business niche that was about to explode on the American landscape.

Show Me Success

Henry and Richard redirected the United Business Company into a new company that specialized in income tax preparation called H&R Block. "Block" replaced the family name of Bloch, because the original name was difficult to pronounce and spell. The business was an instant success, but in order to grow, the brothers had to find other cities in which to expand. Just like the scenario that took place in Kansas City, the federal government eliminated free tax assistance in New York, so they packed their briefcases and headed east to open a new office.

Business was booming in both cities, but the brothers wanted to live with their families in Missouri. They decided to sell the New York operations, where a twist of fate turned the sale into a franchise deal. The prospective buyers couldn't come up with the money, so they agreed to buy a portion of the company, plus pay a portion of the profits to the Blochs. It was a perfect deal for the brothers, who began to replicate this business model across the country. Seven years after opening H&R Block, the company had 206 offices and growing revenues. They took the company public later that year.

The 1970s and 1980s were a time of explosive growth for the company as they took on more clients and bought smaller firms. The number of tax offices in the 1970s blossomed to more than 8,600, aided in part by Bloch's appearances in television commercials. The company expanded their empire by opening income tax schools to keep up with the growing demand for qualified tax experts.

Henry retired as chairman in 2000, assuming the title of chairman emeritus. His day-to-day operations were over, but he continued to play a vital role in the continued growth of the company and in the betterment of the city he called home, Kansas City.

Extra, Extra!

Henry Bloch first appeared in commercials in 1972, which built H&R Block into one of the most widely recognized brands.

The School of Business and Public Affairs at UMKC is named "The Bloch School"

THE BUSCH FAMILY

THE KINGS OF BEER

"Great American Heroes. Real Men of Genius."
—*Anheuser-Busch commercial*

The founder of Anheuser-Busch did not spend his formative years in the Show Me State, but his family legacy is a central part of the history of St. Louis and Missouri as a whole. Adolphus Busch built his company into the largest beer manufacturer in the country and one of the most recognizable names in the world. His descendants have since taken over the reins of the company, remaining a major presence in the Missouri economy and the national business scene.

THE EARLY YEARS

Adolphus Busch was born in Germany on July 10, 1839, the youngest of twenty-one children from a wealthy family with a rich history in alcoholic beverage manufacturing. His father made a fortune dealing in wines and other supplies for breweries in Europe, but Adolphus had his eyes set on America. He left home at eighteen and settled in St. Louis, using his family's wealth to establish a brewer's supply company. He further expanded the family's empire when he co-founded a company in 1866 with his father-in-law, Eberhard Anheuser. That company became known as Anheuser-Busch, Incorporated.

RISE TO FAME

Busch perfected how to sell alcoholic beverages to a mass market while discovering a way to pasteurize beer so it could withstand temperature fluctuations, which enabled his company to distribute beer nationwide. It didn't take long before A-B surpassed their chief brewing rival, Pabst Brewing, to become the largest brewer in the United States.

Adolphus, his wife, and thirteen children lived like royalty, with a palatial mansion in downtown St. Louis, a country estate called "Grant's Farm," two homes in Pasadena, California, a hops farm in Cooperstown, New York, two villas in Germany, and a private railroad car called "Adolphus." He passed away in 1913, leaving quite a legacy for his St. Louis–based family to build upon.

Show Me Success

When the patriarch of the Busch family died, his eldest surviving son, August, inherited the controlling interest in the company. World War II and Prohibition took a toll on the August era though. When the federal government began a crackdown on alcoholic beverages, Anheuser-Busch came up with a strategy to sell alcohol-free beverages and supplies so that buyers could make their own beverages at home. August even spoke to Congress, arguing that ending Prohibition would help America pull out of the Great Depression. Prohibition was ended in 1933, which paved the way for the next generation of Busch descendants to inherit the fast-growing company that had just become publicly traded.

The next family member in line to lead the brewery was Adolphus, III, who took over the top spot in 1934 upon the death of August, Sr. The most notable change in the beer during Adolphus's leadership was the advent of canned Budweiser.

August, Jr., or Gussie as he was known, was next in line, becoming president of the company in 1946. His marketing prowess led to the first-ever sponsorship of a national television show by a brewer, and he spearheaded the purchase of the St. Louis Cardinals. He was also the driving force behind making Budweiser known as the "King of Beers."

His son, August Busch, III, took over as president in 1974, the same year the company reached the 30 million barrel mark. Another Busch, August, IV, took the helm in 2006 and continued to expand the dominance of the brewery through aggressive marketing and advertising campaigns. The company continues to dominate beer sales around the world, with headquarters still in the city where they began, St. Louis.

Extra, Extra!

Anheuser-Busch is the largest beer producer in the world.

According to Forbes Magazine, *the Busch family had a net worth of more than $2 billion in 2004.*

The St. Louis brewery is on the National Historic Landmark Registry.

Bud Light was introduced nationally in 1982.

John W. Brown

William Danforth

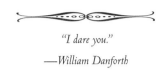

"I dare you."
—*William Danforth*

William Danforth made a name for himself as an ambitious entrepreneur, but he started life in a much different condition. He was a sickly child, but he used his medical problems to change his own life, and the lives of everyone he met. He founded and built Ralston Purina into one of the largest and most successful companies in the world, while empowering others to succeed with his motivational approach to life. He was "dared" as a child to change his life for the better, and he used that same dare to raise others up around him.

The Early Years

William H. Danforth was born around 1870 and grew up in southeast Missouri. The Bootheel section of the state was economically depressed at the time, which led to hard times for many families in the area. The sick young boy was forced to spend many days and nights inside his home reading. One of his teachers became concerned about his health, so she dared him to become the "healthiest boy in class." He took the teacher up on the dare and began the process of changing his life for better health.

He moved to St. Louis to attend Washington University, where he graduated in 1892. His real passion was working with animals, so he looked for a job that would allow him to continue studying their behavior. Eventually, he began mixing feed formulas for farmers in the area, when he realized he could make a great career in animal feed.

Rise to Fame

Two years after graduating from Washinton University, Danforth officially opened a feed business in St. Louis called Robinson Danforth Commission Company, which eventually became Ralston Purina. Much of the area was still farmland, so he had little trouble finding customers to build his blossoming business. His business model was quite successful, so he expanded it to include thirty-two other cities in the United States and Canada. The business was growing rapidly, but World War I interrupted it for a while as he enlisted in the military. He used his time wisely during the war to further develop his business models, which laid the foundation for his company to become a household name.

Show Me Success

Danforth knew that foods had a dramatic effect on health, yet few people knew much about nutrition in the early 1900s. The company introduced a breakfast food called Purina Whole Wheat Cereal at about the same time Albert Edgerly, known as Dr. Ralston, put forth his philosophy on healthy living. Part of Dr. Ralston's health plan was to incorporate whole wheat into your diet, which was espoused in the book *Life Building.* Dr. Ralston had a large following, so Danforth asked him to endorse his new cereal. Ralston agreed, and the two entities were soon synonymous and the company name was changed to Ralston Purina.

The next big breakthrough for the company came during World War I, thanks to an astute observation by Danforth. He noticed that soldiers' spirits were raised whenever they heard the word "chow." He pointed out that the troops were happier and the food seemed to taste better when it was called chow. He figured he could capitalize on the emotions that surrounded the slang term, so he incorporated the word "Chow" into his animal products to entice people to buy them for their pets. Soon, pet foods named Puppy Chow, Cat Chow, and Dog Chow were on store shelves. He combined the new product names with the distinctive red and white checkerboard square design to expand his market presence. These two moves made his company one of the most identifiable in American product packaging. Under Danforth's leadership, Ralston Purina became the largest producer of dry dog and cat foods and a leading producer of cat box filler in the country, and one of the one hundred largest corporations in North America.

His professional career was satisfying, but his real desire was to motivate others. He had built his life on the "dare" principle he learned as a child and used it in almost every aspect of his life. He taught the dare principles in a number of books, the most famous of which was titled *I Dare You.* The philosophy simply stated that each person has not one, but four lives to live: "Physical," "Mental," "Social," and "Religious." Danforth pointed out that all four areas of your life must grow in balance with each other, where the mind should not be developed at the expense of the personality, nor the body at the expense of character. His philosophy proved a success as thousands of people adopted his theories to better their own lives.

His four-square philosophy enabled him to live a long and productive life. He assisted the community in incredible ways, establishing the Danforth Foundation in 1927 as a national educational philanthropy. The foundation continues to give out millions of dollars to individuals and community projects all across the country. His amazing life came to an end on Christmas Eve 1955 at the age of eighty-five.

EXTRA, EXTRA!

Danforth claimed that he never missed a single day of work due to illness.

He made it a point to walk at least one mile every day and get eight hours of sleep a night with the windows open.

Employees of Ralston Purina were given a motivational message every Monday by Danforth himself.

Purina stands for "Where Purity is Paramount."

James Buchanan Eads

Engineer

"The entire work—bridge, tunnel and approaches—are magnificent."
—*Andrew Carnegie*

James Eads was often derogatively called a "non-engineer" by many people of his day because he lacked the technical schooling of most engineers, but his lack of classical training may actually have been a blessing because he never heard about the engineering principles that classical schools taught were impossible. His ideas and designs were scoffed at by these so-called experts, but Eads had the last laugh with the construction of the first major steel bridge across the Mississippi River.

The Early Years

James Buchanan Eads was born on May 23, 1820, in Lawrenceburg, Indiana. The young man bounced around the Midwest while growing up and had very little formal education. Despite his educational shortcomings, he voraciously read any book he could find. The family settled in St. Louis when he was still a boy, and it didn't take long for the motivated young man to land a job in the bustling riverboat industry. By the age of eighteen, he was already working on riverboats. His early years on the river taught him valuable lessons, including the idea that fortunes could be found on the bottom of the river.

Rise to Fame

When Eads was about twenty-two years old, he invented a primitive type of salvage boat that allowed him to dive deep into the river to recover lost items. The diving contraption acted like a submarine where he could walk on the bottom of the river to search for lost bounty. The business flourished as he picked up tons of iron, lead, and other cargo that had fallen from ships. He quit for a while to enjoy the spoils of his labor but was soon back with a business that was larger than ever. He now had ten boats in his fleet, some of which were powerful enough to raise an entire ship from the floor of the river.

His experiences on the water put him on the forefront of history as the Civil War raged across the United States. He proposed to the federal government to construct steam-powered ironclad riverboats to assist Union ground forces to overcome Confederate forts downriver of St. Louis. The Union took up Eads's offer, and he produced seven ships for the Navy in less than one hundred days.

Show Me Success

At the close of the war, Eads was ready to make his next historical mark on the Mississippi River. His theory was that railcar traffic would be vital to the development of the Western United States, but the river posed a major stopping point for the tracks. He presented his idea to a number of cities and governmental groups to build a bridge connecting Illinois and Missouri. Every presentation was met with incredible opposition and often ridicule. Engineering experts said the idea was impossible and impractical, yet Eads continued with the designs. A bridge of this size had never been built, and he faced opposition for his plan to use an unproven material known as "steel" as the major structural component. Political opponents also passed a bill to set a minimum span requirement of five hundred feet on the project so as not to interrupt riverboat traffic, which they believed doomed the project. But Eads beat them at their own game by making spans measuring 502, 520, and 502 feet over the river.

The incredible structure was completed more quickly than anyone imagined, while proving to be stronger than predicted. A huge celebration was held on the opening of the bridge, but it didn't translate into business success for Eads. Railroad companies faced pressure from politicians and other businesses, so they decided to boycott the structure and continue using ferryboats. He was forced into bankruptcy four years after the Eads Bridge opened.

Eads also brought about some damning criticism for his tenacious methods and competitiveness. He is blamed for the loss of many lives in the bridge-building industry because he had found a way to overcome Caisson's Disease, or the "Bends," by slowly lowering workers into the water depths by using a slow-moving elevator car. He failed to publish his information, which experts say could have saved dozens of lives in the Brooklyn Bridge project alone.

Despite widespread contempt for his ideas in America, he became a popular engineer in many other parts of the world. He died at the age of sixty-six on March 8, 1887, in the Bahamas.

EXTRA, EXTRA!

Eads is the first U.S. citizen awarded the Albert Medal of the Royal Society of Arts.

Andrew Carnegie's companies provided some of the steel for the Eads Bridge project.

The Eads Bridge officially opened on July 4, 1874.

His famous family included his mother's cousin, and Eads' namesake, President James Buchanan.

CHARLES EAMES

ARCHITECT, DESIGNER

"The Best Design of the 20th Century"
—Time Magazine *on Eames's Plywood Chair*

World-famous architect Charles Eames made his claim to fame with inexpensive but elegant furniture. In the 1940s and 1950s, he practically redesigned America when it came to home furnishings, toys, movie sets, and houses. Long before the days of decorating shows on cable television, Charles, along with his wife, Ray, were the true superstars of interior design.

THE EARLY YEARS

Charles Ormand Eames was born in St. Louis on June 7, 1907. His early working years built the foundation for his later success. In his early teens, he worked at Laclede Steel Company, which fueled his interest in design and engineering. He enrolled at Washington University for undergraduate studies but dropped out because of frustration with the lack of imagination being taught by the professors. So in 1929, he packed his suitcase to study in Europe, which at the time was known as the cradle of the modern movement in design.

RISE TO FAME

He returned to St. Louis from Europe around 1930 and established the firm of Gray and Eames, but times were getting tough and there was little money in the architectural field in the early days of the Depression. Tough times forced Eames to expand his designs to include household items like furniture and ceramics. The hard times also forced him to expand his horizons, so in 1936 he took a job at the prestigious design program at the Cranbrook Academy in Michigan, where he developed the basis for many of his future designs.

After four years at the Department of Experimental Design, Charles moved to California with his new wife, Ray Kaiser. They worked on a wide range of designs, even branching out to build movie sets. The couple received critical acclaim for their unique designs while becoming a major force in the film industry.

SHOW ME SUCCESS

The next step on the road to fame was an architectural competition. The Eameses entered the Case House Study Program, which was a competition among architects to create inexpensive housing with standard materials from a catalog. Twenty-two of the Eames's thirty-six projects were ultimately built, including Case House Number 8, which was a magnificent home overlooking the ocean in Pacific Palisades, California, which is the design that many say is still his claim to fame.

In addition to his homes, the Eames design firm gained worldwide acclaim for their mass-produced but elegant furniture. They are best known for the Eames chair, constructed of two pieces of molded plywood joined by stainless steel tubing. The furniture-manufacturing firm, Herman Miller, mass produced their molded plywood furniture.

Eames died in 1978, and many of his designs are still being produced and sold today, including his world-famous chair. His products saw an increase in popularity in the early 2000s as baby boomers bought them in bulk, harkening back to the 1950s. Charles Eames did not have a formal architectural degree, but his work continues to have a profound effect on designs around the world.

EXTRA, EXTRA!

Eames forged a close relationship with another famous architect and fellow faculty member in Michigan, Eero Saarinen, the man who designed the Gateway Arch in St. Louis.

Eames's form-fitting shell chair design collaboration with Eero Saarinen, won first place in the Organic Design Competition at the Museum of Modern Art in New York City.

He was elected to the Academy and Institute of Arts and Letters in 1977.

MARY ENGELBREIT

ARTIST, ENTREPRENEUR

"A Vast Empire of Cuteness."
—Wall Street Journal

Mary Engelbreit is first and foremost an artist, but the industry she created around her artwork truly makes her a legend of the business world. She continues to receive high accolades, being called a contemporary Norman Rockwell by *People Magazine.* Her "vast empire of cuteness," as dubbed by the *Wall Street Journal,* began at an early age and has continued to this day as she churns out an amazing number of original works on a yearly basis. In the early 2000s, the "cute empire" had sales of around $100 million a year.

THE EARLY YEARS

Mary Engelbreit was born on June 5, 1952, and grew up in St. Louis. Her artistic abilities began early, where by the age of eleven she was already producing works of art. Her high school guidance counselor at Visitation Academy encouraged her to go college to become a teacher, but Mary had already decided what she wanted to do for the rest of her life. She ignored the advice and skipped both college and design school to begin working immediately on a career in the arts.

RISE TO FAME

After completing school, Engelbreit worked at an art supply store in St. Louis. She also held down jobs at an advertising agency, working as a freelance artist for clients around her hometown, and even as an editorial cartoonist for the *St. Louis Post-Dispatch.*

Mary's desire was to draw illustrations that came from her own memories and imagination. Her big break came on a trip to New York in 1977 when a publisher suggested drawing art for greeting cards. At first, she was crushed by the advice, but she soon realized the idea had some merit. After a few years of working for other greeting card makers, she got frustrated by the bureaucratic ways of large companies that were slow to act and lacked imaginations. So in 1983, she began designing and producing her own cards. By 1985, she was ready for bigger and better things and signed a license with Sunrise Greetings, a major greeting card publisher and distributor. That risky decision was the best business move she ever made and paved the way for worldwide popularity and incredible sales.

Show Me Success

Engelbreit's greeting card line was growing fast, but so was the interest in expanding her blossoming empire. Numerous national companies came calling to use her artwork on a full range of products, including t-shirts, calendars, gift books, mugs, and practically anything they could put a print on. By the mid-1990s her empire was a multi-million-dollar company, and it was time to expand once again. She launched a national consumer magazine called *Mary Engelbreit's Home Companion.*

In 1993, she fulfilled her lifelong dream of illustrating children's books with Hans Christian Andersen's *Snow Queen.* Her dream expanded in 2001 when she signed a contract for more than twenty books starting with her *The Night Before Christmas.* This illustration of Clement C. Moore's beloved poem commanded a spot on the *New York Times* best-seller list for eleven weeks. Soon after, her first animated video based on the book hit the shelves. She went on to illustrate other classic titles, including a collection of Mother Goose rhymes that also became a *New York Times* best-seller as well as a series of original children's books based on her alter ego, Ann Estelle.

The "Vast Empire of Cuteness" continued to grow and included hundreds of books, a national magazine with readership in the millions, a retail and online store, and nearly seven thousand licensed products. Even though the business is worldwide, she still imagines every concept in her head and draws every original illustration with her own hand. In 2005, Mary hit the prestigious honor of $1 billion in lifetime retail sales.

Extra, Extra!

Mary's first studio was a closet in her childhood home.
She sold her first three card designs for $150.
She was eight months pregnant when she decided to start up her own company.

JAMES FERGASON

INVENTOR

His name may not be recognizable to most people, but practically every American looks at his inventions every single day. His Liquid Crystal Displays, or LCDs, are the lights we see in digital alarm clocks, medical imaging devices, computer displays, and many other consumer electronics.

THE EARLY YEARS

James Fergason was born on a farm about four miles from the small town of Wakenda in 1934, near the Missouri River in north-central Missouri. He attended classes in a one-room schoolhouse with other students ranging from first through eighth grade, where he stayed until the seventh grade when his family moved to Carrollton. The "big city" of Carrollton allowed him more opportunities in a school where he graduated in 1952 with 1,957 other students.

His teenage home was only a short drive from the University of Missouri, where he enrolled in 1952 to study physics. He graduated from Mizzou four years later, accepting a commission as second lieutenant in the U.S. Army. The following Sunday, he took another big step and got married.

RISE TO FAME

His first stop after the army was the Westinghouse Research Laboratories in Pennsylvania. At Westinghouse, he perfected his understanding of liquid crystals, which were still relatively new and practically unknown by most Americans. Once he realized the vast uses of this new technology, his interest grew. It was then he made the move to Kent State University, where he joined the Liquid Crystal Institute in the 1960s.

He took over as the associate director of the program where he uncovered the scientific basis that would be the springboard for all modern LCDs. Prior to his discovery, Liquid Crystal Displays were not practical because they used a significant amount of power for hand-held displays, had a short life span, and were hard to see (somewhat like looking at soap on a mirror). But his discovery of the "twisted nematic field effect" changed the way we view technology.

SHOW ME FAME

The LCD was the tool that put Fergason on the inventor's map, but it was only a springboard for more of his vast discoveries. His LCD technology was the basis for a billion-dollar industry, which has been growing with leaps and bounds since the early 1970s.

He founded the International Crystal Company, which provided the scientific basis for digital watch technology through the efforts of the Bulova Watch Company. After proving to be an effective medium for displays in watches and clocks, LCDs were then more widely used in calculators and computer display screens.

His inventions and fame continued to grow in the 1980s and 1990s. As president of Optical Shields Limited, he took a large number of products to market with the use of his LCD technology. In 2001, Dr. James Fergason founded Fergason Patent Properties to develop more patents, and he continues his efforts to this day, looking for new ways to make life easier for all of us.

EXTRA, EXTRA!

*Fergason was inducted into the National Inventor's Hall of Fame in 1998.

*Fergason has been honored by the Intellectual Property Owners Association, Smithsonian Institute, National Inventors Hall of Fame, and the U.S. Department of Commerce.

*He served on the civilian advisory panel for the U.S. Patent and Trademark Office.

*The University of Missouri honored him as a Distinguished Alumni and awarded him the honorary degree of doctor of science in 2001.

Linda Godwin

Astronaut

Linda Godwin grew up in the Bootheel, but she saw the world from a different view: outer space! She rose through the ranks of NASA quickly to become one of our country's greatest astronauts.

The Early Years

Linda Godwin was born on July 2, 1952, in Cape Girardeau and grew up in nearby Jackson where she graduated from Jackson High School in 1970. She stayed close to home through her college years, attending Southeast Missouri State University. She graduated in 1974 with a degree in mathematics and physics. Her next stop was the University of Missouri–Columbia, where she attained a master's degree and a doctorate in physics.

While studying at Mizzou, she took on the additional responsibilities of teaching physics to undergraduate students and taking part in research projects. She conducted research in low-temperature solid-state physics, which included studies in electron tunneling and vibrational modes of absorbed molecular species on metallic substrates at liquid helium temperatures. It took a brilliant mind to understand and master the principles of complex physics. Her research was published, which established her as a force to be reckoned with in the field of science, mathematics, and physics before she was even out of her twenties.

Rise to Fame

Dr. Godwin completed her doctorate at the University of Missouri in 1980 at the age of twenty-eight. That same year she joined NASA in the Payload Operations Division. Her climb within the space agency was steady and impressive. A mere five years after joining the space operations, she was selected as an astronaut candidate. One year later, she graduated to the official title of "Astronaut." She worked in a number of capacities on the ground for NASA before getting called to space in 1991 on the *Space Shuttle Atlantis.*

SHOW ME SUCCESS

Godwin's first role on a space shuttle flight was as a mission specialist. As a mission specialist, she conducted experiments in orbit and worked on the International Space Station. She took part in four space flights, including Space Shuttle Mission No. 76 in 1996, where she took part in a docking mission with the Mir Space Station.

Her space flight in 2001 marked a milestone for space flight, as the crew of Mission No. 108 took part in the twelfth shuttle visit to the International Space Station. In this flight, the crew circled the earth 185 times, traveling 4.8 million miles in just a matter of days.

Dr. Godwin's incredible performance with the space agency has earned her a number of prestigious honors, including the NASA Outstanding Performance Rating, the Sustained Superior Performance Award, and the Outstanding Leadership Award. These are big honors for a small town girl from the Bootheel.

EXTRA, EXTRA!

The Linda Godwin Center for Science and Mathematics at Southeast Missouri State University is named in her honor.

Godwin has spent over thirty-eight days in space, including over ten hours outside the shuttle on a pair of space walks.

Dr. Godwin married fellow astronaut Steve Nagel.

Charles Leiper Grigg

Soft Drink Inventor

"It's An Up Thing"
—*Ad Campaign for 7-Up*

C. L. Grigg was born in a small town that rarely shows up on most state maps. However, his impact still resonates in the food and beverage industry to this day. He invented a number of soft drinks including Whistle and the world-famous 7-Up. Despite the popularity of the drink, Grigg failed to leave behind one very important part of his legacy: the reason for the 7-Up name!

The Early Years

Charles Leiper Grigg was born in 1868 in Price's Branch, which is near Montgomery City. Not much is known about his early years, before Grigg moved to St. Louis to work in advertising and sales for soft drink companies.

Rise to Fame

A short time after Grigg arrived in St. Louis, he landed a job in the soft drink industry. The beverage industry just happened to be an up-and-coming business in St. Louis at the time, and he was in the right place at the right time to take advantage of the shifting marketplace. He first worked for a manufacturing company owned by Vess Jones where Grigg invented an orange-flavored soft drink called "Whistle."

A few years after joining the company, Grigg had conflicts with management, so he left Vess. That split meant he had to leave the rights to his orange soda invention with the company. He took a job at a new soft drink manufacturer, where his primary role was to develop new flavors for sodas. His next soft drink concoction was again an orange-flavored drink called "Howdy."

After yet another successful tenure with a major company, he again left for another business venture, but this time, he was able to take his concoction with him to start his own Howdy Company. Howdy got off to a rough start because of heavy competition from a drink called Orange Crush, which was dominating the market share of orange drinks at the time. So Grigg went back to the drawing board to look for a drink that the beverage market had yet to embrace. This time his focus was on lemon lime carbonated soft drinks.

SHOW ME SUCCESS

In October of 1929, Grigg settled on a formula that not only tasted great but also seemed to have some medicinal benefits. He spent two years testing eleven different formulas before he settled on a formula that he deemed to be the most refreshing and thirst quenching. There were a number of lemon lime drinks sold at the time, but none had developed a following. He called the caramel colored drink, Bib-Label Lithiated Lemon-Lime Soda. The name was difficult to say much less to sell to the public, so it was soon changed to 7-Up Lithiated Lemon-Lime and then again to 7-Up. The reason for the name is still a mystery because Grigg never explained why he shortened the name other than to say that it helped the soda sell better.

The "Un-cola" took a while to catch on, possibly because it debuted a few weeks before the stock market crash of 1929. Grigg was convinced that the public would eventually buy into the product, so he took the unusual step of claiming that the Lithia ingredient in the soda could affect your moods (Lithia is better known as lithium). During the Great Depression, he figured a large number of people would likely need a "pick me up," and the marketing of the drink turned out to be a huge success. By the 1940s, 7-Up was the third best selling soft drink in the world. During this incredible growth, the Howdy Corporation name was eventually changed to the 7-Up Company. Charles Grigg died in 1940, and his son took command of the company.

EXTRA, EXTRA!

*Grigg never told the reason why he named the drink 7-Up. Here are widely circulated theories.

*7-Up was the product of seven ingredients.

*Beverages of the day were often sold in seven-ounce bottles.

*The drink possibly cured mankind's "seven hangovers."

*Grigg won a great deal of money in a craps game thanks to all the sevens that were rolled that night.

George and Phoebe Apperson Hearst

American Industrialists, Tycoons

"Surplus wealth is a sacred trust which its possessor is bound to administer in his lifetime for the good of the community."
—Andrew Carnegie

George and Phoebe Apperson Hearst became famously wealthy from business interests from coast to coast. They made their fame in California, but both had their roots right here on Missouri soil. Their namesake continues today, thanks in part to the fame of their newspaper son, William Randolph Hearst.

The Early Years

George Hearst was born on September 3, 1820, and raised in Franklin County in mid-Missouri. He was said to be illiterate but still managed to graduate from the Franklin County Mining School at the age of eighteen. His poor scholastic work was overshadowed by his ability to read the land and find treasures buried beneath it. After he graduated from school, he worked in numerous mines across the state and even owned a general store in Judith Springs.

Phebe (later changed to Phoebe) Apperson was born on December 3, 1842, near the town of St. Clair. The small town girl attended schools in St. Clair, Steelville, and St. James. Legend has it that when she was just a small girl, George Hearst—a man twenty-two years her senior—moved next door to the family. He left for the California gold rush a short time later, while she became a teacher at a school near the present-day Meramec State Park.

Rise to Fame

Hearst struck it rich as a gold prospector and returned to Missouri a very wealthy man. He moved back to Missouri primarily to take care of his dying mother. But when he moved, the now forty-two-year-old man reunited with the young girl, Phebe, who was now around twenty years old. The two fell in love and were married in 1862. Their first and only child, William Randolph Hearst, was born ten months later.

The couple moved to San Francisco while Phoebe was pregnant, primarily so that George could expand his business interests. He began making money at a rapid pace in the Golden State and made them one of the most affluent couples of the era. Their wealth allowed Phoebe to take their son on lavish trips to Europe, where young William developed the ideas for his famous Hearst Castle.

SHOW ME SUCCESS

George Hearst, ever a mover and shaker, was never one to rest on his laurels or on his enormous amount of money. The next step for him was to turn his success in gold prospecting into success in other business ventures and in politics. He took a giant step forward when a fellow business associate defaulted on a loan to Hearst, which gave the family control of the *San Francisco Examiner.* This paved the way for his son to eventually dominate the publishing industry. With wealth already assured, George turned his attention to politics, as he won a position on the California State Assembly in 1865, but he lost a bid to become governor in 1882. He eventually gained a seat in the U.S. Senate in 1887 and served in that capacity until he died four years later.

Phoebe filled the role as wealthy wife quite well. While in California, she gave large amounts of money to a number of education and arts charities. When her husband was appointed to the Senate, she continued her philanthropic works in Washington, D.C. She was still only forty-nine years old when George died, and she inherited a fortune estimated at $17 million, which would be worth about $750 million today. She spent the remainder of her life helping out causes near to her heart and helped her son become one of the largest publishers in U.S. history. She died in 1919, being called one of California's greatest women in history.

EXTRA, EXTRA!

*Phoebe signed a prenuptial contract when the couple married in 1862.

*The Hearsts were major contributors to the restoration of George Washington's home in Mount Vernon.

*Phoebe was the first woman regent of the University of California.

*George was appointed to the U.S. Senate after the death of John F. Miller.

JOHN W. BROWN

Ewing Marion Kauffman

Entrepreneur, K.C. Royals Owner

"He was not interested in being part of the business or social elite. In fact, he enjoyed playing the role of the outsider."
—Dr. Anne Hodges Morgan

Ewing Marion Kauffman was born to a poor family in a small town, but he died as one of the wealthiest Missourians of all time. His business ethics and values made him a millionaire while making scores of other people wealthy beyond their dreams. He built his business on the principles of "The Golden Rule," while always giving back to others. He earned plenty of money and fame during his lifetime, but it was what he gave back that truly made his life remarkable.

The Early Years

Ewing Marion Kauffman was born on a farm near the small town of Garden City on September 21, 1916. His family spent only a few years in the town before moving to Kansas City when he was still just a boy. His childhood was difficult, as he was bedridden at age eleven due to a heart problem, but he spent his time productively, reading practically every book he could get his hands on. He once estimated that he read up to forty books a month to pass the time.

When Ewing was seventeen, he graduated from Westport High School, but the mid-1930s were a tough time to be entering the workforce. Jobs were scarce, so his family allowed him and a friend to hitchhike to Colorado before starting a career. He took odd jobs along the way to pay for expenses, while also saving money for college. When he returned home, he headed to Kansas City Junior College to get an associate's degree in business.

Kauffman enlisted in the U.S. Navy during World War II soon after graduation. When his time was up in the armed services, he took a job as a salesman with a pharmaceutical company but quit when his territory was reduced. The company cut his sales territory because Kauffman was so successful that he was making more money than the president of the company. He decided not to look for another job. Instead, he made his own mark on the pharmaceutical industry by starting his own company and doing things his way.

Rise to Fame

In 1950, Kauffman started a small pharmaceutical business in the basement of his home in Kansas City. Marion Laboratories, named after his middle name, grew in part to his integrity and the quality of people he surrounded himself with. Like most small businesses, profits were small in the beginning. His first year was tough, with only thirty-six thousand dollars in sales and profits of only about one thousand dollars. He still needed at least one big-name drug to put him on the medical landscape, and Os-Cal was just the drug to do that.

Show Me Success

Os-Cal, or oyster shell calcium, was the breakout drug that Kauffman used to keep his company growing. Numerous other successful drugs and innovative marketing approaches followed, which made his drug company one of the most successful in America. His five thousand–dollar initial investment into the company was churning out $1 billion in sales by the late 1980s. Marion Labs merged with Merrell Dow in 1989, which was then bought out by Marion Roussel Hoechst for $7.1 billion in 1995.

The incredible wealth Kauffman had attained allowed him to pursue other passions, namely owning a major league baseball franchise. He established the Kansas City Royals in 1968 and used his successful business model to build a winning team. The Royals won six division titles under his leadership, two American League pennants, and the World Series Championship in 1985.

Kauffman died in 1993, but the efforts of his Kauffman Foundation continue making an impact. He established the foundation with the same sense of opportunity he brought to his business endeavors and with the same convictions. Kauffman wanted his foundation to be innovative, where they could get to the root of issues in order to fundamentally change people's lives. Today, his legacy continues as the Ewing Marion Kauffman Foundation of Kansas City, which works with partners to advance entrepreneurship in America and improve the education of children and youth.

Extra, Extra!

*Kauffman Stadium in Kansas City is named in his honor.
*Kauffman was honored as the sixteenth point of light in President George Bush's "Thousand Points of Light" tribute.
*Kauffman was named the 1973 Man of the Year by the Kansas City Press Club.
*Kauffman is a member of the Missouri Sports Hall of Fame.
*Kauffman was named the Kansas Citian of the Year by the Kansas City Chamber of Commerce in 1986.

ALBERT BOND LAMBERT

INDUSTRIALIST AND AVIATION PIONEER

Albert Lambert's name will forever be synonymous with Lambert Field in St. Louis, but before he became an aviation visionary, he was primarily known for his fight against bad breath! That's right. Lambert built his fortune on a product called Listerine, which was being sold by his father's pharmaceutical company. He used his business success to make Missouri a worldwide hub for aviation. His influence and vision changed the landscape of St. Louis and the future of flight forever.

THE EARLY YEARS

Albert Bond Lambert was born in St. Louis on December 6, 1874, into a wealthy family. His father was the owner of a Lambert Pharmaceutical Company, which provided the financial means for the young man to attend the prestigious Smith Academy near Washington University. Albert moved to Virginia to attend college where he was a standout athlete on the varsity football team, but his time "out east" was brief, as he returned home to run his father's company before he attained his degree.

RISE TO FAME

Lambert assumed the role of president of the pharmaceutical company, which was already successful under his father's leadership. Albert, however, had his sights set on overseas markets. He expanded the company with factories in France and Germany. His company sold the popular mouthwash Listerine, which used an effective marketing campaign to become one of the most successful American products of all time. The advertising campaign generated a renewed interest in fresh breath and displayed how halitosis could wreck your social standing. It struck a chord with the public, making him and his company extremely wealthy. He stepped down as president a few years later to devote his attention to his real passion: aviation.

Lambert had long been interested in aviation, first with hot air balloons, then later with airplanes. He and some acquaintances established the St. Louis Aero Club in 1907 and built the first airfield in the city of St. Louis. After the end of World War I, he continued his interest in aeronautics by erecting yet another airfield (this one northeast of the city that would later become Lambert Field) and organizing the first National Balloon Race. His success in constructing the airfield led to a business relationship with a young pilot who would put St. Louis on the international aviation map.

Show Me Success

At his airfield, Lambert met a pilot named Charles Lindbergh, who spent time flying out of St. Louis. The two talked about Lindbergh's dream of flying across the Atlantic Ocean and the obstacles he faced. Lindbergh convinced Lambert that he could make the flight, but he needed financial backers to make the trip a reality. Lambert stepped up and put down the first pledge, which brought plenty of publicity for the attempted nonstop flight. The organization backing his flight became known as the Spirit of St. Louis Organization, which also was the basis for the name of Lindbergh's airplane. The buzz surrounding the success of the trip helped pave the way for the expansion of Lambert Field into one of the premier airports in the world.

After the hoopla of international flight, Lambert spent his remaining years living in his mansion across from Forest Park, playing golf, and bankrolling civic projects. Shortly before he passed away in 1946 at the age of seventy-two, he designed more plans for the expansion of Lambert Field. His legacy continues to live on today through his many projects and his namesake airport, embodied in the true Spirit of St. Louis.

Extra, Extra!

He served on the City Council and the St. Louis Police Board.

His interest in attaining a pilot's license was stimulated after taking a flight with Orville Wright.

Lambert was the first person in the city of St. Louis to have a pilot's license.

JOHNNY MORRIS

OUTDOOR SPORTS ICON

"In our family, there was no clear line between religion and fly fishing."
—A River Runs Through It

When most people think of hunting and fishing supplies, there is one name that usually comes to mind: Bass Pro Shops. The man behind that name is Missourian Johnny Morris. He took his love of the great outdoors and turned it into a multi-million-dollar company, which enables people all over the world to enjoy their leisure time more than ever.

THE EARLY YEARS

Johnny Morris was born and raised in the Ozarks, where he also built his fame and fortune. His father was a Springfield business owner, so his son was exposed to running a small business at an early age. That exposure included everything from stocking the shelves, greeting shoppers, and offering good products at fair prices.

After he graduated from Glendale High School, Morris enrolled in Drury College to study business. The business he was interested in was the business of being outdoors. Drury's location in the heart of the Ozarks, and his early business dealings, helped him understand the needs of outdoor lovers when it came to hunting and fishing products. This passion may have seemed like a good hobby to most people, but his knowledge of nature and his good business sense were enough for him to turn his passion into a career.

RISE TO FAME

Morris's career in merchandising started from the back of his father's Brown Derby liquor stores. He was an avid outdoorsman, but he was frustrated that he could not find the equipment he needed for fishing tournaments. He realized that other people were also having the same problem, so he got permission from his father to put up an eight-by-eight-foot display of fishing products inside his father's store. This small business turned out to be a good money-making opportunity, while also serving as a primary stimulus for the Ozarks to become a tourist destination.

Show Me Success

By the early 1970s, Morris was stocking enough supplies to publish a sales catalog. It featured fifteen hundred items and was mailed to people in twenty states. Conservationists, hunters, and fishermen were hooked on his gear, so an expansion was the only way to keep up with the growing demand. Stores popped up across the Midwest, with the granddaddy of them all on the drawing board in southwest Springfield.

The Outdoor World National Headquarters Showroom opened in 1981, which made it one of the largest retail stores in the world. It included a four-story waterfall, live animals, acres of outdoor items, and an upscale restaurant. Word spread quickly about the amazing store, and it soon attracted more than 4 million visitors a year. Additional stores opened around the country, and the catalog expanded to more than thirty thousand items that was sent to a mailing list of 34 million homes around the world.

Morris's business expanded after the success of the Outdoor World shops. He added the luxurious resort, Big Cedar Lodge on Table Rock Lake, Tracker Marine, Top of the Rock Golf Course, and Dogwood Canyon Nature Park. He was also instrumental in building the Wonders of Wildlife Museum in Springfield, right next door to his retail complex. With his success, Morris remained committed to conservation efforts and civic support. His admiration of nature and a love for fishing certainly worked well, which made him Missouri's contemporary natural pioneer.

Extra, Extra!

Morris has received numerous awards, including the Teddy Roosevelt Conservationist Award, bestowed upon him by President George Bush.

Bass Pro Shops Outdoor World in Springfield is Missouri's largest tourist attraction.

THE O'REILLY FAMILY

AUTO PARTS SALES

"Professional Parts People"
—*O'Reilly Advertising Campaign*

The name O'Reilly is seen in front of thousands of auto parts stores across the country and on the hoods of NASCAR and other racing vehicles, but the nationwide fame started in Missouri, where the family continues to call home.

THE EARLY YEARS

The patriarch of the O'Reilly family moved to Missouri in the mid-1800s from Ireland. Michael Byrne O'Reilly settled in St. Louis where he earned a law degree and took a job as title examiner. His son, Charlie Francis O'Reilly, was born and raised in St. Louis and was the driving force behind the auto parts legacy that succeeded him.

RISE TO FAME

Charles Francis "C. F." O'Reilly took a job at an auto supply company in St. Louis where he sold parts throughout the Midwest. One of the cities in his territory was Springfield, Missouri. He realized the area was poised for growth, so he asked the company to transfer him. He eventually became the manager of Link Motor Supply in Springfield where his son, Charles H. "Chub" O'Reilly, also worked. The two helped grow the company into one of the largest auto supply stores in the area in the 1930s.

During company reorganization, the owner of Link Motor pushed the elder O'Reilly toward retirement and tried to transfer his son to Kansas City, but the two balked at the plan. The O'Reillys weren't ready to quit the business, or move, so they decided to start their own store. O'Reilly Automotive, Incorporated, was born and opened to the public in November of 1957.

SHOW ME SUCCESS

O'Reilly Automotive started small, with only one store and twelve employees. Sales and revenues were strong from the start, and expansion followed shortly thereafter. After C. F. passed away, Chub O'Reilly took the reins and forged ahead to grow the company.

As with many family businesses, the children expanded the corporation beyond what their parents ever imagined. This happened not only when Chub took over from his father, but also when Chub's children succeed him. Chub literally raised his children in the business, so they had a good understanding of the company's core business beliefs when it was time for them to take over. His children, Charles H. "Charlie," Larry, Rosalie, and David, were already groomed for business success, which was rapidly happening around them as they grew up.

Just four years after the company was founded, sales reached more than a $1 million. Fourteen years later, that number rose to more than $7 million in sales revenue, with stores in many cities in southwest Missouri. The 1990s and early 2000s were a time of rapid expansion and explosive growth for the company. Not only did the company land a spot on the stock market, but they also began gobbling up smaller stores in the process. O'Reilly merged with Hi/LO Auto Supply, which added nearly two hundred stores. They then expanded again when they bought Mid-State Automotive Distributors.

By the early 2000s, there were around fourteen hundred O'Reilly Auto Parts Stores in twenty-five states with sales approaching $2 billion. Despite the company's nationwide success, the family continues to call the Springfield area home. Chub's four children are still active in the corporation with David O'Reilly the Chairman of the Board. Charlie O'Reilly, Rosalie O'Reilly Wooten, and Larry O'Reilly are retired, but they still retain a spot on the board of directors.

EXTRA, EXTRA!

O'Reilly made their influence felt sponsoring numerous high-profile races, including:

The O'Reilly 300 NASCAR Busch Series.

The O'Reilly NHRA Thunder Valley Nationals.

The O'Reilly 250 NASCAR Craftsman Truck Race.

JOHN W. BROWN

ARTS AND ENTERTAINMENT

ROBERT ALTMAN

FILM DIRECTOR

"Filmmaking is a chance to live many lifetimes."
—Robert Altman

If you have watched television in the past five decades, you have probably been influenced by the work of Kansas Citian Robert Altman. From big budget movies, to TV shows that are a part of television history like M*A*S*H, Altman is truly a legendary Missourian and an American icon.

THE EARLY YEARS

Robert Bernard Altman was born on February 20, 1925, in Kansas City. He was the first-born child of a well-to-do family, who allowed Robert to attend private schools for most of his life. He bounced around various Catholic schools before landing at the prestigious Rockhurst High School. He also spent time at Southwest High School and Wentworth Military Academy in Lexington, where he remained through his first few years of college. After finishing his studies at Wentworth, Altman shipped off to become a B-24 pilot in the Air Force.

RISE TO FAME

Even at the age of twenty, Altman was writing stories and screenplays. His military service put his pursuit of a career in film on hold for a few years, but he was soon back in Kansas City working for the Calvin Film Company around 1950. The company was started by his grandfather, which provided Robert a training ground for which to develop his skills.

He left for California but then returned to Calvin Films numerous times throughout his life. While working in Kansas City, Altman directed a number of films for local companies and a few feature films as well. His first feature was *The Delinquents*, followed later the same year by *The James Dean Story*.

His next step in California was a big one when he was chosen by Alfred Hitchcock to direct a few episodes of *Alfred Hitchcock Presents*. That opportunity opened more doors for the young director, including TV series like *The Millionaire*,

Combat!, and *Bonanza*. He also started his own production firm in 1963. Altman was proving that he had a big career ahead of him.

Show Me Success

In 1969, Hollywood writers were circulating a movie script about a Korean War medical unit. More than a dozen directors had rejected the story, but the dark humor of the script interested Altman. He decided to take the project and turned the movie (which became known as *M*A*S*H*) into a huge box office success. The film won awards at the Cannes Film Festival, was nominated for five Academy Awards, and even won an Oscar. The film also spun off the hit TV show by the same name and was recognized as one of the one hundred greatest American films by the American Film Institute.

He followed the success of *M*A*S*H* with *Brewster McCloud* and a Western called *McCabe and Mrs. Miller*. Actors bought into his philosophy of directing, which earned him the reputation as an "actor's director." That reputation allowed him to assemble a large ensemble cast for his next commercially successful film, *Nashville*, in 1975. *Nashville* won two Oscars and was nominated for three others, including Best Director and Best Picture.

Altman produced nearly a dozen more movies for the big and small screens in the 1980s, but his legacy was again cemented in 1992, when he reached what some say is the pinnacle of his directing career. *The Player* took a critical look at Hollywood and the hypocrisy of the movie industry. It was a box office success and a big hit with the Academy of Motion Picture Arts and Sciences. The movie was nominated for three Oscars, including yet another nod for Best Director.

During his more than five decades directing films, he has remained a maverick by doing things his own way. He went against the methods that directors had been using for years, while refining the way films are made and the way they are watched. Many of the techniques he perfected early in his career were seen as revolutionary but are now standard practice in many areas of filmmaking. His revolutionary approach to the genre not only makes Altman one of the most successful directors in American history, but also a true pioneer in America's most popular form of entertainment. Altman died in 2007 from leukemia, with an amazing thirty-eight feature films under his direction.

Extra, Extra!

During World War II, Altman came up with the idea of dog tattooing, and even tattooed President Truman's pet.

The 1993 movie Short Cuts *earned Altman his third Oscar nomination for Best Director.*

M*A*S*H and Nashville *were selected for historic preservation by the United States National Film Registry.*

SCOTT BAKULA

ACTOR

"Leaping about in time, I've found that there are some things in life that I can't change, and there are some things that I can. To save a life, to change a heart, to make the right choice. I guess that's what life's about."

—Sam in Quantum Leap

Scott Bakula is best known as the star of TV shows *Quantum Leap* and *Star Trek: Enterprise*, but he also has an impressive amount of work in many other areas of performing arts. He has worked on stage, on TV, in movies, and even sang on several albums and with the St. Louis Symphony. However, he will forever be remembered as Dr. Sam Beckett and Captain Jonathan Archer and his adventures in time in science fiction classics.

THE EARLY YEARS

Scott Bakula was born in St. Louis on October 9, 1954, and grew up in the suburb of Kirkwood. His early plans had him following in his father's footsteps to become a lawyer, but the lure of the stage kept pulling him in a different direction.

He grew up in a musical family, where he sang and played musical instruments throughout his school years and performed in community theaters across the St. Louis area. His first big break came before heading off to college when he sang on stage in front of thousands of people with the St. Louis Symphony.

Bakula graduated from Kirkwood High School in 1973 then headed off to the University of Kansas to study law. He changed to major in theater but stayed at KU just a short time before he tried his luck as a full-time actor.

RISE TO FAME

Scott moved to New York in the mid-1970s, where he took stage-acting jobs to pay the bills. He was gaining valuable experience while impressing fellow actors and directors as a great actor and a great person. In 1983, he made his name on

Broadway as Joe DiMaggio in *Marilyn, An American Fable*. As his reputation grew, Bakula appeared in plays across the country.

He appeared in the Off-Broadway production of *Three Guys Naked from the Waist Down* and in *Nite Club Confidential*. He once again returned to Broadway in *Romance/Romance*, where he won critical acclaim and solidified his reputation as one of the best actors in the industry.

Show Me Success

Bakula appeared regularly on TV around 1986 in shows like *I-Man, Matlock, My Sister Sam*, and *Designing Women*. But his true "big break" came when he landed the lead role on the new show *Quantum Leap* in 1989. The science fiction drama put him in front of millions of viewers each week, on the cover of magazines, and on the stage again, only this time accepting awards for his acting.

Quantum Leap lasted five years and earned him four Golden Globe nominations for Best Actor in a Drama Series, including a win in 1992. He also received four Emmy nominations for his work as Dr. Samuel Beckett. His Missouri roots also shined through with five consecutive honors for excellence by the Viewers for Quality Television organization.

When the series ended, Bakula continued working both in front of the camera and behind as a producer. Over the next decade, he starred in some of the biggest shows on television and in the theaters, which included the award-winning *American Beauty* in 1999. He forever endeared himself to his sci-fi fans when he landed a role as Captain Jonathan Archer with *Star Trek: Enterprise* in 2001. The show again became a hit for Bakula. When the series ended in 2005, Bakula took on starring roles in *The New Adventures of Old Christine, American Body Shop*, and *Blue Smoke*, which continues to make him one of the most bankable stars in Tinseltown.

Extra, Extra!

His feature film debut was in Sibling Rivalry *in 1991, co-starring with Kristie Alley.*

Bakula was nominated for Favorite Male Performer in a New Television Series in People's Choice Awards in 2001.

He received a Tony nomination in 1988 for his starring role in the Broadway musical Romance/Romance.

Jesse Barnes

Artist

"If people say my paintings bring them closer to their roots, then that's fine with me."
—*Jesse Barnes*

The paintings of Jesse Barnes are some of the most popular and valuable works of art being produced today. His paintings garner a significant amount of world-wide recognition. He was even given a prestigious honor of being commissioned to produce a painting to benefit the 2002 Olympics in Salt Lake City. Even with worldwide fame, he continues to make his home and produce his artwork in the Ozark hills, right where it all started.

The Early Years

Jesse Barnes was born in Jefferson City in 1936 and moved to Springfield when he was two years old. He attended school in Springfield but dropped out before graduation to help support his family. Jesse's artistic ability developed early, and people gained interest in his artwork before he was even a teenager. His first original oil painting was bought by his elementary school principal when he only ten years old.

Rise to Fame

Jesse refined his craft through his early years as he grew up through "self-taught" trial and error. Hallmark commissioned prints during this time as he worked with the craft guild. Through the guild, he displayed his works at malls throughout the Midwest and at Silver Dollar City. His paintings of country settings made him one of the most popular artists in the Branson amusement park, as visitors repeatedly asked where they could find the "light" painter.

Show Me Success

Word about Barnes's unique style spread, and "The Light Painter" was soon a famous name among art circles. His first Limited Edition Print, *Night Before Christmas*, was released in 1983 and proved to be a major success. The print was originally offered for seventy-five dollars but is now sold in art stores for thousands of dollars, if you can find one. He developed a cult-like following, with fans standing in line for hours to buy the prints on the day they are released.

Since the famous style debuted in 1983, Barnes has released over seventy-five Limited Edition Prints and has been named to the USArt Hall of Fame. He has also created prints for the Bradford Exchange for Limited Edition Collector's Plates. He still lives in his hometown of Springfield and continues to paint in a small room in his basement. His work is inspired by life in the Ozarks and his travels across the country, but Jesse stays true to his roots by choosing to make Missouri his home.

Extra, Extra!

Barnes owns the copyright to the title "The Light Painter."

At least one owl is included somewhere in almost every painting he produces.

ROBERT BENNETT

COMPOSER

"Ev'rythin's up to date in Kansas City
They've gone about as fur as they c'n go!"
—Lyrics to "Kansas City"

Robert Bennett is one of the most prolific composers in Broadway history. He orchestrated the musical scores for more than three hundred Broadway shows, while arranging and conducting and learning to play practically every instrument in the orchestra. Broadway is his claim to fame, but he worked on several Hollywood film scores as well. His amazing amount of success in several genres puts him in the history books as one of the more successful composers and musicians of all time.

THE EARLY YEARS

Robert Russell Bennett was born on June 15, 1894, in Kansas City but spent a few of his early years on a farm just south of the city. The family moved to the farm when he was just a child with hopes that the fresh air would cure his polio. While in the country, he was home schooled, with music taking up a large portion of his education.

He showed an amazing aptitude in music early in life. At the age of three, he performed parts of a Beethoven sonata he heard his mother play on the piano. In fact, both of his parents were musicians, with his mother a piano teacher and his father a performer with the Kansas City Philharmonic. He was so well versed in every instrument that if any member of his father's local band was absent, the younger Bennett could step in and play. When he was in his mid-twenties, Bennett moved to New York City to see if he could make it in the Big Apple.

RISE TO FAME

Bennett began working in New York soon after he arrived, primarily side jobs as a musician and copyist. World War I set him back for a few years, but it also turned out to be a stepping-stone for him. In the army, his duties included scoring musical arrangements and conducting the army bands. It kept him away from the Broadway musical scene for a while, but it did give him experience working with large bands on a tight budget.

After the war, Bennett returned to New York with greater skill and more experience. He got married and moved to Paris on a Guggenheim Fellowship to study with famous composers. Four years later, he was back in New York, and he put his new skills to the test. He won a symphonic contest, which boosted his confidence, fattened his wallet, and drove him to succeed as a composer on Broadway.

SHOW ME SUCCESS

Over Bennett's next three decades on Broadway, he scored more then three hundred arrangements for the stage, including *Show Boat, Annie Get Your Gun, Kansas City, Oklahoma,* and *The Sound of Music.* Practically everywhere you went between 1930 and 1960, you were sure to hear his arrangements. He racked up numerous honors and even had twenty-two different shows appearing on stage at the same time.

Bennett used his success on the East Coast to open doors in Hollywood during the late 1930s. He again had the magic touch to turn ordinary films—*The Hunchback of Notre Dame* and *Swingtime*—into masterpieces.

Bennett died in 1981 and left behind one of the biggest musical pedigrees in history. He rarely had to make adjustments to his arrangements, despite the fact that he churned them out at astonishing speeds. Few people outside the inner circle of music recognize his contribution to popular culture, but he was truly a musical giant that few will ever match.

EXTRA, EXTRA!

Bennett won an Oscar in 1955 for his work on Oklahoma!

He won a Special Tony Award in 1957 for his immense body of work on Broadway.

His first "official" appearance as a conductor was at the age of eleven.

GEORGE CALEB BINGHAM

ARTIST/POLITICIAN

"In an age when the camera was not widely available, Bingham provides an interesting insight into his fellow citizens in Missouri and their way of life."
—Critique by Nicola Hodge and Libby Anson

THE EARLY YEARS

George Caleb Bingham was born on March 20, 1811, in Virginia to a prosperous family. When he was about eight years old, the family fell on hard times and lost their farm, which forced them to look for a new place to live. At that time, there was a land rush taking place in central Missouri, so the family settled on a piece of land near the Missouri River in the town of Franklin.

His mother set up a school, but floods in the Missouri River bottom forced them to pick up their belongings once again, and they moved to the other side of the river in Arrow Rock. Here, his mother reestablished the school while his father opened an inn. The inn proved to be important to Bingham's development as an artist. The nine year old was inspired by a traveling artist who lived at the inn for a period of time after he tracked down Daniel Boone for a portrait. That artist also allowed Bingham to serve as his assistant for the portrait, further stimulating George's interest in the arts.

RISE TO FAME

Bingham had no real career direction early in life, so he took some pretty diverse jobs. He worked for a while as a lawyer, then later as a minister, despite having no formal training in either. None of his career choices held his interest like painting. But in the early years, his passion for the arts didn't pay the bills.

He pursued his dream of painting by working on portraits of wealthy residents of mid-Missouri. He had a good degree of success, so he decided to try his luck in a bigger city like St. Louis. His paintings were considered good, but there wasn't enough work for him to make a decent living. Bingham decided he needed formal schooling to become a successful artist, so he headed to Philadelphia to attend art school. At school, he learned the skills he needed to paint realistic pictures of everyday life. It was this skill that would ultimately take him to the top.

SHOW ME SUCCESS

When Bingham returned from Philadelphia in the late 1840s, his passion was rekindled to make his mark in the art world. His first painting during this phase in his life turned out to be his best according to some art critics. *Fur Traders Descending the Missouri* defined his style and was the first step toward becoming a famous artist. He followed that piece with several others that finally brought him some much-needed money and a reputation as one of the greatest living artists of the day.

Bingham's style changed during the Civil War. His changing attitudes about politics also changed the focus of his artwork, and changed the course of his life as well. He became increasingly active in politics and even served as the Missouri State Treasurer for a few years. His political activity practically erased his memories as an artist during his lifetime.

He died in 1879, several years after his last popular work of art. His popularity saw a resurgence in the 1930s when his most famous work, *Fur Traders Descending the Missouri,* was purchased by the Metropolitan Museum of Art in New York. The St. Louis Art Museum also honored the Missouri native with an exhibition that placed him in the history books as one of the all-time greats from the Show Me State.

EXTRA, EXTRA!

Bingham had a studio in the basement of the U.S. Capitol for a while, where he hoped to paint famous politicians.

He went bald after a bout with sickness on a riverboat from St. Louis to Liberty. From then on, he wore a wig.

His apparent win for a Missouri House seat was overturned by Democratic lawmakers that put his opponent into office. He defeated that same lawmaker two years later to claim the seat.

VINSON COLE

OPERA SINGER

"I learned that having a beautiful voice wasn't enough so I worked very hard to cultivate all aspects of my career."
—*Vinson Cole*

Vinson Cole is a world famous tenor who has performed all over the globe. He began his singing career for churches and civic organizations around Kansas City but rose to fame in operatic performances that made the musical world buzz.

THE EARLY YEARS

Vinson Cole was born in 1950 and spent his entire childhood and early twenties in the Kansas City area. He was born to a musical family, with a mother who was a child performer on the radio in the 1930s and a grandmother who led the children's choir at the church his family attended. Since his grandmother was the musical leader of the choir, Vinson took an early interest in singing. His talent was noticed by another member of the church who took him to sing for her voice teacher, who happened to be the head of the voice department of the Kansas City Conservatory. The young boy had a great deal of talent, thus he started taking voice lessons and was encouraged to develop his vocal talents. As a boy soprano, he made his operatic debut in Menotti's *Amahl* and *The Night Visitors* at a local high school.

Cole graduated from Southeast High School and enrolled at the University of Missouri–Kansas City as a voice performance major. He knew he wanted to be an operatic singer, so he pursued it with great fervor throughout his college years. After graduating from UMKC, Cole realized that he needed further training, so he moved to Philadelphia to study at the Philadelphia Musical Academy with the famous Metropolitan Opera star Licia Albanese. After one year at PMA, he went to the famed Curtis Institute of Music to study with Margaret Harshaw, one of the most respected voice teachers of our time.

RISE TO FAME

Vinson was performing on the stage before he was a teenager and made a name for himself in opera companies in Kansas City and Philadelphia. He worked as an apprentice with the Santa Fe Opera Company while at the Curtis Institute, where he performed major roles including the lead as the tenor soloist in the *Verdi Requiem*. Success in Santa Fe led to his official operatic debut with the San Francisco Opera Company in *Mascagni's L'Amico Fritz*. This show was a critical success, and Vinson Cole became one of the operatic world's rising young stars.

SHOW ME SUCCESS

Cole was getting professional recognition outside the United States in his late twenties and thirties. He was poised for greatness, and his dream of performing in Europe came true when he auditioned for the world's most famous conductor Herbert von Karajan. Von Karajan immediately signed him up to record and sing the Italian Tenor in Strauss's *Der Rosenkavalier* at the Salzburg Festival. His collaboration with this conductor was extremely important to the progress of his career, which opened doors for him to work with many of the famous conductors of his time.

Cole has sung romantic lead roles at many of the top opera houses with some of the top orchestras in the world. Vinson is truly an international star redefining the roles he plays and the way opera fans experience a performance.

EXTRA, EXTRA!

When not traveling the world, Cole is a professor of voice at the University of Washington in Seattle.

He is on the faculty of the Aspen Music Festival and School during the summer months.

He has been honored with numerous awards including the Alumni Award from the Conservatory at UMKC, plus the Seattle Mayor's Arts Award for outstanding individual achievement and commitment to the arts.

Marlin "Jim" Davis

Actor

"The boys will take care of all business deals while we're gone, punk. Don't worry about it."
—Jock Ewing's last lines on Dallas

Jim Davis was born in one of the smallest towns in the state of Missouri but made a name for himself in one of the biggest cities in the world. As a star on the TV show *Dallas*, he portrayed Jock Ewing, a wealthy oilman and the father of one of the most notorious TV villains of all time, J. R. Ewing.

The Early Years

Marlin Davis was born on August 26, 1909, and grew up in the small town of Edgerton, which lies midway between Kansas City and St. Joseph. After high school, he stayed close to home by attending William Jewell College in Liberty. He still didn't know what he wanted to do for a living after he left the school, so he bounced around with odd jobs like a tent rigger for the circus and a salesman for an oil company. The oil job eventually took him to California, where he again changed careers. This time it was for keeps as the bright lights of Hollywood put stars in his eyes.

Rise to Fame

His tough midwestern upbringing gave him a rugged appearance and a steely persona, which were immediately noticed by talent scouts in California. He was 6'2", good looking with piercing eyes, had the looks of a cowboy, and the gravelly voice to match. This was a perfect combination of characteristics that TV executives were looking for in the 1940s, as Westerns were the top draw in theaters.

Marlin landed roles that suited his persona, especially those of a frontiersman and cowboy, but also of the tough guy and villain. He appeared in dozens of movies and commercials before landing a big role in 1952, where he played a bad guy against one of the biggest stars of the era.

SHOW ME SUCCESS

The Big Sky was released in 1952 starring Kirk Douglas. Douglas's nemesis in the movie was none other than the big guy from Missouri, Jim Davis. Davis starred as the conniving, evil, and murderous counterpart to Douglas's good guy. The movie, and Davis in particular, received critical acclaim, which solidified him as one of the best character actors of the day.

Dozens of movie roles followed, but it wasn't until 1978 when he would reach the pinnacle of his career. Davis landed the role of the family patriarch in the new drama *Dallas*. The prime time TV program turned out to be one of the biggest shows of all time, with tens of millions of people watching every week to see what happened at South Fork Ranch.

Davis played the role of Jock Ewing, the man who built an oil empire and made his family one of the richest in the world. He was perfect for the role and finally became a household name at the age of sixty-three. Tragically, he only appeared on the show for two years, after he passed away in 1981.

Jock was such an integral part of the program that the producers didn't know what to do with his character after he died. They first thought about replacing him, but instead sent his character to South America to drill for oil for a year so they could make a decision about what to do with his storyline. Producers ultimately decided that there was no way Davis could be replaced, so his character was killed off in a plane crash in the 1982 season.

EXTRA, EXTRA!

One of Davis's most famous commercials was for Carnation Non-Dairy Coffee Creamer.

His only child, Tara Diane, died at age sixteen in a car crash.

He is buried with a picture of his daughter and actress Victoria Principal, who many say reminded him of his daughter.

CLIFF "UKULELE IKE" EDWARDS

PERFORMER, SINGER

"When You Wish Upon a Star, makes no difference who you are."
—Lyrics of Ukulele Ike

Ukulele Ike rose to fame in the early 1900s by recording some of the most popular songs of all time. Many of these songs we know by heart, yet we don't know the name of the man who sang them. He appeared in over one hundred movies and performed on albums that have sold more than 70 million copies. He is the voice of Jiminy Cricket and the voice of "When You Wish Upon a Star." He is credited with developing a new style of singing, but he died penniless after a series of personal misfortunes that caused most of his fame to disappear.

THE EARLY YEARS

Cliff Edwards was born on June 14, 1895, in Hannibal to a poor farming family in northeast Missouri. Little is known about his early years, but it is known that he showed an amazing amount of musical talent at an early age. During a family trip to St. Louis, he was first exposed to voice recordings on vinyl records, which was fascinating to him. Until this time, the only music he had been exposed to were religious songs in church, but hearing this new type of music stimulated a musical interest that he tried to emulate back to the farm in Hannibal. Despite being in an area with few musical influences, he never lost interest in the music that he heard on that trip. By the time he was a teenager, he was back in St. Louis performing in theaters and saloons.

RISE TO FAME

Edwards gained a relative amount of stardom as a singer in St. Louis during the early 1900s. Simultaneously, he developed the ability to play ukulele. His vocal range was an amazing three octaves, and he could do things with his voice that very few people had ever heard. He created a unique style of singing called "effin," where he mimicked the sound of a kazoo while singing.

In his late teens, he traveled with carnivals to make a living. The big city was a new experience for him, so he figured he needed a better stage name to make a living. It was during this time that he picked up the name "Ukulele Ike." It was also during this time that he teamed up with a pianist named Bobby Carleton who had written a song called "Ja Da." That tune became one of the biggest selling songs of the 1920s and established Ike as a major singing sensation.

Show Me Success

Ukulele Ike was steadily climbing the entertainment ladder when he landed a breakout role on Broadway. He took a part on George Gershwin's production of *Lady Be Good,* where he stole the show. His success on Broadway soon opened the door for movies. In 1929, at the age of thirty-four, Ike became the first performer to sing "Singin' in the Rain" in the movie *The Hollywood Revue of 1929.* It seemed that everything Ike recorded became a major hit, so the Hollywood studios capitalized on his famous name and bankable status as a movie star. He played in more than one hundred movies after that, which made him one of the highest paid and most successful actors of the era.

His next career move combined his on-camera experience with his amazing voice. In 1940, Walt Disney Studios picked him to be the voice of Jiminy Cricket in *Pinocchio.* His voice was perfect for the role and the song, "When You Wish Upon a Star." His performance earned him an Academy Award for Best Song. The song also came to symbolize the Disney empire from that moment on.

Despite the millions of dollars he earned as a Hollywood star, his career and life seemed to fall apart as his fame faded. He struggled with gambling and drinking addictions, he failed to pay taxes and alimony, and he soon found himself destitute. When he died, the city of Hannibal offered to pay to bury him in his hometown, but the Actor's Guild stepped in with Disney Studios to pay for his burial in California. His fame and fortune were lost, but his voice continues to entertain new generations of fans, even if they don't know his name.

Extra, Extra!

Ike was named a Disney Legend in 2000.

He was the voice of Jim Crow in Dumbo, famous for his performance of "When I See an Elephant Fly."

In 2000, Ukulele Ike was inducted into the Ukulele Hall of Fame.

SARA EVANS

COUNTRY MUSIC SINGER

"Cause I'm almost home . . .
Back in Missouri, yeah!"
—*Sara Evans "Back in Missouri" lyrics*

Sara Evans proves that a small town girl can remain true to her roots to become one of the biggest-selling musicians of all time. She took a common route to Nashville, but her story turned out different than most. Her stunning good looks and amazing vocal range took her to the top, thanks in part to music videos that showcased the best of both assets.

THE EARLY YEARS

Sara Evans was born on February 5, 1971, in Boonville but grew up on a farm near the small town of New Franklin. The family discovered her musical ability when she was four years old, and they were soon on the road playing practically anywhere they could get her a performance. The show turned into a family act with her two brothers playing the instruments while Sara sang lead vocals.

When Sara was old enough to drive, she made the thirty-mile trip to Columbia to play in a country bar called the Country Stampede. She was one of the most popular acts at the popular nightspot for college students and locals. After graduation from New Franklin High School, she packed her bags and headed to Nashville to see if she could make a living out of her dreams.

RISE TO FAME

Sara arrived in the Country Music Capital of the World in 1991 with her mind set on a recording contract. She worked part time at a Holiday Inn when she met a man named Craig Schelske. The two fell in love and moved to Oregon the next year where they were soon married. They moved back to Nashville in 1995, only this time Sara was older and more prepared for success. She recorded songs once again, in hopes of a record contract.

Show Me Success

She finally landed a record deal with RCA, but it took a few years before she hit the charts. Her first album didn't catch on with country music fans, possibly because they were too heavily influenced by pop and rock music. She finally scored her first hit on her second album, *No Place That Far,* which received a Country Music Association Award nomination, but she was still relatively unknown in the music world.

Evans stayed true to her own personal music style with the release of her third album in 2001. *Born to Fly* turned out to be a huge success. It went double platinum and earned Evans her first CMA nomination for Album of the Year. She also won the award for Music Video of the Year for the title track.

Her next album, *Restless,* was released in 2003 and provided Evans with more accolades, including the Academy of Country Music nomination for Album of the Year. She followed that success with another album in 2005, *Real Fine Place.* Two thousand and five marked another milestone after she received a fourth straight nomination for Female Vocalist of the Year.

She was nominated in 2006 for the CMT Female Video of the Year for "A Real Fine Place to Start." She also won the Female Vocalist of the Year for *Radio and Records* and the Top Female Vocalist Award by the Academy of Country Music. In 2007, she was nominated by the CMT Music Awards for Female Video of the Year for "You'll Always Be My Baby" and won the BMI Country Awards 50 Most Performed Country Songs Award for the same song.

A bitter divorce in 2007 stirred up lawsuits and scandals, but Sara continues to be one of the most popular stars in country music and in pop culture. Her unique style makes her one of only a few artists who have been able to attain such crossover success. She continues to rack up fans and incredible record sales, which makes her one of the biggest music stars ever from the Show Me State.

Extra, Extra!

*Sara performed at the Republican National Convention in 2004.

*People Magazine *named her one of the world's most beautiful people.*

Sara comes from a large family, the third of seven children.

SHANDI FINNESSEY

MISS USA, PERFORMER

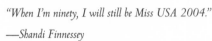

"When I'm ninety, I will still be Miss USA 2004."
—*Shandi Finnessey*

Shandi Finnessey is a tall, strikingly beautiful woman who receives attention no matter where she goes. The accomplished musician, author, academician, and model put a number of promising careers on hold while competing in pageants, but the hard work definitely paid off. In April of 2004, the St. Louis girl was seen around the world winning the title of Miss USA. She has since parlayed that honor into a job as co-host of a game show seen across the country.

THE EARLY YEARS

Shandi Finnessey was born on June 9, 1978, in St. Louis and grew up in the suburb of Florissant. The six-foot-tall blonde bombshell graduated from Incarnate Word Academy in 1996 and began her college studies at Lindenwood University in St. Charles. As a college student, she gained attention for her stellar academic performance and her skills playing piano and violin. In addition to her success at school, she made waves in the modeling industry and in pageants across the Show Me State.

RISE TO FAME

While finishing up her degree in psychology in only three and a half years, Shandi was perfecting her stage presence for the Miss Missouri Pageant. In 2002, just hours before her birthday, she was crowned Miss Missouri, which meant she had to put her studies on hold to compete for the title of Miss America. In September of 2002, she took the stage in Atlantic City, winning the preliminary evening-wear competition but coming up just short of winning Miss America.

JOHN W. BROWN

SHOW ME SUCCESS

She still had one year of eligibility to compete in the Miss USA Pageant, so she headed back to the stage in Poplar Bluff, winning Miss Missouri USA 2004 and earning another shot at a national pageant title. On April 12, 2004, in Los Angeles, Shandi was crowned Miss USA, which earned her a chance to compete for the Miss Universe title. She was in contention for the crown until the very end, finishing as First Runner-Up. Shandi continued her motivational speaking and charitable work after passing the crown to the next Miss USA.

Since her success on the pageant circuit, Shandi has made a name for herself on televisions game shows and reality shows. She was a co-host on the shows *Playmania* and *Lingo* on the Game Show Network. She followed those performances with a memorable appearance on "Dancing With the Stars." She was the local favorite but was the second person voted off the show in the 2007 season. The amazing resume continues to expand, but it seems the native Missourian has seemingly already conquered the world, all before turning thirty.

EXTRA, EXTRA!

Shandi authored the book The Furrtails *in 2002.*

She appeared in one episode of Donald Trump's hit show, The Apprentice 3.

She was the grand marshal of the Macy's Thanksgiving Day Parade in 2004.

Isadore "Friz" Freleng

Cartoon Animator

"Varmint, I'm a-gonna blow you to smithereens!"
—Yosemite Sam

If you ever watched Sylvester the Cat, the Pink Panther, Yosemite Sam, or Speedy Gonzalez, then you can thank another Missourian for impacting your life. Friz Freleng worked with fellow Missourian, Walt Disney, and with Warner Brothers to develop some of the best-known cartoon characters of all time. Friz entertained generations of children and adults and is immortalized with a star on the Hollywood Walk of Fame.

The Early Years

Isadore Freleng was born on August 21, 1905, in Kansas City. He began painting and drawing when he was very young, and by the time he graduated from high school he was already a talented illustrator. He worked with Walt Disney Studios in the 1920s and then landed a job with Warner Brothers animations a few years later. At Warner Brothers, he made his mark on American culture and changed the way people watched animated television.

Rise to Fame

At the age of twenty-four, Freleng animated the first-ever cartoon for Warner Brothers called *Sinkin' in the Bathtub*. He worked on the relatively new medium of animation throughout much of the 1930s, developing his skills and inventing characters that are still recognized today.

Another skill that put him ahead of all the other animators of his day was the ability to match his animations to a musical score. The combination made the finished product more enjoyable to the audience and made him a valuable commodity in Hollywood.

Freleng worked with Warner Brothers for three decades, producing many of the best Bugs Bunny, Daffy Duck, and Sylvester and Tweety cartoons the studio ever released. He also invented a number of characters, including Sylvester the Cat, Yosemite Sam, Porky Pig, Rocky and Mugsy, and refined the characteristics of Bugs Bunny.

When WB closed their animation department in 1964, Freleng had amassed nearly three hundred productions for the studio. So he partnered with David De-Patie to form DePatie-Freleng Enterprises. The pair produced large amounts of animated shows, including the development of the Pink Panther.

Freleng became one of the most awarded producers, directors, and animators in history. He won five Academy Awards, numerous Emmy Awards, and was even honored with a star on Hollywood's Walk of Fame in 1992. He died in 1995, but the cartoons that he produced more than fifty years ago are still viewed on television today.

EXTRA, EXTRA!

Freleng admitted that he, himself, was the inspiration for the gun-slinging character Yosemite Sam.

He served two terms as a Television Academy governor.

Freleng stated in 1989 that his favorite animated character was the Pink Panther.

JANE FROMAN

ACTRESS, MUSICIAN

"To Jane Froman, a great soldier, who, though, wounded herself, didn't forget us wounded."
—*Tribute from G.I.s to Froman*

Jane Froman was a musical pioneer and legend of the early 1900s. She defined the era with her class and dignity, coupled with an amazing voice that many called the best they had ever heard. In fact, when the famous musical producer Billy Rose was asked to name the ten best female singers, he replied, "There is Jane Froman and nine others."

THE EARLY YEARS

Jane Froman was born on November 10, 1907, in University City but moved shortly thereafter to the small town of Clinton. She spent a short time in the western Missouri town before moving to Columbia with her grandmother, where she spent the rest of her childhood. Her father disappeared one night in Atlanta and the case was never solved. A large number of stressful events in her childhood caused her to develop a speech impediment at the age of five, and she stuttered for the rest of her life, except when she was singing.

After high school, she received her associate's degree from Christian College, (later known as Columbia College) and then attended the University of Missouri–Columbia to study journalism. Her amazing voice was getting a great deal of attention from teachers and musical professors in college, who encouraged her to pursue a career in music. At Mizzou, her grades were suffering and her musical abilities were not being fully developed, so her mother sent her off to study at the Cincinnati Conservatory of Music at the age of twenty-one.

RISE TO FAME

Her next stop on the road to fame was at the age of twenty-three, when she auditioned as a singer for Cincinnati radio station WLW. Listeners to the station were amazed at what they heard. Calls to the station came in droves as listeners voted her the top girl singer of the day. From that moment on, she was a bona fide star with musical scouts from all over the country asking her to perform. In just a matter of years, she went from college student to one of the top radio performers in the country.

Show Me Success

Her first credited movie role was for a short film called *Kissing Time* in 1933. The movie didn't get a lot of attention from critics or the public, but it gave her needed experience to move on to bigger and better productions. Her first big break came when she got a job on a radio program starring Bing Crosby. That job opened the door to more radio work while allowing her to work on television shows and in movies.

She traveled and performed across the country in the late 1930s and built a legion of fans everywhere she went. Her popularity hit its peak during World War II when she traveled to Europe with the USO to entertain the troops. But on February 22, 1943, she sustained serious injuries when her plane crashed in Portugal. Severe injuries, crutches, and rattled nerves still were not enough to keep her off the stage. She performed nearly one hundred shows in Europe, further cementing her status as one of America's most beloved entertainers. Her career continued into the 1950s and 1960s, as she starred in *The Jane Froman Show* and the classic variety show, *Toast of the Town*.

After thirty-four years on stage, Froman moved back to Columbia where she spent the rest of her life. Even though she was "officially" retired, she continued to perform around the Show Me State and raise money for charities like her Jane Froman Foundation. She also did quite a bit of charitable work in Arrow Rock for the Jane Froman Music Camp, which helps children develop their musical abilities. She died in 1980 from cardiac arrest. She is forever memorialized in her home state though, as the Missouri State Senate passed a resolution recognizing her as one of Missouri's all-time greats.

Extra, Extra!

Clinton, Missouri, named July 25, 1973, Jane Froman Day.

The life-altering crash and her amazing performances afterward were chronicled in the award-winning movie, With a Song in My Heart, *starring Susan Hayward as Froman. Jane's voice was electronically dubbed into the film.*

Columbia, Missouri, declared the centennial of her birth, November 10, 2007, Jane Froman Day.

JOHN GOODMAN

ACTOR

"Doing Roseanne made me famous. To this day, people will call me Dan Conner. They'll shout out, 'Where's Roseanne?'"
—John Goodman

John Goodman made his mark on popular culture through a long line of acting and comedic credits. He is often viewed as the modern-day "everyman" with flaws and strengths that people around the world relate to. He was the affable husband of Roseanne Barr on the show *Roseanne* and the star of numerous movies. Goodman often jokes that he is actually from L.A., meaning "Lower Affton."

THE EARLY YEARS

John Stephen Goodman was born on June 20, 1952, and raised in the St. Louis suburb of Affton. He graduated from Affton High School in 1970, where he was a high school football star. His ability on the field earned him the chance to play at Southwest Missouri State University in Springfield, but a knee injury ended his playing days and forced the "big man on campus" to find a different activity to focus his energy. The stage allowed him to perform in front of an audience, which proved to be just the right touch for the popular student.

RISE TO FAME

Goodman focused his time studying drama after his football days were over with fellow students Kathleen Turner and Tess Harper. He graduated with a degree in theater in 1975 and then hopped on an Amtrak train for New York to pursue his dream of professional acting. Goodman picked up a few acting jobs, including ads for car dealers, Burger King, and Campbell's Chunky Soup. He also landed roles on the stage in children's theater and in Off-Broadway shows including *A Midsummer Night's Dream*.

His stage acting got the attention of directors and producers, which led to two Broadway shows, *Loose Ends* in 1979 and *Big River* in 1985. He even landed a spot on the classic 1980s film *Revenge of the Nerds*, which made him an instant cult favorite. This exposure made Goodman a marketable character actor with a unique look and style.

SHOW ME SUCCESS

Goodman first became a nationally known celebrity with the sitcom *Roseanne.* He played the role of Dan Conner in a show that was a ratings success for eight consecutive seasons. He earned seven Emmy nominations and a Golden Globe Award for his work on the show.

John's talents also expanded to movie theaters in the critically acclaimed *Raising Arizona* and *The Big Lebowski.* He also continued to rack up awards on the small screen, as he received an Emmy nomination for *Kingfish: A Story of Huey P. Long* and for his role in the CBS production of Tennessee Williams' *A Streetcar Named Desire.*

Goodman continues to be one of the most in-demand character actors today. He has often said that no matter what he does for the rest of his career, people will only want to talk about *Roseanne.* He also expanded his business interests in his hometown when he bought a restaurant and a radio station in the St. Louis area. He left Missouri for Hollywood several decades ago but continues to make an impact on the people of the Show Me State.

EXTRA, EXTRA!

His character on Roseanne *ranked thirteen on the list of the "50 Greatest TV Dads of All Time."*

He earned a Golden Globe Award nomination for the movie Barton Fink.

One of his more memorable roles was that of Fred Flintstone in The Flintstones *movie.*

BETTY GRABLE

ACTRESS, PERFORMER, MILLION DOLLAR LEGS

"There are two reasons why I am successful in show business. And I am standing on both of them."
—*Betty Grable*

World War II will forever be remembered for a myriad of events and images, some of which are the pictures of a famous Missourian performing for the soldiers at the most remote locales. Betty Grable is an American movie icon and a piece of Americana as the voluptuous pin-up girl with the million-dollar legs.

THE EARLY YEARS

Ruth Elizabeth Grable was born on December 18, 1916, to a family on the south side of St. Louis. Her father was a successful businessman, which allowed the family to live in relative luxury in the Forest Park Apartment Hotel. Her family's stature also allowed the girl to attend the prestigious Mary Institute prep school. Her mother was intent on training the young girl for stardom, which included enrolling her in dance classes and encouraging her to take saxophone and singing lessons.

The family went to California on vacation when Betty was about thirteen years old. Shortly after the trip, her mother decided it was in the family's best interest for her and her daughter to move to Tinseltown so the young girl could pursue an acting career. Soon after arriving in Los Angeles, Betty enrolled in performance classes at the Hollywood Professional School, the Albertina Rosch School, and the Ernest Blecher Academy. She was still young, but casting directors noticed her amazing talent.

RISE TO FAME

Betty's first professional job required her to break the law in order to perform. The law in California stated that performers had to be at least fifteen years old to perform in the chorus, but she was only thirteen when she landed a role in *Let's Go Places*. When producers found out that she falsified documents, she was terminated and forced to wait a few years before taking any more chorus jobs.

In the meantime, she continued to take classes and refine her talents. The same year, she also landed a role in *Whoopee!* under the leadership of Hollywood icon Sam Goldwyn. The movie proved to be a big stepping-stone for the actress. Numerous opportunities followed, including roles in two movies with Ginger Rogers and Fred Astaire.

Show Me Success

In 1937, Betty was in her early twenties and had a new husband and a new job as the leading lady in *Down Argentine Way.* The movie made her an international star about the same time World War II was beginning to break out around the globe. She continued to perform, only now for American troops. Her famous pose in a white swimsuit graced the walls of barracks all over the world and on the ships that carried soldiers to the front lines. She also became an unofficial symbol of what was waiting for the men at home when the war was over.

Over the next several decades, Grable became one of the most prolific and successful actresses of all time, performing in hundreds of films. She solidified her place in Hollywood lore with outstanding performances in *Pin Up Girl, How to Marry a Millionaire,* and *Guys and Dolls.* Her career came to a sudden halt when she was diagnosed with lung cancer in 1972. She died less than one year later.

Extra, Extra!

*In 1943, Twentieth Century Fox had Betty's legs insured with Lloyd's of London for the record $1.25 million.

*The treasury department recorded Grable as the highest earning American woman in 1946–1947, earning about three hundred thousand dollars annually.

*Grable was listed as one of the top ten box office stars for twelve years.

ROBERT GUILLAUME

ACTOR

"Do not use any facet of yourself that you perceive as a handicap as an excuse. Be prepared to go over, through and around."
—Robert Guillaume

Robert Guillaume played one of the most memorable TV characters of the 1980s, while doing his part to break down racial stereotypes. Guillaume has received critical acclaim for his singing voice, stage acting, and TV and movie roles. His amazing talent has also earned him numerous awards, including a pair of Emmy's for his signature role on television.

THE EARLY YEARS

Robert Guillaume was born by the name of Robert Williams on November 30, 1927, and grew up in downtown St. Louis. He was raised by his grandmother, who also nurtured his promising career as a singer. He showed amazing musical abilities in school but was expelled by St. Joseph's High School and eventually landed in the army in 1945. He returned two years later to graduate from St. Joseph's. He enrolled at St. Louis University, and then Washington University to major in music.

While at Wash. U., he won a scholarship to study at the Aspen Music Festival. This turned out to be a big break for the young man because it put him in front of influential people in the entertainment industry. He turned the scholarship into a paying job, as producers snatched him up for a role at the Karamu House Theatre in Ohio. It was about this time that he changed his name from Williams to Guillaume to reflect his French-Indian heritage.

RISE TO FAME

After spending time refining his talents at Karamu, he packed his bags for a tour of Europe with an up-and-coming producer named Quincy Jones. The experience greatly expanded his abilities, which put him into position for a number of musical and acting roles upon his return to the United States. He spent most of the next decade on stage, performing in musicals such *Kwamina*, *Porgy and Bess*, and *Othello*. Less than a year after starring in *Guys and Dolls*, he got his shot at nationwide stardom on a new television series that took the TV world by storm.

Show Me Success

Guillaume became a weekly fixture on TV in 1977 on the primetime show *Soap*. He played the sarcastic butler, Benson DuBois, for two years. He was a standout star on the show, which allowed him to take the character to a spin-off show, aptly named *Benson*. He starred on the show for seven years, ultimately winning two Emmys for his role as Benson.

The *Robert Guillaume Show* was his next big role in the late 1990s, where he played a marriage counselor named Edward Sawyer. At the same time, he played the role of a television executive on *Sports Night*. His career and life slowed down after he suffered a stroke during the taping of *Sports Night*.

He went into semi-retirement but continued to appear in several movies after the incident. His stardom allowed him to break down racial stereotypes on his award-winning shows, and he continues to make an impact on our society to this day, both on and off the camera.

Extra, Extra!

*You can hear his voice as the baboon Rafiki in the movie The Lion King, where he won a Grammy for his performance.

* He supplied the voice for Eli Vance in the video game Half-Life 2.

*He worked as a streetcar driver while attending college in St. Louis.

Jean Harlow

Actress, Pin-Up Girl

"In the first sitting I fell in love with Jean Harlow. She had the most beautiful and seductive body I ever photographed."
—Charles Sinclair Bull (portrait photographer)

Jean Harlow was the original Blonde Bombshell, famous for movies, pin-up posters, and her ability to make front-page news of Hollywood magazines with everything she did. "The Platinum Blonde," as she was called from a 1931 movie of the same name, was the ultimate sex symbol and tabloid darling. She was also the precursor to today's troubled young stars, with money to burn, multiple marriages, and a life cut short by tragedy.

The Early Years

Harlean Harlow Carpenter was born on March 3, 1911, and spent her early years in Kansas City and the surrounding area. Her father was a successful dentist, so the attractive young girl grew up in comfortable surroundings when many people were struggling to make ends meet. She was often sick as a youngster, which included meningitis at age five and scarlet fever at age fifteen, which was a precursor to an illness that afflicted her in the twenties.

She was a teenager when her parents divorced, which is when she and her mother moved to Los Angeles to begin their new lives. It didn't take the young girl long to grow up in the big city. She met a successful banker, married him, and moved to Beverly Hills, all before she was seventeen.

Rise to Fame

Harlow yearned to be a movie star, but her husband and her father tried repeatedly to thwart her efforts. She landed a small part in the movie *Moran in the Marines*, but her husband's opposition to her career choice forced her to put acting on hold for a while. She eventually became frustrated by his efforts to control her future, so she left him and took roles as a production extra. By this time, she had registered her name with an acting agency as Jean Harlow, and the name stuck.

154

She was still young (only nineteen by the time she was married and separated), beautiful, and full of ambition. She had the right combination of sexual allure and tenacity to make her a star, which is exactly what producers in Hollywood helped her achieve.

Show Me Success

Harlow was still an unknown actress when the eccentric moviemaker Howard Hughes picked her for the lead role in the movie *Hell's Angels*. Her blonde hair was an instant draw, sending peroxide sales soaring as women tried to copy her look.

The exposure she received from women for the hairstyle and men for her seductiveness made her an overnight success. She soon picked up plenty of movie roles, with money rolling in to the tune of tens of thousands of dollars per appearance, which was a huge sum in the early 1930s. Over the next seven years, she appeared in more than twenty movies, which included starring roles in *The Public Enemy* with James Cagney and *Red Dust* with Clark Gable.

When she was twenty-six, her life took a tragic turn. She had just started shooting the movie *Saratoga* with Clark Gable. She began getting sick on the set, but doctors were unable to determine what was causing her ailments. She was hospitalized in the middle of shooting the movie, and she died a short time later from uremic poisoning on June 7, 1937. The film was completed with long-angle camera shots and a body double. *Saratoga* went on to be the highest grossing film of 1937 as fans packed theaters to see how the producers finished the movie without her.

Extra, Extra!

*She was married two times during her short life, plus she was engaged to actor William Powell from Kansas City when she passed away.

*She was ranked twenty-two on the American Film Institute's "100 Years, 100 Legends" list.

*She appeared on the cover of LIFE Magazine in 1937, making her the first movie actress with that honor.

DON JOHNSON

ACTOR

"You've got to know the rules before you can break 'em. Otherwise, it's no fun."
—Sonny Crocket in Miami Vice

Don Johnson is one of the best-known actors of our generation, but many people don't even realize the *Miami Vice* star grew up in a tiny town in southwest Missouri. He has performed in nearly fifty movies and TV shows and even released a pair of musical albums. He was constantly on the covers of magazines, especially during his fashionista days on *Miami Vice*. And who would have thought that a guy from Flatt Creek, Missouri, would start a fashion trend that took the world by storm.

THE EARLY YEARS

Donnie Wayne Johnson was born on December 15, 1949, and grew up in the small town of Flatt Creek, which is actually just a small cluster of homes near Galena. His father worked on the family farm in the remote area, trying to make a living for the growing family. Both of his grandfathers were ministers, so it was natural that Don grew up performing in the church. His first taste of the spotlight came at age five, when he sang solos in front of the congregation.

Don and his family packed up their bags when he was young and moved to Topeka so his father could take a job with an aircraft company. Seven years later, Don was back in Flatt Creek after his parents divorced and his father moved back to take care of the farm. Don left again as a teenager and graduated from high school in Wichita in 1967. He enrolled in the theater department at the University of Kansas but left after two years to train at the San Francisco American Conservatory Theater.

RISE TO FAME

Don performed around San Francisco in a play called *Your Own Thing*. One night in 1968, the famed actor Sal Mineo attended one of the performances and was impressed with Johnson. He told Don that he was producing a play called *Fortune*

and Men's Eyes and wanted him to read for a part. Don nailed the audition and starred in the critically acclaimed show. His reviews were so strong that other producers and directors wanted him to star in their productions.

His career was exploding when he went to a casting call for a new show, tentatively called *Dade County Fast Lane*. He read for the part of Sonny Crocket but didn't hear back from the producers. Johnson decided to take a role in another film, which was also shooting in Florida. After the movie wrapped, the call finally came where producers asked him to read again for the part, this time with other potential co-stars. And the rest is television history.

Show Me Success

Johnson read for the part of Sonny Crocket with a number of fellow actors, including Philip Michael Thomas. When the two auditioned together, producers knew they finally had the right chemistry. The two were paired up as co-stars for the show, which was now called *Miami Vice*.

When the show debuted in 1984, it made Johnson an overnight megastar. He was the hottest actor in Hollywood, and he single-handedly changed the way American men dressed. His unique style of flashy linen blazers, pastel shirts, baggie pants, and no socks were a hit. Johnson also released a pair of musical albums during his five-year run with *Miami Vice*. His performance made him a worldwide star, a wealthy young man, and the winner of a Golden Globe.

When the showed wrapped up production, he sought another challenge in the entertainment industry. He took another role, similar to Sonny Crocket, as the detective Nash Bridges in the show of the same name in 1994. In the meantime, he expanded his empire by starting his own production company.

He continues to star on the big and small screens. He was awarded a star on the Hollywood Walk of Fame in 1996 for his acting prowess. It seems that everything Johnson touched over the past two decades has been a hit, which proves that he is one of the most bankable stars in Hollywood.

Extra, Extra!

Don opened an upscale restaurant in 1999 in San Francisco called Ana Mandara.

Don's role in A Boy and His Dog *earned him the honor of Best Actor of the Year by the Academy of Science Fiction and Horror Films.*

He was kicked out of a business class during his senior year of high school, which forced him to take a drama class to graduate.

KEVIN KLINE

ACTOR

"I think every American actor wants to be a movie star. But I never wanted to do stupid movies, I wanted to do films. I vowed I would never do a commercial, or a soap opera, both of which I did as soon as I left the Acting Company and was starving."
—Kevin Kline

Kevin Kline is one of the most accomplished actors of our time, winning critical acclaim and numerous awards in movies and on Broadway. He has starred alongside some of the biggest names in movie history. His star on the Hollywood Walk of Fame proves that he is truly one of the biggest stars to ever come from the Show Me State.

THE EARLY YEARS

Kevin Delaney Kline was born on October 24, 1947, and grew up in the St. Louis suburb of Clayton. He attended Priory High School, where he showed amazing aptitudes in extracurricular activities including music, athletics, and foreign languages. His skill at mastering dialects and languages impressed his teachers so much that they pushed toward a career in foreign services. But his love was for performance, so he headed off to study for a career on the stage.

Kline enrolled at Indiana University after graduating from Priory in 1965. He began college as music performance major but switched to drama when he realized he didn't have the discipline for a career in music. Acting turned out to be the right choice, as he was accepted at the prestigious Julliard School in New York. He gained valuable experience as he toured the country with an acting company, which set the tone for the next career step on Broadway.

RISE TO FAME

Kline was steadily working as an actor in New York when his first big breakthrough came at the age of thirty-one. He landed the Broadway role of a narcissistic womanizer in *On the Twentieth Century*. That role provided Kline with a Tony Award, which was followed two years later with another Tony for *The Pirates of Penzance*.

Tony and Drama Desk Awards can constitute a successful career, but Kline was still a relatively unknown talent to most Americans outside the world of theater. However, a pair of movies in the early 1980s made him one of the biggest stars on the big screen.

SHOW ME SUCCESS

Sophie's Choice in 1982 turned out to be his first shot at Hollywood stardom. The movie was a surprise hit and earned Kline a Golden Globe nomination. He followed that success the following year with the major hit *The Big Chill*. The Baby Boomer classic made him one of the most in-demand actors of the day. Over the next six years, Kline churned out fabulous performances, including roles in *Silverado*, *Cry Freedom*, and *A Fish Called Wanda*, where he won an Oscar for Best Supporting Actor in 1988.

Kline's success continued in the 1990s with the major hit *Chaplin*. His following role as the president of the United States—and the president's body double—in the hit movie *Dave*, earned him another Golden Globe nomination. He stayed in the spotlight with another Golden Globe nomination for *In & Out* in 1997, and in one of the biggest-budget films in history, *Wild Wild West* with Will Smith. He continued to be a major draw in theaters with the 2006 remake of *The Pink Panther*, opposite Steve Martin.

Kline showed his dedication to the acting craft and to his hometown by helping start the Kevin Kline Awards. The annual honor ceremony began in 2006 to recognize outstanding theater performances in the St. Louis area.

EXTRA, EXTRA!

*Kline was a member of the first graduating class at Julliard Drama School with William Hurt and Patti LuPone.

*He turned down the role of Batman in the 1989 version of the movie.

*He met his wife, Phoebe Cates, during an audition for The Big Chill. *The two later starred together in* Princess Caraboo.

Brad Kroenig

Model

Brad Kroenig is one of those faces you recognize in magazines yet seem to know little about. In the early 2000s, he was one of the top fashion models in the world, commanding forty thousand dollars a day for a photo shoot. The St. Louisan is a reluctant celebrity, yet hangs out with the likes of Mike Tyson, Tom Cruise, and Paris Hilton. Throughout 2004 and 2005, Brad was ranked as the top male model in the world by an industry ranking service. Not bad for a South County boy who didn't really want to get into the modeling industry in the first place.

The Early Years

Brad Kroenig was born on April 23, 1979, and grew up in the St. Louis suburb of Oakville. He excelled in basketball and soccer at Oakville High School, which earned him a scholarship to play soccer at Southern Illinois University–Edwardsville. He transferred after two years to Florida International University in Miami, which was also the modeling capital of the world at the time. The combination of being in the right place at the right time with the right "look" soon took him from the soccer field to the runway in just a matter of months.

Rise to Fame

Brad was good-looking with a chiseled body, so a friend at the university urged him to meet with the modeling agencies on South Beach. Most prospective models have to meet with a number of agents before finding one that will sign them, but Brad was accepted by practically every agency he visited. He ended up signing with the world-famous Ford Modeling Agency. In the span of a year, he went from relative obscurity to worldwide popularity. His formal university education was put on hold just three months after being "discovered," as he turned his attention to the business of modeling.

Show Me Success

Brad rose through the modeling ranks at remarkable speed. He graced the covers of dozens of major fashion magazines and appeared in ad campaigns for Ralph Lauren, Tommy Hilfiger, and Perry Ellis. He was suddenly the most sought after male model in the world and commanded millions of dollars a year.

Brad spent the next few years on top of his industry, bouncing around the world on a weekly basis. Despite his huge success, he claims to have no interest in launching an acting career. He said his true passion isn't fashion, but rather real estate, where he points out that his "real" career will begin after he retires from the high-profile modeling career.

Extra, Extra!

*Brad's mother claims that he drove home from college almost every night because he was homesick.

*Abercrombie and Fitch was his first major ad campaign that put him on the walls of stores across the country.

Cedric "The Entertainer" Kyles

Actor

"I was always considered funny. I went to college and studied, sang. I really thought I was going to be a singer. That's where the 'Entertainer' comes from."

—Cedric, during an interview with Blackfilm.com

You may not know the name Cedric Kyles, but the odds are you know the stage name of Cedric "The Entertainer." Cedric has always been a funny guy and was able to turn that great sense of humor into an incredible career. From the stage to the screen, the St. Louis native has certainly put his mark on pop culture.

The Early Years

Cedric Kyles was born on April 24, 1964, in Jefferson City. He moved to St. Louis when he was young and spent the rest of his childhood and teenage years there. Even as a child, friends and family say he was funny in practically every situation. He continued his comedic ways in school and was named the Most Popular and Most Humorous student in his class at Berkeley High School.

Kyles put his comedy career on hold after graduation from college at Southeast Missouri State University in Cape Girardeau as he began a job as an insurance adjuster for State Farm Insurance. He pursued his passion to be on stage on the weekends, performing at comedy clubs throughout the St. Louis area.

Rise to Fame

Kyles always dreamed of being a performer, not only as a comedian but also as a singer. When he was twenty-six, friends urged him to take the stage at a comedy club where the Johnny Walker National Comedy Contest tryouts were taking place. He won the contest, which earned him a chance to perform in Chicago.

There, he won the competition, a little money, and the chance to travel the country doing his act.

His next big break came after being in the right place at the right time, when the right person was there to see his act. Cedric, now known as "The Entertainer," stopped by a comedy club in Dallas. The headlining act wasn't very entertaining, so Cedric took the stage on a whim. He was an instant hit with the crowd, which just happened to include comedian Steve Harvey. The two hit it off immediately. When Harvey landed his own TV show, "The Entertainer" was invited along for the ride.

SHOW ME SUCCESS

His pairings with great comedians paved the way for success in the late 1990s. *The Steve Harvey Show* debuted in 1997, with Cedric Kyles playing Cedric Jackie Robinson. He was a hit on the show and won numerous awards. The next year, Cedric teamed up with big-name comedians Bernie Mac and D. L. Hughley for a comedy tour called *The Kings of Comedy*. The tour sold out almost every night and took in nearly $40 million over two years.

The exposure of his TV show and the comedy act made him a bankable star in Hollywood. He landed a part in *Ride* in 1998 and in *Big Momma's House* in 2000. That same year, the movie version of *The Kings of Comedy* hit theaters, which gave the Missouri native even greater exposure. He followed the success of these performances with starring roles of his own in *Barbershop* and *Johnson Family Vacation*.

Cedric turned his love for entertaining people into a multimillion-dollar entertainment empire. He continues to be one of the highest paid and most in-demand actors in Hollywood. He even set up a foundation to fund scholarships for underprivileged kids in his hometown. His sense of humor and hard work ethic have allowed him to achieve worldwide fame, but his humble roots and contribution to society prove that "The Entertainer" still knows where he came from.

EXTRA, EXTRA!

Many people first saw Cedric as the "Smooth Dancing Lover" in commercials for Budweiser.

Cedric won the Richard Pryor Comic of the Year Award from BET in 1994.

He won four NAACP Image Awards for Outstanding Actor in a Comedy Series for his role on The Steve Harvey Show.

The premiere for the movie Barbershop was held at the Esquire Theater in Richmond Heights, Missouri.

His voice can be heard in Dr. Doolittle 2 and in the children's cartoon The Proud Family.

KIMORA LEE-SIMMONS

MODEL, TELEVISION HOST, ENTREPRENEUR

"The First Lady of Hip Hop"
—Kimora's unofficial title

Kimora Lee-Simmons began her meteoric rise to stardom before she was even a teenager, and she has never had a chance to sit back and relax. She has traveled the globe as one of the world's top models, hosted her own television show, appeared on the big screen, and even created her own line of clothing and accessories.

THE EARLY YEARS

Kimora Lee was born on May 3, 1975, in St. Louis. She grew up quickly, literally, where she was nearly six feet tall as a young teenager. Her height and unique looks of Japanese and African American descent were soon paying dividends as she started working as a model at age twelve. Despite the heavy time commitment of being a teenage model, she still graduated from Lutheran North High School in St. Louis. After completing her education, she hit the road full time and built a multimillion-dollar empire in the process.

RISE TO FAME

At the same time she was learning the basics of education in middle school, Simmons was also getting a real-world business education. Famous fashion icon Karl Lagerfeld took an interest in her when she was only thirteen as he personally picked her to be a model for Chanel. It was a big step for the two, but the gamble turned out great for both Chanel and Simmons. She graced the covers of magazines and walking the biggest catwalks in Europe and America, all before she could legally drive a car!

SHOW ME SUCCESS

The fashion world and Hollywood were becoming synonymous during the 1980s and 1990s, where stars in each field were successfully crossing over. This was the perfect combination for Kimora, who was already a superstar model with savvy business skills. Her modeling success translated into TV shows like *Fashionably Loud* on MTV, *America's Next Top Model* on UPN, and as co-host of the nationally syndicated talk show, *Life and Style*. Movies were next on her list as she landed a part on the successful movie *Beauty Shop* in 2005. She also helped develop a reality show for Style Network titled *Kimora: Life in the Fab Lane* in 2007.

Kimora enjoyed great financial success with her numerous entertainment ventures. Her insatiable work ethic also drove her to become the creative director of a line of clothing called Baby Phat. She and her husband, hip-hop mogul Russell Simmons, became some of the biggest names in the entertainment world. Phat Farm was sold in 2004 to the Kellwood Company of St. Louis for an estimated $140 million, which allowed Kimora to become president and creative director of the Baby Phat clothing line. Only in her early thirties, she has already proven her success in modeling, fashion, music, television, movies, cosmetics, jewelry, books, and housewares.

Extra, Extra!

*Kimora's foundation provides scholarships for disadvantaged students at Lutheran North High School in St. Louis.

*She won a prestigious Tony Award in 2003 for work as executive producer on Russell Simmons Presents Def Poetry Jam on Broadway.

*Model/actress Tyra Banks was the maid of honor at her wedding.

*Kimora and Simmons filed for divorce in 2006.

KATHLEEN MADIGAN

COMEDIAN

"Living with kids is like living with bums. They chase you around going, 'Hey, can I have a dollar, some food, I'm missing a shoe and need a ride.'"
—*Kathleen Madigan*

Kathleen Madigan has been recognized as one of the funniest people on the comedy circuit today. Her unique perspective on current affairs makes her one of the most in-demand stand-up comics and public speakers in the country. The St. Louis woman has churned out hilarious comedy specials, which places her on the top of the charts as one of the biggest entertainers in Show Me State history.

THE EARLY YEARS

Kathleen Madigan was born on September 30, 1965, and grew up in a large family in the St. Louis suburb of Florissant. After graduating from McCluer North High School in 1983, she moved on to Southern Illinois University–Edwardsville, where she studied journalism.

RISE TO FAME

Kathleen put her journalism degree to good use after graduating from SIUE, as she worked in the St. Louis area with the *Suburban Journals* and for the Missouri Athletic Club publications department. At the same time she was working for the MAC, she attended "open mic" nights at local comedy clubs. Her comedic stories were reflections of real-life experiences and the news of the day, and audiences instantly related to the stories she was telling. Suddenly, she was getting a fan base that drove for miles to hear her unique brand of stand-up comedy.

Around the same time she was becoming popular on the local comedy circuit,

Madigan was also becoming frustrated with the news business. She formulated a plan to make a career out of "making fun" of news, instead of reporting on it. Her year and a half of experience in traditional journalism was more than enough, so she struck out on her own to see if she could make a living doing comedy.

Show Me Success

Kathleen made the jump to be a full-time comedian in 1988 and instantly landed national exposure on the show *Stand-Up Spotlight* on VH-1. She followed that with another popular show, the *½ Hour Comedy Hour*, where her talent was showcased in front of a national audience.

In 1996, at the age of thirty-one, Madigan won the honor of Best Female Standup Comedian at the American Comedy Awards. She also signed on to host her own comedy special on HBO called *Kathleen Madigan Live*. During this time she was also making the rounds by appearing on Comedy Central, *The Late Show with David Letterman*, *The Tonight Show with Jay Leno*, and on *Late Night with Conan O'Brien*. She was also showcased in TV shows like VH-1's *Greatest Celebrity Feuds*, E! Entertainment's *100 Greatest Celebrity Oops!*, *Last Comic Standing*, and as a comedic contributor to news shows and magazines all over the country.

Despite her humble beginnings and tough times on "open-mic" nights around St. Louis, Kathleen Madigan has truly made a name for herself as one of the most popular and entertaining performers of our generation.

Extra, Extra!

Kathleen is a regular on the TV show Hollywood Squares.

She won the mid-Missouri Hoops Shoot Championship when she was in school.

She was a contributing writer for the 2004 Emmy Awards.

VIRGINIA MAYO

ACTRESS

"I really wanted to be a dancer, but I ended up as an actress and I got to perform next to some of the greatest actors of our time."

—Virginia Mayo

Virginia Mayo spent nearly sixty years in the public eye as one of the most successful actresses in history. She appeared in dozens of movies with some of the biggest names of Hollywood. She was called "one of the most beautiful women to ever appear on camera" and was one of the first stars honored with a star on the Hollywood Walk of Fame.

THE EARLY YEARS

Virginia Clara Jones was born on November 30, 1920, and was raised in St. Louis. Her family had deep roots in the Show Me State, dating back several generations. Her father was a local newspaper reporter and her aunt ran an acting school, which she began attending at the age of six. After graduating from Soldan High School in 1937, she immediately put her acting skills to the test. She landed her first professional acting and dancing jobs shortly after graduation at the St. Louis Municipal Opera, or the Muny.

RISE TO FAME

She had a large amount of success on local stages, but she expanded her skills by traveling the country with a stage act known as Pansy the Horse. As her fame grew, she changed her name to Virginia Mayo. Around the same time, she gained the interest of the Hollywood icon Samuel Goldwyn. He signed her to a contract where she was able to work on larger budget productions with much bigger stars.

Signing with one of the biggest studios in Hollywood opened doors for her she never imagined. Her first job under Goldwyn was in 1942 at the age of twenty-two. It was a small part in the movie *Jack London*. She landed additional small acting roles when producers realized that her incredible beauty was an instant drawing card for a movie. Audiences were coming to the theater just to get a glimpse of her on screen, which led to bigger and better roles in a wide variety of productions.

She starred in a half-dozen films between 1944 and 1946 before finally hitting it big in 1947 with *The Secret Life of Walter Mitty*. Her pairing with Danny Kaye was music to the ears of studio executives who used the couple as co-stars in three additional films. At the pinnacle of her career in the late 1940s and early 1950s, she was the top money-making star for Warner Brothers. Mayo packed theaters with hits like *White Heat* with James Cagney, *The Princess and the Pirate* with Bob Hope, *The Silver Chalice* with Paul Newman, and *The Girl from Jones Beach* with an up-and-coming young actor named Ronald Reagan.

Starring roles for Mayo started drying up in the 1960s, but she continued to act as a supporting character for several more decades. Contemporary audiences enjoyed her acting in shows like *Murder She Wrote*, *Remington Steele*, and *The Love Boat*. Six decades of working as an actress produced one of the most amazing resumes in Hollywood history. Virginia Mayo died in January 2005, with her legend already in the history books as one of the greatest screen icons in American history. She earned a number of awards for her acting, but her biggest claim to fame was being one of the first names to appear on the Hollywood Walk of Fame.

EXTRA, EXTRA!

Her great-great-great grandfather founded East St. Louis, Illinois.

Her stage name of Mayo came from a Vaudeville act where she performed with two men known as the "Mayo Brothers" who dressed up in a horse costume.

MICHAEL McDONALD

SINGER, MUSICIAN

". . . his mixture of tenderness and passion is so relentless, he can infuse just about any lyric with conviction."
—*Stephen Holden*, Rolling Stone Magazine

Michael McDonald is certainly one of the biggest names in music, with one of the most distinctive voices, and it all started right here in the Show Me State. He became a worldwide star with Steely Dan and the Doobie Brothers, but he went on to even larger success as a solo artist. His songs are instantly recognizable, and he continues to impact new generations of fans with an incredible legacy of hit music.

THE EARLY YEARS

Michael McDonald was born on February 12, 1952, in St. Louis and was raised in the suburb of Ferguson. He started performing on stage before he was even in high school with the band Mike and the Majestics. He performed with a number of bands around the St. Louis area throughout his years at McCluer High School, but he dreamed of bigger fame. At age eighteen, he made the move to California to pursue a full-time music career.

RISE TO FAME

Michael spent two years on the West Coast without finding much work. He was making demo records and networking with influential music industry insiders when he learned that the group Steely Dan was looking for a singer and musician. He tried out for the band, nailed the audition, landed the job, and was soon thereafter traveling the world with the group.

McDonald enjoyed a great deal of success with the group but was playing a secondary role. After working with Steely Dan for three years, he found out that the Doobie Brothers were looking for a new member to replace singer and musician Tommy Johnston. Another member of the "Doobies" suggested giving Michael a shot, and the rest, they say, is musical history.

JOHN W. BROWN

Show Me Success

The Doobie Brothers released the song "Takin' It to the Streets" in 1976 with Michael on lead vocals. The song was a huge hit, which put him on the map as an artist and on music magazines everywhere. The band had a winning combination with McDonald on the microphone, providing them with numerous hits and sold-out concert tours. That success also helped Michael and the band win multiple Grammys, but Michael was looking for another change to expand his abilities, so he struck out on his own and pursued a solo career.

McDonald continued his string of success when he released his first solo album in 1982. He was one of the most popular artists on the radio, not only with his fans but also with other musicians. In addition to his solo work, he performed duets with stars like Kenny Loggins, Christopher Cross, Aretha Franklin, and James Ingram.

Even though musical styles have changed over the years, McDonald continues to reinvent himself and remains one of the most dynamic and unique performers in the music industry. His legion of fans, both in and out of the business, was never more evident than at a tribute concert to McDonald in 2000 when musicians Kenny Loggins, Boz Skaggs, James Ingram, Patti LaBelle, Steve Winwood, and others performed his songs to a sold-out auditorium in Los Angeles.

He has found a fan base in rock music, easy listening, rhythm and blues, and smooth jazz. He has spent nearly four decades on top of the charts, which places him in a category very few artists will ever achieve.

Extra, Extra!

*What a Fool Believes *in 1977 is one of his biggest albums ever and won four Grammys including Song of the Year and Record of the Year.*

McDonald teamed up with the Doobie Brothers in 1995 for a reunion tour.

PAT METHENY

MUSICIAN

"Right from the start, one of the major tenets of the group was that we wanted to go beyond song-form type material whenever we could."

—*Pat Metheny*

Pat Metheny is one of the most intriguing musicians of the past four decades. As a solo artist and also as a part of the Pat Metheny Group, he continues to defy musical categories. He has been called one of the most influential people in jazz music, but that statement doesn't quite capture his impact. His amazing style of blending musical genres has impacted almost every aspect of music that people enjoy today.

THE EARLY YEARS

Pat Metheny was born on August 12, 1954, in Kansas City and grew up in the suburb of Lee's Summit. His musical family exposed him to a wide variety of musical influences as a child, which made a huge impact on his development. He was playing the trumpet at age eight and then switched his focus to guitar at age twelve. He proved to be such an adept musician that, by the time he was in his teens, he was already playing with some of the best musical groups in the Kansas City area.

RISE TO FAME

Unlike many musicians who finally get stage experience in their twenties, Metheny was already a stage veteran in his teens. By the age of eighteen, he was already teaching classes at the University of Miami to students much older than him. Not only was he the youngest teacher in history at the Florida university, he also became the youngest teacher at Boston's Berklee College of Music at age nineteen.

At age twenty, he was already well known in musical circles, but he did not have household name recognition. He spent the next three years touring with Gary Burton and playing for packed houses all over the country while releasing

JOHN W. BROWN

small solo albums. The exposure as a backup artist expanded his horizons and gave Metheny the experience he needed to move to the next level: the frontman of a band. He released his first solo album *Bright Size Life* in 1975 and began a "constant musical tour" that has consumed his life over the past thirty years.

Show Me Success

Metheny was always fond of large musical arrangements, so he made the bold move of adding a large number of musicians to his act and formed the Pat Metheny Group in 1977. Part of his unconventional approach to music was to add instruments that weren't normally associated with jazz, including the twelve-string guitar, the guitar synthesizer, and the forty-two-string Pikasso guitar. The popular sounds helped develop an immense following, with the band releasing an album nearly every year since the mid-1970s to keep their fans happy.

His style is so unique that many music aficionados claim he is the most copied performer in the industry. His success can also be measured by the amazing number of awards he has won. He racked up three gold albums and an amazing sixteen Grammy Awards, including seven years in a row for seven consecutive albums. His Grammys include awards for Best Rock Instrumental, Best Contemporary Jazz Recording, Best Jazz Instrumental Solo, and Best Instrumental Composition.

Metheny and The Pat Metheny Group continue to churn out albums in the 2000s, making him one of the most resilient and biggest selling artists over the past three decades. He also ranks as one of Missouri's greatest entertainers of all time.

Extra, Extra!

His older brother, Mike Metheny, is also a professional musician.

Pat received an honorary doctorate from Berklee College of Music.

NELLY

RAPPER, MUSICIAN

"Sing it loud
I'm from the Lou' and I'm proud!"
—Nelly's "Country Grammar"

When it comes to performers that have redefined the musical industry over the past decade, St. Louis's Nelly definitely tops the list. He debuted to a national audience in 2000 and quickly rocketed to the top of the A-list of star power. He dominates almost every area of pop culture these days, from music to movies to fashion. On his rise to the top, he took the time to pay homage to his hometown by wearing St. Louis–emblazoned clothing in his music videos and on the stage in front of millions of people. He became a "one-man" chamber of commerce for the city and made St. Louis a hotbed of musical talent. He is one of the biggest stars in Missouri history and the future looks even brighter for this entertainment and business icon.

THE EARLY YEARS

Cornell Haynes, Jr., was born on November 2, 1974, in Austin, Texas, but grew up in St. Louis. Like many young men, he ran into trouble as he grew up when he started hanging out with the wrong crowds. So his mother decided to move to the suburban University City.

University City High School was known for its strong sports programs, and Cornell excelled on the field. He was a great baseball player and was even scouted by major league baseball teams. While refining his baseball skills, he was also writing rhymes and rapping with his friends. While attending tryouts with major league baseball teams, his new group, the St. Lunatics, was getting popular. When the baseball dream subsided, he turned his focus to music, which proved to be one of the best moves he ever made.

RISE TO FAME

Nelly and some close friends formed the St. Lunatics in the mid-1990s and produced a regional hit, "Gimmie What You Got." The song received quite a bit of airplay but failed to translate into a major record deal. The group tried their luck in

Atlanta, which was a hot spot for hip-hop artists in the late 1990s. Their group managers decided that Nelly could be the standout star of the group, so it was decided he should try to land a record contract by himself, and then bring the others along once he made it big. The plan was ambitious, but it worked. Nelly signed with Universal and went into the studio as a solo artist to produce his first major label album.

Show Me Success

Country Grammar was released in 2000 and was an instant success. It rocketed to the top of the charts by selling more than a quarter of a million copies in its first week of release. It also became the summer anthem for a generation of music fans. *Country Grammar* went on to sell 9 million copies and stayed on top of the charts for seven weeks, making it one of the biggest selling albums in history. Not only did the album put Nelly on the music scene, but he also put St. Louis on the rap music map by using the city as the backdrop for many of his music videos.

Nelly was such an intriguing figure that he was appearing on TV shows everywhere, including MTV, VH-1, and even at the Super Bowl halftime show. His face was on the cover of music, fashion, fitness, and entertainment magazines. He used the exposure to launch his own clothing line and energy drink. He expanded the empire even further by becoming part owner of the Charlotte Bobcats of the NBA, buying a controlling interest in a NASCAR team, and even starting his own recording label, Derrty Entertainment.

Despite his solo success, he stayed true to his promise to bring his friends along for the ride. The St. Lunatics went back into the studio and released their first major album in 2001, which was also a success.

His universal appeal allowed him to sell nearly 30 million albums and to star in movies. Nelly followed his first solo album with another disc in 2002 called *Nellyville*, which also hit the top of the charts and proved that he was definitely more than a one-hit wonder. His role in the movie remake of *The Longest Yard* won critical acclaim and once again proved that everything Nelly touches turns to gold.

Nelly is a true American icon and one of the most influential performers in America today, but to many Missourians his continued efforts to honor his state and hometown in front of millions of people are much more important.

Extra, Extra!

*He put his energy into raising money for leukemia research after his sister Jackie Donahue was diagnosed and ultimately died from the disease.

*He received a star on the St. Louis Walk of Fame in 2005, the youngest person to get the honor.

Jane Novak

Actress

The more famous of the Novak sisters, Jane, starred in a number of movies opposite the biggest male lead actors of the early 1900s. She amassed an impressive array of roles at a time when sound was first being incorporated into movies. When "talkies" became more prevalent, her career faded away, along with much of the money she made from her time as a star. She continued to get small roles until she was nearly sixty and then stayed out of the limelight for another thirty years until her death.

The Early Years

Jane Novak was born on January 12, 1896, and grew up in the city of St. Louis. She attended Notre Dame convent where her interest in acting was first stimulated. She performed in a St. Louis acting group for a short time before heading off for Hollywood. In fact, legend has it that her career actually took off when a director saw her photo on the make-up table of her famous aunt, actress Anne Seymour.

Rise to Fame

Jane wasted little time getting to California and was given a contract by the Kalem Company when she was only a teenager. That contract gave her the green light to appear in a number of films, which mainly included low-budget silent films. The pay wasn't much—only about ten dollars a week—and the allure of being a "broke" Hollywood star quickly faded. That's when she transferred to the Vitagraph Production Company, where she was able to make more money by appearing in bigger productions with bigger co-stars.

Show Me Success

Novak's new employer placed her in films that generally cast her as the rugged, western-style heroine. She starred with acting legend William S. Hurt in a number of popular films around 1920. Over the next decade, she appeared in nearly forty films, which won her critical praise and a legion of fans.

During the 1920s, Jane also made a small fortune by investing her acting money wisely. She lived the life of the young, rich, and famous until the stock market crash wiped out most of her net worth. The advent of movies with sound further knocked her career off track during the 1930s. She appeared in only two films in the 1930s and only a few more in the 1940s.

Novak died in 1990 at the age of ninety-four, largely forgotten by most movie fans despite appearing in ninety-two films.

EXTRA, EXTRA!

She was a niece, by marriage, of actress Anne Seymour.

She published a cookbook in 1974 titled Treasury of Chicken Cookery.

Her sister Eva appeared in 119 movies but is generally regarded as less of a movie star than Jane.

VINCENT PRICE

ACTOR

"I don't play monsters. I play men besieged by fate and out for revenge."
—*Vincent Price*

Vincent Price will forever be known as one of the great horror movie actors of all time, but his real persona was vastly different from what the big screen shows. He was described as a "consummate gentleman," a collector of fine arts, and a fan of gourmet cooking. He was the ultimate villain on camera, and the ultimate nice guy off camera.

THE EARLY YEARS

Vincent Leonard Price was born on May 27, 1911, and lived his entire childhood in the St. Louis area. He was born to a wealthy family with a father who owned the National Candy Company. Vincent attended the Community School and prestigious St. Louis Country Day School before studying at Yale University.

Price's first job after graduating from the Ivy League school was as a teacher. He wasn't ready for the business of education, so he quit after only one year, which is when he headed to England at the age of twenty-two to study at the University of London. He was working toward a degree in fine arts when the acting bug bit him and changed the course of his life toward a career on stage.

RISE TO FAME

Price got his first on-stage experience at the age of twenty-three in a pair of productions, which included the leading role of Prince Albert in *Victoria Regina*. That play later transferred to Broadway, and Price went with the show. He stayed with the production for three years in the Big Apple while branching out to other areas of performance. He picked up speaking jobs on the radio, including a role on Orson Welles' *Mercury Theater*. After his stint in New York, he moved to Hollywood to try his hand at movie acting. The trip paid immediate dividends as he landed roles in hit movies like *The House of Seven Gables*, *Laura*, and *Champagne for Caesar*.

Price was one of the leading actors in Hollywood during the late 1940s and early 1950s, both as a romantic leading man and in horror films. He always had the biggest success playing a frightening villain. He used his reputation for fright to land a role in his breakout movie *House of Wax* in 1953. The movie used a new type of filmmaking technology called 3-D to enhance the horror scenes.

The popularity of that film led to more leading roles in *The Fly*, *The Return of the Fly*, and *House on Haunted Hill*. During this time he expanded his acting repertoire in comedies like *Casanova's Big Night* with Bob Hope and in epics like *The Ten Commandments*. The 1960s were equally successful for Price as he continued to establish himself as the master of horror. He played in dozens of productions, including *The House of Usher*, *The Pit and the Pendulum*, and *The Masque of the Red Death*.

As he approached the age of sixty, he slowed down and pursued his passion for fine arts and gourmet cooking. He still worked in Hollywood, just not on the big screen. He wrote a number of books about classical and fine art and even coauthored cookbooks with his second wife. Many younger movie fans may not recognize his big screen roles but will forever remember his appearances on Michael Jackson's "Thriller" and Alice Cooper's "The Nightmare." He played one last memorable role in 1990 in the blockbuster movie *Edward Scissorhands* with Johnny Depp.

Price died three years after his last big role at the age of eighty-two. He left an amazing body of work with more than one hundred films. He will forever have a reputation as a villain in the movie theater, but the Missouri-born actor proved that he was a man of many assets, most importantly, a man with a passion for life.

EXTRA, EXTRA!

*Vincent's grandfather invented baking powder.

*Price is the "evil voice" on Michael Jackson's song "Thriller," which is the biggest-selling album of all time.

*Price attended the opening night of the first production of Richard O'Brien's The Rocky Horror Picture Show.

CHARLES RUSSELL

ARTIST

"One of the premier artists of the American West, Charles M. Russell lovingly preserved the rugged splendor of the frontier."
—inscription on St. Louis Walk of Fame

When many people think of the western United States, they likely envision the scenes painted by artist Charles Russell. He grew up in St. Louis but found fame with his depictions of the "True West" in paintings, drawings, and sculptures that still capture the imagination of people all over the world.

THE EARLY YEARS

Charles Marion Russell was born to a well-to-do family in St. Louis in 1864. He spent his early years at the family's country estate, Oak Hill, which is near the present-day Tower Grove Park in south St. Louis. The area was sparsely populated in the mid-1800s, which gave him a taste of remote spaces with plenty of room to dream. Even as a child he was enamored with the Wild West. He listened intently to the fur trappers' tall tales about the West as they made their way through St. Louis. Russell even made clay models of the animals he heard the trappers tell stories about though he had never actually seen the animals in person. When he turned sixteen, he decided to pursued his passion so he moved west for a life on the open range.

RISE TO FAME

Russell first moved to Montana to become a professional cowboy. He landed a job as a cattle wrangler in 1882 where he spent his days on the range and his evenings rolling cigarettes and drawing scenic pictures. His job consisted of riding horses and roping cattle. Fellow cattle workers said that he wasn't very good at being a cowboy, but they were impressed with his stories and drawings.

When cowboy jobs started drying up in the decade after he arrived in Montana, he turned his attention to becoming a full-time artist. He had little success during the first three years as a professional artist, but when he married Nancy

Cooper in 1896, she took the reins of the business. It was the combination of her business savvy and his artistic ability that made him one of America's favorite artists.

Show Me Success

Even though the West was his inspiration for painting and sculpting, Russell found little success selling his works there. The couple moved to New York where there was more interest in fine art, and more importantly, more money to spend on art. He worked as an illustrator for several years before his first big break came at a one-man art show in 1911.

His depiction of life on the range and the mystique that came along with it were a hit with New York art fans. His success at the New York gallery opened the door for other exhibitions in London. Now a bona fide star in art circles, he sold prints and other pieces of art at an amazing rate, and sometimes for amazing amounts of cash.

During his life, Russell produced more than three thousand pieces, including paintings, drawings, and sculptures. Throughout his works, it can be seen that Russell knew his subject intimately, and very few artists have, or will ever, be able to capture the West so perfectly. His artwork helped show easterners the West, which is fitting since he grew up in the city known as the "Gateway to the West."

Extra, Extra!

Will Rogers called Russell the best storyteller he ever heard.

His first job on the range was tending to sheep, which he didn't feel was fit for a cowboy.

David Sanborn

Musician

"I do this because I love it, and at the end of the day, the fact that I can make a living at all doing this, I'm grateful for."
—*David Sanborn*

St. Louis has always been known as a hotbed for jazz, which is fitting since one of the best-known contemporary jazz performers of all time hails from the area. David Sanborn is perhaps the most prolific performer of all time in the genre of smooth jazz. His songs are played on stations around the globe on radio, satellite, and even on television programs. David Sanborn is truly one of the best when it comes to contemporary saxophone music.

The Early Years

David Sanborn was born on July 30, 1945, in Tampa, Florida, but moved to the Show Me State when he was a child. He grew up in the St. Louis suburb of Kirkwood, where his musical abilities were discovered early. He suffered from a bout with polio, which actually was the stimulus for his ability to play saxophone. As a part of his physical therapy, doctors suggested that he pick up a wind instrument to help his lung capacity. As he recovered, he continued to work on his musical skills. He was so adept on the instrument that by the time he was twelve he was allowed on stage at a local club to back up musical legend Albert King.

After graduating from high school, Sanborn headed to Northwestern University but later transferred to the University of Iowa. Soon after making the move, he got married and had a child. These life-changing events made him realize it was time to expand his career prospects in order to pay the bills, so he sought out bigger venues to showcase his talent.

Rise to Fame

Even though Sanborn was only in his early twenties, he already had a decade of experience playing on stage. A friend encouraged him to try out for the Paul Butterfield Blues Band, which he did, and ended up getting the job. He toured with

 John W. Brown

the band for a while, which gave him more experience and the opportunity to travel the country.

He spent most of the 1970s as a traveling studio performer and ensemble musician for a number of acts. During this time, he played with some of the biggest names in music, including David Bowie, Paul Simon, James Taylor, the Rolling Stones, the Eagles, and Stevie Wonder. He was a man in high demand and already had four of his own albums on store shelves. But as the 1970s came to a close, Sanborn decided it was time to reach out for a bigger solo career and see if he could make it on his own.

SHOW ME SUCCESS

The 1980s turned out to be a major turning point in his career. He released his breakout album, *Hideaway*, in 1980. The following year he released *Voyeur*, which won Sanborn his first Grammy. He won four more Grammys in the 1980s, making him one of the most honored musicians of the decade. His popularity reached into the TV world as well, as he performed with Paul Schaffer's band on *Late Night with David Letterman*, and even started his own TV show, *Night Music*.

The 1990s provided him with even more success. He was already an established star on smooth jazz radio, and he began incorporating other artists to play on his albums. His unique style allowed him to infuse other genres of music while keeping his core fans happy. He paired up with an orchestra on the album *Pearls*, toured with rock great Eric Clapton, and won another Grammy for *Inside*.

Sanborn continues to dominate the airwaves in the 2000s, selling millions of albums and packing arenas around the world. His collaborations with other stars, and an amazing body of solo recordings, make him one of the most influential saxophonists in jazz, pop, and R&B over the past few decades.

EXTRA, EXTRA!

The saxophone solo in James Taylor's classic remake of "How Sweet It Is" was performed by David Sanborn.

He recorded the theme song for the hit TV show L.A. Law.

Sanborn performed at Woodstock with the Paul Butterfield Band.

He appeared in the movie Scrooged with Bill Murray.

St. Louis Rap Scene

Murphy Lee

Murphy Lee was born and raised in St. Louis. He is a solo rap artist and a member of the St. Lunatics with fellow Missouri legend, Nelly. Murphy Lee has achieved success as a solo artist, a group member, and as a part of ensemble casts. He hit the charts with collaborations on the songs "Air Force Ones" and "Shake Ya Tailfeather." His solo album, *Murphy's Law,* was a major success, spawning the hit, "What da Hook Gone Be?" He also shared the honor of winning a Grammy for Best Rap Performance by a Duo or Group in 2004.

Chingy

Chingy has earned success as a group member and solo artist over the past few years on the rap scene. He hit the charts in 2003 with his song, "Right Thurr," keeping St. Louis rappers at the top of the charts. The song received a large amount of airplay in the southern United States originally, but it eventually reached the whole country and landed at No. 4 on the Billboard Hot 100 chart. He followed the success of the first hit with the songs "Holidae Inn" and "One Call Away," and then the album *Powerballin.* He expanded his success with collaborative efforts with other major stars. In 2005, he teamed up with Janet Jackson for "Don't Worry," followed in 2006 with Tyrese in "Pullin' Me Back," Jermaine Dupri with "Dem Jeans," and Amerie in 2007 on "Fly Like Me." He has also branched out into acting, appearing in *My Wife and Kids, The George Lopez Show,* and *Scary Movie 4.*

J-Kwon

When J-Kwon was thirteen, he was kicked out of the house by his mother and forced to live in the backseat of a car. He fell into a dangerous life of selling drugs in south St. Louis, but a St. Louis music producer took him under his wing and mentored the young man in the music business. Before he was even out of his teens, J-Kwon took the music world by storm with the song "Tipsy," produced by music producers Trackboyz. His first album, *Hood Hop*, climbed the charts and made him one of the most in-demand rappers of the time.

JACK WAGNER

ACTOR, MUSICIAN, GOLFER

"I decided that I have much more control over what I do on stage than whether or not my golf ball goes out-of-bounds when it hits a tree."

—*Jack Wagner*

Jack Wagner has been a mainstay on television for several decades, from daytime soaps to nighttime dramas. He is also a singer and hit the charts with one of the biggest songs of the 1980s. The multitalented star also shines on the golf course, where he has been recognized as one of the best golfers in the entertainment industry.

THE EARLY YEARS

Jack Wagner was born on October 3, 1959, and was raised in the town of Washington. As a teenager, he became one of the best golfers in the Show Me State, winning the Missouri Junior Championship. Jack also excelled in every other activity he tried, including football, basketball, schoolwork, music, and drama.

After graduating from high school, he headed a few miles down the road to attend East Central College in Union. He played golf at the junior college and won the Missouri State Junior College Golf Championship in 1980. The next year he set off for the University of Missouri–Columbia for one year before trying to land a golf scholarship at the University of Arizona. He didn't get the golf scholarship, but he landed a full scholarship for drama at the Arizona college.

RISE TO FAME

Wagner completed his studies at Arizona and moved to Hollywood. He lived the life of a struggling actor for a few years where he worked as a tour guide, waited tables, and in retail sales.

His first big break came at the age of twenty-three when he landed a part on the daytime soap opera *A New Day in Eden*. As the saying goes in Hollywood, it's much easier to get work when you are working, and the saying came true for Wagner. He soon had a small part on *Knot's Landing*, and a bigger role on the horizon.

Show Me Success

The year after his part on *Knot's Landing*, he landed a high-profile job as Frisco Jones on *General Hospital*. The role was a perfect combination of a number of his passions, and he soon had critical acclaim and legions of fans for both his acting and his music. Exposure on the radio and TV helped send his first hit song, "All I Need," straight to the top of the charts.

In 1991, Jack took on another role with the daytime soap opera *Santa Barbara*. The role lasted only a short time because the show was cancelled two years later. But the timing was perfect. The next year, he was added to the cast of the hit television show *Melrose Place* as Dr. Peter Burns. The show won numerous awards and kept Jack in the public eye as one of the most popular actors of the late 1990s.

When *Melrose* halted production in 1999, he spent a few years doing live theater. During this time, he also decided to combine his two main passions, golfing and television, into a new TV show. The show on ESPN, called *Off Course*, allowed Wagner to interview other celebrities during a round of golf. It was the perfect combination of all of his skills, but the show lasted only a short time.

In 2003, Jack made the move back to daytime soaps with a role on *The Bold and the Beautiful*. He won an Emmy nomination for his portrayal of Dominick Payne, proving that after two decades in the public eye, he is still a force to be reckoned with in the entertainment world.

Extra, Extra!

* Jack is consistently one of the top golfers in the world on the Celebrity Players Tour.

* Jack released his first album in twelve years, Dancing in the Moonlight, *in 2005.*

Porter Wagoner

Singer, Entertainer

"I stand in awe of Porter Wagoner. I think of him as a visionary."
—Buddy Miller

Porter Wagoner is one of the true legends of country music, selling millions of albums, packing concert venues, and staying true to his humble roots. He started his career by playing guitar for anybody that would listen and built a following of millions that watched his every move. His career has taken him from grocery store performances to the Grand Ole Opry to the New York Stock Exchange.

The Early Years

Porter Wagoner was born on August 12, 1927, and grew up around the southern border of Missouri near West Plains. He taught himself to play guitar by listening to the radio and mimicking the songs he heard. He became an accomplished musician by the time he was out of high school, but there were few opportunities to showcase his talent in the Ozarks. That's when he turned his attention to getting a "real" job to pay the bills.

He got married when he was nineteen, and soon after his marriage, he formed a band called the Blue Ridge Boys. They played small venues across southern Missouri but made very little money. To supplement his income, he worked at a grocery store. It was at this store that Wagoner got his music on the radio. To draw people into the store, the owner convinced local radio station KWPM to broadcast their morning show from the butcher block while Porter cut meat, and music, for customers.

Rise to Fame

Soon after the success of the show in the grocery store, Springfield radio station KWTO hired the twenty-four-year-old entertainer to appear on their airwaves. His time in Springfield was shorter than anyone expected as he was soon thereafter signed to a contract with RCA Records.

After signing the record contract, Wagoner quickly made an impact on country music. The same year he joined RCA, he had his first No. 1 song, "A Satisfied Mind," which meant he had to move his growing family to the Country Music Capital of the World, Nashville.

Show Me Success

In the mid- and late-1950s, Wagoner was a bona fide star, and TV executives were looking for ways to capitalize on his popularity. He hosted the *Porter Wagoner Show* in 1960, which aired for the next twenty-one years and encompassed nearly seven hundred episodes. The show was broadcast to millions of viewers each week, which also helped increase album sales.

Wagoner was getting more popular than ever, and the awards rolled in. He had several Grammys and numerous top ten hits. Dolly Parton was added to his show in 1967 to expand its popularity. The duo went on to record more than a dozen top ten hits, including "Please Don't Stop Loving Me," which peaked at No. 1 in 1975.

Because of his popularity, Wagoner became the unofficial spokesperson for the Grand Ole Opry, while also acting as an Opryland tourist ambassador in the 1990s. He was immortalized in 2002 when he was elected to the Country Music Hall of Fame and honored again in 2006 for fifty years of service to the Grand Ole Opry. He continued making music into his eighties with *Wagonmaster* released shortly before his death in 2007, climbing all the way to No. 63 on the album charts. He died of lung cancer in Nashville in October of 2007 with a memorial held at the Grand Ole Opry.

Extra, Extra!

*Wagoner rang the opening bell at the New York Stock Exchange while representing Gaylord Entertainment, the parent company of the Grand Ole Opry.

*He appeared in the Clint Eastwood film Honkytonk Man.

*Wagoner and Parton were named the Country Music Association's Duo of the Year for three years in a row.

*One of the main highways through West Plains is named Porter Wagoner Boulevard.

DENNIS WEAVER

ACTOR

"To get what you want, stop doing what isn't working."
—*Dennis Weaver*

Dennis Weaver, a Missouri-born actor, performed some of the most recognizable acting roles of all time. He portrayed "Chester Goode" on *Gunsmoke* and "Marshal Sam McCloud" on the show *McCloud*. His dedication to the Old West shines through his acclaimed acting roles and in his commitment to preserving the environment in the American West.

THE EARLY YEARS

Dennis Weaver was born on June 4, 1924, and grew up in Joplin where he was a star athlete at Joplin High School and at Joplin Junior College (which is now Missouri Southern State University) before attending the University of Oklahoma on a track and field scholarship. At Oklahoma, he set numerous school records in track and even tried out for the U.S. Olympic team in the decathlon. He placed sixth in the 1948 Olympic Trials, but only the top three contestants made the Olympic team. After his attempt at track and field stardom was over, he moved to New York to pursue his passion for acting.

RISE TO FAME

His first role on Broadway came as an understudy in the production of *Come Back, Little Sheba*. When the show hit the road for a national tour, Weaver took over the role of "Turk."

He was also accepted by the Actor's Studio, where developed his skills and made contacts with other up-and-coming actors. These contacts paid off in 1952 when he landed a contract with Universal International Studios. The parts didn't pay enough in the early years, so he supplemented his income with various odd jobs including delivering flowers and selling vacuum cleaners.

SHOW ME SUCCESS

In 1955, the course of Weaver's career changed dramatically when he auditioned for a role on a new Western TV show called *Gunsmoke*. He read for the part of "Chester" and immediately landed the co-starring role. The show was a huge success and led to an Emmy for Weaver.

Weaver longed for greater challenges and exposure, so he guest-starred on other television series, including *Twilight Zone*, *Alfred Hitchcock Theatre*, and *Playhouse Ninety*. After nine years on *Gunsmoke*, Weaver felt that he had exhausted the creative potential connected with Chester. When NBC guaranteed him twenty-four shows as the star of *Kentucky Jones* in 1964, he decided it was time to leave *Gunsmoke* to take on a new challenge.

The next big step in his acting career came in 1970 when he took the starring role as Sam McCloud in the new series *McCloud*. He again proved to be an outstanding actor and garnered more honors, including three Emmy nominations.

The 1980s and 1990s proved that Weaver was still one of the top actors in Hollywood, not only in the rugged western roles he came to define but also in comedies, as a leading man, and even as a country music artist. This combination of skills solidified his reputation as a great performer in practically every genre of entertainment. He died in 2006 after a life full of success and adventure. He was awarded with a star on the Hollywood Walk of Fame, inducted into the Western Performers Hall of Fame, and has a star on the Dodge City Trail of Fame.

EXTRA, EXTRA!

His top pay on Gunsmoke was nine thousand dollars per week.

He sold vacuum cleaners to supplement his acting income during the early years.

From 1973 to 1975, he was president of the Screen Actors Guild.

Was the voice of cowboy Buck McCoy on the animated show The Simpsons.

MEDIA AND BROADCASTING

JIM BOHANNON

SYNDICATED RADIO HOST

"One of the 100 Most Important Radio Talk Show Hosts in America."
—Talkers Magazine

Named one of the most influential talk radio hosts in the country for several years straight, Jim Bohannon has made a significant impact on radio and is often referred to as the man who succeeded Larry King. His larger-than-life persona started in a much more humble manner, growing up as just a regular kid in the Missouri Ozarks.

THE EARLY YEARS

Jim Bohannon was born on January 7, 1944, in Corvallis, Oregon. Jim was just a few months old when his family moved to Lebanon, Missouri, which is where he spent the rest of his childhood. He graduated from Lebanon High School in 1962 and then moved forty-five minutes away to attend college at Southwest Missouri State University in Springfield.

Bohannon took an early interest in broadcasting. He picked up his first on-air job in 1960 at the age of sixteen at his hometown radio station KLWT-AM. During his college years at SMSU, he honed his skills as a disc jockey at KICK radio and as a news reporter at KWTO-AM.

After he finished college, he shipped off to Vietnam where he spent one year with the 199th Light Infantry Brigade. Upon completion of his duties, the U.S. Army sent him back to Washington, D.C., where he launched a career asking questions of the rich and powerful in our nation's capital.

RISE TO FAME

Soon after Bohannon returned to the United States, he took a position at WGAY radio station. It was an odd fit for him because the station played easy listening music. His news interests eventually pulled him away from the music format and back into talk radio when he landed reporting jobs at news radio stations WTOP and WRC.

In 1980, he packed his bags and headed to Chicago for a morning show at WCFL. The high-profile job expanded his expertise and exposure, but it wasn't enough to keep him content. He picked up a side job in the afternoons at CNN's Chicago bureau, filing stories to be seen around the country. The exposure he received from those two positions in the third-largest media market in the country set the stage for his next big move.

Three years after he moved to Chicago, he took a job as a reporter with the Mutual Broadcasting Network. That network just happened to carry the world-famous *Larry King Radio Show.* Bohannon made such a positive impact on the listeners that he was soon the primary fill-in host when King was gone. It was incredible exposure, and now people around the country were beginning to know the name Jim Bohannon. He was offered his own syndicated show in 1993 when Westwood One bought out Mutual and moved Larry King to a daytime position, leaving the evening position open for the *Jim Bohannon Show.*

SHOW ME SUCCESS

The *Jim Bohannon Show* was an immediate success. Millions of listeners related to his easygoing manner and intelligent political discussions. Never one to rest on his success, he picked up additional hosting duties for a daily news magazine at Westwood One and a weekly feature radio show as well.

In addition to his legions of listeners and fans, the awards and honors were starting to rack up. He was inducted into the Radio Hall of Fame in Chicago and put on the Wall of Honor in his hometown of Lebanon. Topping things off, Bohannon was inducted into the national Radio Hall of Fame in 2003.

Despite his worldwide success, Bohannon continues to make southwest Missouri a part of his life. He took the unprecedented step of broadcasting his syndicated show from the Ozark Empire Fairgrounds in Springfield, giving the area additional national exposure. In fact, this small-town Missouri boy saw such exponential growth of his program that the *Jim Bohannon Show* ranked as the fifth most listened-to talk program in the country!

EXTRA, EXTRA!

*Jim is one of the specialty voice announcers that can be heard on CBS's Face the Nation.

*Bohannon was nominated for the National Association of Broadcasters Marconi Radio Award for the Network Syndicated Personality of the Year.

*Bohannon and his wife, Annabelle, went to high school together but didn't see each other again for thirty-three years. They "re-met" at a book signing in Columbia, Missouri, and were married a few years later.

 JOHN W. BROWN

JOE BUCK

SPORTS BROADCASTER

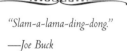

"Slam-a-lama-ding-dong."
—*Joe Buck*

"Go crazy folks! Go crazy!"
—*Jack Buck*

Joe Buck is one of the nation's most prominent sports broadcasters of all time. A listing of his great career and amazing accomplishments would not be complete without also including the part his father played in his legacy. Jack Buck was known as the Voice of the St. Louis Cardinals for decades. But Jack was raised in Massachusetts, so he was not eligible for this book. It is imperative, however, to mention him in his son's biography because Jack had a tremendous impact on his family, the broadcast industry, and Missouri history. As is often the case with successful children of successful parents, Joe picked up where his father left off and took the family name to even greater heights.

THE EARLY YEARS

Joseph Francis Buck was born on April 25, 1969, in St. Petersburg, Florida, but was raised in the city of St. Louis. His childhood was not what most people would consider normal, as he traveled with his father around the country broadcasting games for Major League Baseball and the National Football League. Jack was the broadcaster, but he was often a bigger star than many of the players. Joe graduated from the prestigious Country Day High School in St. Louis, and then headed off to college at sports-crazed Indiana University.

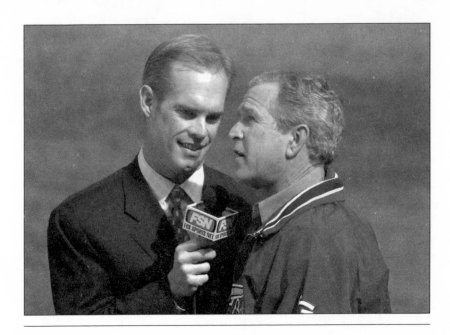

RISE TO FAME

Joe Buck got into broadcasting almost as quickly as he entered college. In 1989, he took up the job of play-by-play announcer for the Louisville Redbirds, who just happened to be the minor league affiliate of the St. Louis Cardinals. He also worked as a reporter for ESPN's coverage of the minor league All-Star Game. When he graduated from college, it was time to head to the big leagues. He followed in his father's footsteps, broadcasting games for the St. Louis Cardinals on KMOX radio and KPLR-TV.

SHOW ME SUCCESS

At the age of twenty-five, Joe was calling games that the best broadcasters in the industry only dreamt of. He made a name for himself after he accepted a job with Fox Sports, which was in the early stages of acquiring sports broadcasting rights across the country. At Fox Sports, he announced NFL games, which broadcast his voice into the homes of millions of people every Sunday afternoon. Joe built on his success throughout his late twenties and early thirties, becoming the lead announcer for the NFL on Fox shortly after joining the network. A few years later, he put another line on his resume when he did play-by-play for a Super Bowl game in 2004.

Baseball was his first love and the continuing connection to his father's legacy. He took over the duties as primary announcer for Fox's Major League Baseball rotation in 1996. This made him one of the highest paid and most recognizable sports announcers in the country. At the age of thirty, he had the honor of doing play-by-play for the World Series, which made him the youngest person ever to call a World Series game on television. Perhaps one of the highlights of his young career was in 2006 when he as able to say, "St. Louis has a World Series winner," after the Cardinals won the series against the Detroit Tigers.

Joe has become one of the most successful broadcasters in American history and is still in his thirties. His father may have opened doors for him, but Joe continues to prove that his success is due to his own merits.

Extra, Extra!

Buck is only the third announcer to handle a television network's lead MLB and NFL coverage in the same year.

He has won numerous sports Emmy Awards for Outstanding Sports Personality for play-by-play.

Buck has two brothers and five sisters, some of whom are also in the broadcasting industry.

HARRY CARAY

SPORTS BROADCASTER

"Holy cow!"
—*Harry Caray*

Harry Caray is best known as the broadcasting voice of the Chicago Cubs. Before he moved to the Windy City though, he was just another St. Louis boy who loved baseball. He grew up poor in the heart of St. Louis but went on to capture the hearts and minds of sports fans all over the country thanks to catch phrases like "Holy cow" and his renditions of "Take Me Out to the Ballgame."

THE EARLY YEARS

Harry Christopher Carabina was born on March 1, 1914, in St. Louis. He grew up in a rougher section of the city on LaSalle Street, which, ironically, is near the spot where Busch Stadium now stands. His father died when he was an infant, and his mother died when he was only ten. So as a child he lived with his aunt in Webster Groves, where he attended and graduated from high school.

He was an exceptional athlete during his school years and even played with semi-professional baseball teams. Unable to move up the ranks to the majors, he instead turned his focus to talking about sports on the radio.

RISE TO FAME

Carey's first radio audition took place when he was only nineteen and fell into the role of broadcaster quite naturally. Much like life in the minor leagues, broadcasting required that he bounce around the minor leagues of media in cities like Joliet, Illinois, and Kalamazoo, Michigan.

He made the jump to the big leagues when he landed a broadcasting job with the St. Louis Hawks basketball team. At around this time, he also picked up announcing jobs for the University of Missouri football team and the Cotton Bowl games. His next jump made him a staple of the St. Louis area radio waves and a household name in one of the best sports cities in the country. He was only in his mid-twenties, but he was holding down two major broadcasting jobs as the announcer for both St. Louis professional baseball teams, the St. Louis Cardinals and St. Louis Browns.

The Browns were coming off a World Series appearance in 1944, but they were still the second-favorite team in the city, losing the World Series to the city's favorite team. Coupled with low attendance and declining interest in the club, he decided to focus solely on the Cardinals. So from 1945 to 1969, he was the play-by-play announcer for the St. Louis Cardinals, announcing the highlights of players like Stan Musial, Dick Groat, and Ken Boyer.

Caray was a star in the city of St. Louis, but difficulties with Cardinals ownership and an offer from the Oakland Athletics in 1970 led him to the West Coast. His one-year stint in Oakland was followed by a job with the Chicago White Sox, and finally the Chicago Cubs in 1982.

Show Me Success

Harry Caray's flamboyant style, "over the top" broadcasting calls, trademark thick-rimmed glasses, and unusual Seventh Inning Stretch singing performances made him more than just the Voice of the Cubs; he was a national icon. He was the ultimate fan with a style all his own, and the fans loved it.

In addition to the hoards of people who hung on his every word, he was also racking up quite a few honors from his peers. In 1989, Caray was inducted into the broadcasters wing of the Baseball Hall of Fame in Cooperstown, New York. He was also named the "Baseball Announcer of the Year" seven years in a row by *The Sporting News*. He had an amazing string of attending every opening-day game for forty-one years before a stroke sidelined him in 1987.

Caray held the play-by-play announcer job for the Chicago Cubs until his death in 1998. Like another famous Missouri broadcasting legend, Jack Buck, his son picked up where he left off. Caray's son Skip, and grandson Chip, have both migrated to the broadcast booth and continue Harry Caray's legacy.

Extra, Extra!

Caray was teamed up in the broadcasting booth was another Missouri legend, Jack Buck.

Even after his death, his namesake restaurants keep his legacy alive.

EUGENE FIELD

WRITER, COLUMNIST

"Wynken, Blynken and Nod one night
Sailed off in a wooden shoe
Sailed on a river of crystal light,
Into a sea of dew."
—*Eugene Field*

Eugene Field lived a short life, but his legacy has endured for nearly 150 years. The Missouri native became known as the country's first columnist and the "poet of childhood." He left behind an impressive compilation of writings that are known around the world, with few people realizing that Missouri was part of his early influences.

THE EARLY YEARS

Eugene Field was born in September of 1850 in St. Louis to a family with East Coast roots. Eugene's father, Roswell, played an important role in American history as the attorney for the Scott family in the Dred Scott legal case that played out in court in the city of St. Louis. Field's mother died when Eugene was young, and he was sent to live in Massachusetts with a cousin. His father died when Eugene was a teenager.

After his father's death, Eugene bounced around to several colleges, ending up at the University of Missouri–Columbia. The legacy he left at the university was not so much that of a scholar but rather that of a practical joker, and he dropped out without attaining a college degree. Eugene's education came from life experiences; in large part from a European trip he took soon after his father's estate was settled. Formal schooling eluded him, but his unique look at life as a "Road Scholar" made him a star of his day.

RISE TO FAME

Field began his journalistic career as a reporter for the *St. Louis Evening Journal* at the age of twenty-three. He took the job in part to make some extra money while he waited for his fourteen-year-old girlfriend, Julia Comstock, to turn sixteen so they could marry. After the marriage, he spent the next decade moving around the Show Me State writing for a number of publications, including the *St. Joseph Gazette*, *St. Louis Times-Journal*, and *Kansas City Times*. His editorial and gossipy writings were popular in every city in which he worked, but the readers were unaware of who the author really was.

Field left Missouri in 1881 for a job in Colorado at the *Denver Tribune* where his column was again very popular. Two years later, he took a job at the *Chicago Daily News* where he had free reign to write about any topic he chose in a column called "Sharps and Flats." The column became a "must read" for audiences, and Field finally found a city where he could plant his roots.

SHOW ME SUCCESS

"Sharps and Flats" was such a hit that Field became known as "America's First Columnist" (aka, "The Father of the Personal Newspaper Column"). He became more of a local celebrity than a newspaper writer, especially when he wrote about the actors of the day. His insight into their lives made the stars seem more real to the readers. That column is often regarded as a precursor to the celebrity media culture we have today. In addition to actors, Chicagoans were also passionate about their sports heroes. Field took the same approach to writing about the sports stars, humanizing them for the readers and giving himself the reputation as one of baseball's biggest fans.

Many people think of Field solely as a children's author, despite the fact that children's literature was but a small part of his writings. His poems have stood the test of time and are still widely read today, including "Wynken, Blynken, and Nod," "The Duel," and "Little Boy Blue."

Field died in his sleep from a heart attack in 1895 at the age of forty-five. He lived a short life, but he left a legacy as a great Missourian, an amazing children's poet, and America's first newspaper columnist.

EXTRA, EXTRA!

The Eugene Field House Historic Site is open to the public on Broadway in south St. Louis.

A large number of schools across the Midwest are named in his honor.

He and his wife had eight children, five of whom reached adulthood.

ROBERT HEINLEIN

SCIENCE FICTION WRITER

"Always listen to experts. They'll tell you what can't be done and why. Then do it."
—*Robert Heinlein*

Robert Heinlein's name may not be recognizable to most people, but those who know his works regard him as a great. Heinlein was a prolific author with a contingent of science fiction fans who hung on his every word and couldn't wait for his next story to be published. There have been few like him in the history of publishing, earning him the title "Dean of Science Fiction Writers."

THE EARLY YEARS

Robert Anson Heinlein was born on July 7, 1907, in the small town of Butler. He and his six brothers and sisters moved to Kansas City when he was about three and lived there throughout his childhood. He had an amazing interest in astronomy as a child that was stimulated in 1910 with the appearance of Halley's Comet. He was only three when the comet raced past the earth, but from that point on he was hooked on space.

He graduated from Central High School in 1925 and was eventually accepted into the U.S. Naval Academy. A case of tuberculosis led to a discharge from the Navy, which allowed him to study physics and mathematics at UCLA. He also became interested in politics during this time following the "EPIC" (Ending Poverty In California) political movement. He was so inspired by the movement that he ran for the California legislature.

RISE TO FAME

After his election defeat, he turned his attention to writing. In 1939, *Life-Line* was published in a magazine and earned him seventy dollars. The book was a product of Heinlein's imagination about the political movements of the day. It seemed like easy money because he was simply writing about a topic in which he was well versed.

From that time on, he churned out an amazing number of stories, often under different names so he could have multiple stories appear in a single issue of magazines. One of the defining characteristics of his stories was a precise understanding of astronomy and science, which he wove in and out of the storylines.

World War II forced him to put writing on hold for a few years, but the job he took during the war expanded his understanding of space even more. He worked as an aircraft engineer at the Naval Aircraft Factory near Philadelphia where he designed high altitude space suits, which were later incorporated into his books. After the war, he resumed his writing and produced some of the best works in science fiction history.

SHOW ME SUCCESS

Juvenile science fiction books was one area that Heinlein expanded. These books were much like his earlier works except the heroes were younger and the stories lacked the sexual content. He published *Starship Troopers* in 1959 in the juvenile science fiction genre, which many people consider his best work. The book made him a star and was adapted for numerous movies including the 1997 version that was a big hit with audiences.

Despite his success, Heinlein was frustrated with publishers because they often carved up his storylines to make them more sellable. So he decided to write a book titled *Stranger in a Strange Land*, where he satirized the religious, political, and sexual attitudes of the day. The timing of the book was perfect because America was on the verge of the turbulent 1960s, and he captured the controversial issues in the science fiction realm. *Stranger in a Strange Land* became a cult classic and the best-selling book in science fiction history. The success of that book finally gave him the freedom to write stories the way he wanted without worrying what editors would do to the manuscript.

Over the course of his writing, Heinlein won a total of four Hugo Awards for best novel of the year and was the first recipient of the Grand Master Nebula Award by the Science Fiction Writers of America. Over his six decades of writing, he was able to make science fiction mainstream and is still regarded by many as the man who paved the way for widespread acceptance of stories like *Star Wars* and *Star Trek*.

EXTRA, EXTRA!

*Heinlein published his last novel on his eightieth birthday.

*Heinlein was cremated and his ashes thrown from the deck of a warship in the Pacific Ocean near Santa Cruz.

*He was a college fencing champion while in the Naval Academy.

AL HIRSCHFELD

ILLUSTRATOR

"Artists are just children who refuse to put down their crayons."
—Al Hirschfeld

Al Hirschfeld often claimed that he was not a celebrity, just a man who saw celebrities in unique ways. Despite his denials, his drawings in the *New York Times* made him a Broadway fixture for decades and a star in his own right. He drew world-famous caricatures of the biggest names of stage and screen, which were often coveted by the stars themselves. His amazing talent allowed him to travel the world, but his start was right here in the Show Me State.

THE EARLY YEARS

Albert Hirschfeld was born on June 21, 1903, in St. Louis. He and his two siblings were raised in the area just north of Forest Park where he was heavily influenced by the arts. His family moved to New York when he was twelve where he continued his love affair with the arts. He was so enamored with the culture that he enrolled at the Art Students League and became the artistic director at a motion picture studio at the age of eighteen.

Hirschfeld eventually worked his way into a job at Warner Brothers, but he longed to study overseas. So when he was twenty-one, he headed to Paris to expand his understanding of the world and perfect his craft. During his trips home from Europe to visit family, he often caught a few plays. On one particular trip in 1926, he went to a show and sketched a picture that changed his life forever.

RISE TO FAME

Hirschfeld and press agent Richard Maney attended a show starring a French actor named Sacha Guitry. Hirschfeld took out his program and drew a picture of the woman. Maney was so impressed by the drawing that he asked if Hirschfeld could reproduce the drawing on a clean sheet of paper so Maney could reprint it in the newspaper. When the picture appeared in the *New York Herald-Tribune*,

Hirschfeld was suddenly a working artist! Newspapers across the city were clamoring for his drawings, with stars even begging for their own pictures to be drawn. His popularity continued to climb when the *New York Times* came calling in 1929. He remained at the *Times* for the rest of his professional life.

SHOW ME SUCCESS

For the next seventy years after joining the *Times*, Hirschfeld was a staple on Broadway and at opening nights all over the city. He perfected his craft of drawing in the dark during the shows in a very intricate manner. He used a system of notations that allowed him to create the caricature in perfect detail after he left the show. The drawings became a status symbol for many Broadway and Hollywood stars, and his works were as much a part of the show as the performance itself.

His daughter, Nina, was born in 1945, which began another phase of his artwork that was closely watched by loyal fans. He inserted her name into the lines of almost every drawing after her birth. In fact, the one time he failed to include her name in a drawing, people were so upset that they overwhelmed him with responses about the omission. From that point on, the number of times her name appeared in drawing was printed in a corner of the picture, which made the drawings a "word search" game for loyal fans.

Hirschfeld racked up accolades and honors from people all over the world, including a special Tony Award for his depictions of stage actors. A film documentary about his life also garnered an Academy Award nomination. He wrote several books and collaborated on a musical called *Sweet Bye and Bye*, but his lasting legacy will always be that of the *Playbill* on Broadway. He died in his sleep at age ninety-nine, as a true star that made his living drawing other stars. It is rightly pointed out by one Broadway critic that "there are just two forms of fame on Broadway: seeing your name in lights, and more significantly, to be drawn by Hirschfeld."

EXTRA, EXTRA!

*The New York Landmarks Conservancy named Hirschfeld as one of six people considered New York City Landmarks.

*In 1991, Hirschfeld designed a booklet of stamps for the U.S. Postal Service showcasing comedians Stan Laurel and Oliver Hardy, Edgar Bergen and Charlie McCarthy, Jack Benny and Fanny Brice, and Bud Abbott and Lou Costello.

MARY MARGARET McBRIDE

RADIO HOST

"It's one o'clock and here is Mary Margaret McBride!"
—Opening line of McBride's radio show

One of the pioneers of talk radio, Mary Margaret McBride blazed a path that few women—or men for that matter—had taken. She grew up in small-town Missouri, but she made her mark in the Big Apple. She worked with and socialized with the biggest stars of the era, making her one of the biggest names in the country in the early 1900s.

THE EARLY YEARS

Mary Margaret McBride was born on November 16, 1899, in Paris, Missouri. She grew up on a farm in northwest Missouri before enrolling at William Woods College in Fulton. At the time, William Woods was still just a prep school, which she used to get ready for the University of Missouri–Columbia. Mizzou was becoming known for its top-notch journalism program, and McBride took advantage of the learning opportunities. She graduated with a degree in journalism in 1919 and set off for a career in the media.

RISE TO FAME

After graduation, McBride took a job in Ohio with the *Cleveland Press*. She worked in Cleveland for about five years before she was offered a job at the *Evening Mail* in New York City. New York was the center of the publishing universe, so it was easy for her to pick up additional work as a freelance writer. Her hard work and excellent skills opened doors for her to write for prestigious magazines like *Good Housekeeping* and *The Saturday Evening Post*.

Her folksy style and motherly approach were a hit with readers. Radio stations took interest in her abilities and her name value, and soon she was working with the powerhouse radio station WOR under the name "Martha Deane." The daily advice show for women became popular as fans soaked up every word of her grandmotherly advice (even though she was only thirty-eight at the time).

Show Me Success

The CBS Radio Network hired McBride in 1937, just three years after debuting on WOR. She dropped the name of Martha Deane and went back to Mary Margaret McBride. Her show was a mixture of advice, entertainment, celebrity news, politics, and news of the day. She interviewed the top newsmakers from every segment of society, which made her one of the top radio celebrities in the country in the 1940s, 1950s, and 1960s.

McBride also started a television show in 1948, but it never gained popularity with the viewing audience. The show was dropped soon after it started but was a precursor to today's advice shows like *Oprah* and *The View*.

McBride also wrote numerous books and a syndicated newspaper column. After her syndicated radio days were over, she moved to a small town in upstate New York where she continued broadcasting, sometimes from her living room. She died in 1976 and left behind a legacy as one of the first true multimedia superstars.

Extra, Extra!

*She only accepted advertisements on her radio show for products she endorsed. She rejected all tobacco and alcohol ads!

*During the 1940s, she took the bold step of having black guests on her show, which was done very little during that time.

*She interviewed several big-name personalities, including Harry S Truman, Eleanor Roosevelt, Frank Lloyd Wright, Bob Hope, Tennessee Williams, and Joe DiMaggio.

RUSS MITCHELL

NEWS ANCHOR

"What I miss about Missouri the most would be the people. You don't really appreciate that until you've spent some time walking down the streets of places like New York City. Even though I've been gone for quite some time now I still call Missouri home."
—*Russ Mitchell*

There are only a handful of network anchor jobs in the country, and St. Louisan Russ Mitchell is one of a few people skilled enough to handle that position. He was a familiar face on local television stations in Columbia, Kansas City, and St. Louis before the rest of the country got to know him as a network anchor at CBS News.

THE EARLY YEARS

Russell Edward Mitchell was born at Jewish Hospital on March 25, 1960, in St. Louis and grew up in the St. Louis suburb of Rock Hill. He graduated in 1978 from Webster Groves High School, then headed off to the prestigious journalism school at the University of Missouri–Columbia.

RISE TO FAME

Russ took his first television broadcast job after college at KMBC-TV in Kansas City. He worked as a reporter at the ABC affiliate for a short time before a big career jump to Dallas, which just happened to be one of the largest media markets in the country. He was only twenty-three years old and working in a high-profile anchor position at WFAA-TV. He stayed in Texas from 1983 to 1985 and then returned to his roots to accomplish a career goal by taking a job in his hometown of St. Louis.

Mitchell began working for KTVI-TV in 1985, which at the time was

the ABC affiliate in St. Louis. He moved to the CBS affiliate, KMOV, in 1987 where he became a well-known public figure and award-winning broadcaster. During his time at KMOV, he picked up the 1989 award from the UPI for Best Reporter in Missouri and a pair of Emmy Awards for his on-air reporting.

People at the network level were taking notice of his tremendous talent and easygoing on-air personality. After only seven years back in the Show Me State, he took the career jump of a lifetime by taking a job in New York with CBS News.

Show Me Success

Mitchell made the difficult transition from local news to network correspondent in 1992 and made an immediate impact. He was seen in homes from coast to coast, working on shows that included *Eye to Eye*, *Up to the Minute*, *CBS Evening News with Dan Rather*, *CBS Evening News Saturday Edition*, and the *CBS Early Show*.

He became the anchor of *The Saturday Early Show* on CBS when the show debuted in 1997. While holding down that job, he also anchored the *CBS Evening News Saturday Edition* and was a correspondent for *CBS News Sunday Morning*. He was promoted in 2006 to news anchor and host of the *CBS Early Show*, where he continues to rack up loyal fans and numerous awards.

Extra, Extra!

Professional honors:

*2001 Sigma Delta Chi Award for spot news coverage of the Elian Gonzalez case.

*1997 Emmy Award for coverage of the crash of TWA's Flight 800.

*1995 National Association of Black Journalists News Award.

ERICH "MANCOW" MULLER

RADIO SHOW HOST

"My show is revolutionary, not evolutionary. I keep reinventing myself, not like the other dinosaurs in this business right now."
—Mancow

Mancow is a famous radio talk show host known not only for his wild antics on the air but also for his publicity stunts off the air. He was a stage actor, small-market radio DJ, and promotions director for radio stations before making it big in shock-talk radio. His show is often a lightning rod for controversy and multimillion-dollar fines. His success has translated into millions of radio fans, national television appearances, and even book publishing.

THE EARLY YEARS

Erich Muller was born on June 21, 1967, in Kansas City. His first love in perfor-mance was acting as he appeared on stage in more than one hundred professional plays. Muller stayed close to home after graduation from high school to attend Central Missouri State University. Warrensburg was also where he got his first taste of radio at KOKO-AM. His responsibilities consisted of running the mixing board and playing commercials during Larry King's syndicated radio program.

RISE TO FAME

During Muller's senior year at Central Missouri State, he was a full-time student holding down a full-time job as promotions director and weekend radio person-ality at KLSI-FM in Kansas City. Despite the overloaded schedule, he graduated from CMSU with degrees in public relations and theater.

After graduation, he moved back to Kansas City for a radio show of his own. His hard work paid off when he landed a high-profile position as morning drive host on KBEQ-FM, Q-104. The show had low ratings when he took over, but the *Holy Moly and Maxx Show,* as it was called, was a ratings success and quickly helped the station rise to No. 1 in the city. Because of that large amount of ratings suc-cess, bigger opportunities presented themselves. From Kansas City, Muller took a giant leap to one of the biggest radio markets in the country: San Francisco.

Show Me Success

Muller, now known as "Mancow" on the radio, hit the airwaves with a splash on Wild 107 in San Francisco. The show was again a big success, drew large ratings, and brought the station plenty of publicity. But a stunt by the morning crew brought the station more attention than they wanted, along with more than a million dollars in fines.

Mancow was able to shut down the Golden Gate Bridge in the middle of the morning rush hour while his morning sidekick got a haircut. The stunt was designed to poke fun at President Bill Clinton, who was accused of shutting down air traffic in San Francisco while he received a haircut on Air Force One. Mancow's stunt got the attention he wanted, making national news headlines and making the name Mancow known across the country.

At the age of twenty-eight, he left San Francisco for another radio job, this time during morning drive in Chicago. He landed at WKQX, Q-101, where he hosted *Mancow's Morning Madhouse.*

The *Madhouse* has been a lightning rod for criticism and FCC penalties despite the fact the Muller claims on the air to be a very spiritual person. He is quick to point out that *Mancow's Morning Madhouse* is a show, meaning that the character you hear on the air is not necessarily a true reflection of who he really is. In his mind, he is an actor. He has faced millions of indecency fines over the years, yet he attends church and reads the bible regularly.

His legions of fans are now spread across the country thanks to the syndication of his show, which allows him access to be on shows like *Oprah, Jerry Springer,* and *Hard Copy.* Thousands of his loyal fans finally got to see him on TV in 2004 when he became a regular correspondent for the network television show *Fox and Friends.*

He may be a dichotomy to many people who listen to his show, but the youth actor-turned-radio show superstar is doing exactly what he says he was born to do: Entertain you.

Extra, Extra!

The name "Mancow" came from the half-man, half-cow he portrayed in a play at CMSU.

Muller was performing in the stage version of On Golden Pond *as a child when Henry Fonda stopped by to watch the show. Fonda later went on to make a film version of the show.*

He wrote a book called Freedom Road: Journeys with My Father.

He appeared in Lee Jeans and Wal-Mart ads as a child.

Richard Marlin Perkins

Zoologist, Broadcaster

"Hello, and welcome to Mutual of Omaha's Wild Kingdom."
—*Marlin Perkins's introduction to his weekly show*

If you watched television in the 1960s and 1970s, the odds are you watched Marlin Perkins on Mutual of Omaha's *Wild Kingdom*. Perkins exposed an entire generation of people to the amazing characteristics of wild animals and how people and nature can work together in harmony. He went around the world to showcase the most amazing animals on the planet. He wrestled giant boa constrictors in the wild, tracked crocodiles, and dodged a stampede of elephants. His love of nature gave all of us a better understanding of the wild animals around us.

The Early Years

Marlin Perkins was born in Carthage, Missouri, on March 28, 1905. He lived there for a short time before his mother died, when he moved in with his aunt on a farm in Pittsburg, Kansas. It was on the farm where he showed an interest in animals and actually created his own personal zoo consisting of snakes, frogs, and other "creatures." He lived there for nine years before returning to live in Carthage with his father, Joseph Dudley Perkins, a prominent judge in Jasper County.

He continued to collect all sorts of animals during his teenage years, which was spent between Carthage and Pittsburg. After graduation from high school, he headed to the University of Missouri–Columbia to study zoology and gain an even greater understanding of the animals he loved.

Perkins didn't stay at Mizzou very long. The world-famous Saint Louis Zoo was only two hours away, and he was more interested in learning from the animals firsthand. At the age of twenty-one, he took a job with the ground crew at the Zoo so he could be closer to the animals.

His love of snakes proved to be a valuable skill right from the start of his new job. He informed the zoo director that he wanted a greater role in taking care of the reptiles. The Reptilian Department was small, with only six animals, so the director put him in charge of the exhibit. Marlin took that small role and turned it into a major success. Soon the reptile collection under his care was one of the zoo's most popular attractions. Two years after his entry-level appointment, Perkins was the curator of Reptiles with a collection of animals that expanded to five hundred over the next eleven years.

Perkins showed that he was capable of taking care of animals while getting others interested in them as well. He was ready to spread his wings to bigger challenges, so he took a job in 1938 as the director of the New York Zoological Gardens in Buffalo. Six years later, he was hired in Chicago as the director of the Lincoln Park Zoo.

While working at the zoo in Chicago, he took his love for animals to the small screen. His live TV show called *Zoo Parade* made him a national celebrity in 1945. His natural charisma and gentle manner with the animals was a hit with audiences from coast to coast. Not only was the audience entertained, but Marlin was also fulfilling a personal mission of educating people about the habitat and behavior of these wild animals.

Show Me Success

Perkins returned to St. Louis in 1962 to take over as the zoo's director and immediately began working on a new television program. Under his leadership, he made the Saint Louis Zoo one of the premier zoological parks in the country, while also building his show into one of the most successful nature shows in history. Mutual of Omaha's *Wild Kingdom* debuted in January 1963, less than one year after he moved back to St. Louis. The show was produced for twenty-seven years and racked up four Emmy Awards. The show also became the first television series to receive the Parent Teacher Association's "Recommended for Family Viewing" designation.

Perkins retired from the zoo in 1970, but he remained in the St. Louis area

until his death at his home in Clayton in 1986. Until his death, he worked on ecological projects around the country, but primarily in the Show Me State. His amazing life was memorialized in 1993, when the Saint Louis Zoo founded the Marlin Perkins Society to carry on his dream for conserving endangered species and nurturing their existence.

EXTRA, EXTRA!

* *Mutual of Omaha's* Wild Kingdom *was shown on two hundred stations in North America and in more than forty countries worldwide.*

*Marlin was the zoologist for Sir Edmund Hillary's expedition in 1960 to climb Mount Everest in the Himalayas.

*Perkins was given honorary doctorate degrees from the University of Missouri–Columbia, Northland College in Wisconsin, Rockhurst College in Kansas City, MacMurray College in Illinois, and College of St. Mary in Nebraska.

STONE PHILLIPS

NEWS ANCHOR

Stone Phillips is one of the most recognizable faces, and voices, in the news industry today. He has made a name for himself on the anchor desk, covering major events all over the world and with special reports on NBC News. The award-winning journalist has been a witness to some of the world's biggest stories, including drug trafficking in South America and the destruction in war-torn Beirut. He has interview newsmakers like Jeffrey Dahmer, Donald Trump, George Bush, Boris Yeltsin, Michael Jordan, and Jack Kevorkian. This Missourian has truly had a front-row seat to history.

THE EARLY YEARS

Lester Stockton Phillips was born on December 2, 1954, in Texas City, Texas, but grew up in St. Louis. He graduated from Parkway West High School, where he was a standout athlete and student, which landed him a spot at Yale University.

While at Yale, he continued to star in the classroom and on the field. He was the starting quarterback on the Yale Football team that won the Ivy League Championship in 1976. He brought home the championship trophy for the Bulldogs and won the university's F. Gordon Brown Award for outstanding academic and athletic leadership. Phillips graduated with honors from the Ivy League school in 1977 with a degree in philosophy.

RISE TO FAME

After graduation, Phillips taught remedial reading and math in Atlanta, Georgia, at the Fulton County Juvenile Detention Center. He was also working as a waiter when he landed a job at the NBC affiliate in Atlanta, WXIA-TV. Over the next

year and a half, he worked his way up the ladder as a news producer and reporter. He made the amazing jump two years later to network television when ABC News hired him as an assignment editor in their Washington, D.C., bureau. In 1982, just five years after graduating from college, Phillips was promoted to correspondent for the network.

Show Me Success

Phillips entered the national scene in a major way in 1986 when he landed a job with ABC's *20/20* news magazine. His exposure expanded greatly when he was tabbed to be a substitute host on *Good Morning America*. In 1992, he made the jump to rival NBC, where he anchored *Dateline NBC* from its inception until 2007. He has also served as a substitute anchor on *Today*, *NBC Nightly News with Tom Brokaw*, and *Meet the Press*.

Phillips has won a plethora of awards for his outstanding work, including two Emmys for broadcast journalism. He also was honored with the Sigma Delta Chi Award for Public Service from the Society of Professional Journalists, which is one of the highest honors bestowed upon journalists, proving that he is truly one of the best of his generation.

Extra, Extra!

Phillips was also a member of the Yale senior society Scroll and Keys.
Other honors include:
The Investigative Reporters and Editor's Gold Medal.
The Robert F. Kennedy Journalism Award.

Three National Headliner Awards.

216　　　JOHN W. BROWN

Irma Rombauer

Cookbook Author

"It is definitely number one on my list . . . the one book of all cookbooks . . . that I would have on my shelf if I could have but one."
—Julia Child on The Joy of Cooking

The Joy of Cooking is one of the biggest-selling cookbooks in history, penned by a woman from Missouri. Irma Rombauer risked her entire life savings to publish the book that she knew would be popular with women of the 1930s. It offered an inexpensive and carefree method of bringing a meal to the table in a format that had rarely been seen. Her gamble was right, and the book has now been in print continuously since 1931.

The Early Years

Irma von Starkloff Rombauer was born in October 1877 in St. Louis. Not much is known of her early years except that like many women of the late 1800s she married young, started a family, and stayed at home while her husband worked. She played the role of faithful wife and hostess and likely never imagined she would have to work outside the home to make a living. Her life changed instantly in 1930 when her husband died unexpectedly and left her without an income and very little savings to pay the bills. She turned to the two things she knew really well: entertaining and teaching others how to cook.

Rise to Fame

Irma's personal collection of recipes and cooking techniques was immense. She knew the collection would be of great use to women who needed a no-frills and inexpensive way to put a meal on the table. She had collected recipes for most of her life, so she decided to write and publish a book that showcased what she had learned over the past fifty years as a homemaker. She gathered all of her recipes, and all the money she could scratch together, and assembled the book. Irma wrote while her daughter, an art teacher, provided illustrations. By the time the book was done, it was more than one thousand pages. She self-published the book in 1931 and hoped it would bring in just enough money to sustain her.

Show Me Success

The Joy of Cooking was a huge success, much to the surprise of many people in the publishing industry. It did so well with book buyers that major book publishers quickly took notice. The Bobbs-Merrill Publishing Company bought the rights to publish the book five years after the first printing. The large publishing house expanded the exposure of the book around the country and provided some monetary relief for Irma and her family.

Rombauer's gamble had paid off, as families were using her techniques to entertain guests around the world. *The Joy of Cooking* has now sold more than 15 million copies, and it continues to be published today, more than seventy years after it first hit store shelves.

Extra, Extra!

Sales of the 1943 edition made The Joy of Cooking the nation's most popular cookbook.

Irma's daughter, Marion Rombauer Becker, became a co-author of the book in 1951 and continued publishing the book to adapt it to changing tastes.

John W. Brown

SARA TEASDALE

POET

"No one worth possessing can be quite possessed."
—Sara Teasdale

Sara Teasdale lived a short but productive life as one of the greatest poets ever to come from the Show Me State. Her poems often revolved around women's issues, especially how women cope with love, nature, and death. She was one of the most widely read authors of the early 1900s and became a voice for women at a time when there were few female voices for them to listen to.

THE EARLY YEARS

Sara Trevor Teasdale was born on August 18, 1884, and grew up in St. Louis. She was born to a wealthy family in St. Louis's fashionable Central West End. She had a brother and sister, but she was raised much like an only child because her siblings were nearly twenty years older than her.

Teasdale's early education was top notch at prestigious schools like Mary Institute and Hosmer Hall. She first began seriously writing poems in her late teens and joined a group of young women writers who called themselves "The Potters." This literary support group provided an opportunity to publish her writings in a magazine called *The Potter's Wheel*. She was often sick, so the time she spent at home in bed gave her ample opportunities to write and reflect on issues that became the central themes of her works.

RISE TO FAME

The Potter's Wheel also provided the public their first exposure to Teasdale's style of writing. However, she longed for bigger and better things. With the help of her parents' money, she published a batch of poems in 1907. This was just the beginning of the prolific amount of writing she churned out over the next few decades.

Her first professional book of poems was published four years later, titled

Helen of Troy and Other Poems. Critics and readers were impressed with the themes and the intensity of her subject matter.

Teasdale was now a well-known writer in the United States and around the world. She wrote about the strength and frailty of women, morality, and of course, love. But it took a marriage in 1915 to a St. Louis businessman to provide her with the inspiration that made her famous beyond her expectations.

Show Me Success

Soon after her marriage to Ernst Filsinger, she released her third collection of poems. Around this time the couple moved to New York where she spent the rest of her life. At the age of thirty-three, she had a prolific collection of book titles to her name and her collection of writings titled *Love Songs* won the Columbia Poetry Society of America Prize. That prize was one of the biggest awards for writers in the early 1900s and was in essence the forerunner of the Pulitzer Prize for Poetry.

Teasdale completed several more books of poetry after the prestigious honor, but her health declined steadily. She often traveled to England for inspiration, but she usually returned home exhausted and depressed. Fifteen years after winning the Columbia prize, she died from an overdose of sleeping pills in 1933 at the age of forty-eight in New York City. A number of additional writings were released after her death, some of which were praised as the best writings of her career.

Extra, Extra!

One of her classmates at Hosmer Hall was Zoe Byrd Akins, who won the Pulitzer Prize for Drama.

She is buried in Bellefontaine Cemetery, the resting place of many famous Missourians.

John W. Brown

WALTER WILLIAMS

"FATHER OF JOURNALISM"

"His greatest contribution to journalism was the Journalist's Creed. It changed journalism from a trade to a profession."
—Bill Taft, Missouri Press Association historian

Little did anybody expect that a young man from Boonville (who never graduated from high school) would change the world of journalism, but that's exactly how it happened. Walter Williams not only changed the code of ethics by which journalists do their jobs, but he also founded the world-famous school of journalism at the University of Missouri. The small-town Missouri boy made such an impact on society that he has often been called the "Father of Journalism Education."

THE EARLY YEARS

Walter Williams was born to a large family in Boonville in 1864. His innocent days of childhood came to an end at the age of fourteen, when both of his parents died. This tragedy forced him to drop out of school and get a job to support his family. He found work at the local newspaper, the *Boonville Topic*, where he made seventy cents per week. It was a tough job for a young teenager, but it provided him with the opportunity to make a living and to learn a skill: writing.

RISE TO FAME

Since Williams was a good worker at the *Topic*, the publisher allowed him to write a few stories for the paper. He showed such an amazing amount of maturity and skill that when the company merged with the *Boonville Advertiser* a few years later, the twenty-year-old Williams was hired to be the editor. He continued to learn the trade and was able to become a part owner of the paper only two years after the merger. A short time later, he impressed his working peers to such an extent that he was named the president of the Missouri Press Association.

At the age of twenty-six, Williams was lured to Columbia to edit the *Columbia Herald*. He loved the city and became increasingly convinced that the University of Missouri should offer a program in journalism for aspiring reporters and editors. He felt that journalism would never reach a high set of standards if journalists weren't trained properly. Still, he faced opposition from many Mizzou faculty members, because at the time, newspaper jobs were seen as vocations and not professions. The Board of Curators eventually relented in 1905 and established the program with Williams acting as the first dean of the College of Journalism.

SHOW ME SUCCESS

Interest in the new school was initially strong with students, as well as with practicing journalists across the country. The School of Journalism was finally established in 1908 with only three faculty members and ninety-seven students. One of Williams' first tasks was to make the program as functional as possible by giving the students "real-life" experience. He established the *University Missourian* (now the *Columbia Missourian*) newspaper as a working lab for the students. It seems obvious today that a working newspaper on the campus was a great idea, but it was again met with opposition by people who thought a state-supported paper was unfair competition to the private sector.

Not long after the University of Missouri established the journalism program, numerous other schools across the country started similar programs. Williams, however, was concerned that these other institutions would not keep the same high professional standards that he did. So he decided to write a set of rules that would guide professional ethics. Williams penned the Journalist's Creed in the early 1920s to put forth a high set of standards for the profession. The creed continues to be the backbone of professional ethics that journalists follow today.

During the Depression, the curators once again turned to Williams for help by naming him the president of University of Missouri. His high level of integrity and his vision for the university guided the school through a difficult time for everyone, especially colleges and universities. Cutbacks and school closures were common, but he argued for the continued support of the school. In fact, while requesting pay increases for faculty members, Williams cut his own salary. Due largely to his stellar reputation and commitment to higher education, he sustained the university in the face of certain peril.

He died in 1935 at the age of seventy-one in Columbia and was honored in papers across the globe as the man who changed journalism. Oddly enough, the man who was called the Father of Journalism Education never attended college.

EXTRA, EXTRA!

Williams spoke to leaders all over the world to promote journalism, including Adolf Hitler, long before the atrocities of World War II.
Joseph Pulitzer helped Williams push for the School of Journalism.
KOMU, a commercially affiliated TV station partially run by students, opened in 1953.

JOHN W. BROWN

LANFORD WILSON

PLAYWRIGHT

Lanford Wilson is a Pulitzer Prize–winning playwright and a pioneer of the Off-Off-Broadway theater movement. His early years were spent in small towns in the Ozarks, often the central theme of his plays. His massive amount of stage productions continue to make him a force in the theater industry, and his success continues to make him a force on societal issues facing the country, especially in the genre of gay literature.

THE EARLY YEARS

Lanford Eugene Wilson was born on April 13, 1937, in Lebanon, Missouri. He stayed in the small southwest Missouri town until he was about five years old when he and his mother moved to Springfield after his parents divorced. When his mother remarried, they moved to a farm near the small town of Ozark, where they stayed until he graduated from high school in 1955.

Wilson moved to San Diego not long after he graduated to reunite with his father and attend San Diego State University. As depicted in a later auto-biographical writing, *Lemon Sky*, the reunion didn't go so well, so he moved to Chicago. He took a playwriting class at the University of Chicago, which struck a chord with the young man and stimulated an interest that turned out to be a lifelong passion.

RISE TO FAME

Wilson stayed in the Windy City for six years, where he worked jobs at an advertising agency and as an actor while developing his skill at playwriting. To really make it big in theater, though, he knew he had to try his luck in New York City. He moved to Greenwich Village in 1962 at the age of twenty-five and immediately embraced the culture. He got involved with a group of local writers and actors at the Caffe Cino coffeehouse, which acted as a staging ground for the avant-garde theater movement. It allowed playwrights and actors the chance to hone their skills in a supportive environment before trying their hand at bigger venues. His first play, *So Long at the Fair*, was produced at this cafe in 1963.

Wilson wrote, produced, and acted in plays over the next several years in the Off-Off-Broadway circuit. He finally reached the "big-time" in 1968, when his play, *The Gingham Dog*, made it to Broadway. It was a major milestone for the young man to finally have a hit show in the Big Apple, but it was just the start for the prolific playwright.

Show Me Success

While Wilson enjoyed the success of producing plays for other production houses, he longed for something he could call his own. So in 1969, he and four associates founded the Circle Repertory Company. Their first major success was a 1973 play titled *Hot L Baltimore*, which Wilson wrote. The play drew enormous crowds, won critical praise, and played for more than one thousand performances before heading off to Broadway.

Wilson also wrote an autobiographical play called *Lemon Sky*. It was the story of a young man who comes to terms with his homosexuality as he tries to reconcile with his father who abandoned him when he was only five. The reconciliation proves to be unsuccessful, and the gay themes of the play made Wilson a frontrunner in gay literature.

Over the next few decades, Wilson churned out nearly twenty full-length plays and dozens of short plays. One of the most famous was released in 1979, titled *Talley's Folley*, which won the Pulitzer Prize for Drama and made him one of the most successful and powerful writers and producers on the stage. In addition to the Pulitzer Prize, he was also honored with four Obies, two New York Drama Critic's Circle Awards, The Institute of Arts and Letters Award, and the Brandeis Creative Arts Award. He continues to write and produce plays in New York, where he is an outspoken advocated on gay rights issues and where he is still one of the biggest names in theater.

Extra, Extra!

Wilson learned Russian in order to translate the writings of Anton Chekhov.

He is often compared to fellow Missourian Tennessee Williams for his themes of crumbling illusions and alienation.

Talley's Folley used Lebanon, Missouri, as the backdrop for the story.

John W. Brown

SPORTS HEROES

FORREST "PHOG" ALLEN

BASKETBALL COACH

"You can't coach basketball, Forrest, you play it."
—Dr. James Naismith

Short and simply, Phog Allen is a basketball legend. In fact, by the time he was finished coaching, he had more wins than any coach in college basketball history. He became known as the "Father of Basketball Coaching," compiling an amazing record of 771–233 in nearly fifty years on the bench. He was instrumental in making basketball an Olympic sport and left a legacy that few coaches have matched.

THE EARLY YEARS

Forrest Clare "Phog" Allen was born on November 18, 1885, in Jamesport, Missouri. He graduated from Independence High School near Kansas City, where he was an outstanding basketball player. Despite the fact that he was only about six feet tall, he took his amazing on-court abilities to the University of Kansas and won the honor of All-American twice, while also coaching the team during his final year on the squad.

RISE TO FAME

After graduating from KU, Allen took a coaching job at Baker University in Baldwin City, Kansas, for two years. He compiled a record of 46–2, a winning percentage almost unheard of for a new coach. The outstanding success opened doors for more coaching jobs, including a position at Haskell Institute and then at Warrensburg Teacher's College (Central Missouri State University). He amassed an amazing record at Warrensburg of 107–7 during his six years at the school. After achieving such phenomenal success at smaller universities, he finally was offered a major coaching position at the school where he made his name as a player.

JOHN W. BROWN

SHOW ME SUCCESS

Phog Allen officially took over the helm as head coach at the University of Kansas in 1920. His impact on the game as coach was swift. The Jayhawks under his helm won the national championship a mere three years after his arrival. Over the next nearly forty years at the university, he racked up nearly six hundred wins.

Allen died in 1974 and it has been more than a half-century since he last coached, but his impact on the game is still felt today. He spearheaded an effort to make basketball an Olympic sport in 1936 and then led the team to the gold medal sixteen years later. He also founded and became the first president of the National Association of Basketball Coaches (NABC). His professional honors include the Helm's Foundation "Basketball Man of the Year" in 1952, the NABC National Coach of the Year in 1950, and a second national championship with the Kansas Jayhawks in 1952.

EXTRA, EXTRA!

His college basketball coach at the University of Kansas was Dr. James Naismith, the inventor of basketball.

He was a leading proponent behind the formation of the NCAA basketball tournament.

He was a charter inductee into the Naismith National Basketball Hall of Fame.

Allen Fieldhouse at the Kansas University is named in his honor.

ANTHONY BONNER

The "Big Man from St. Louis" was one of the top forwards in the NBA during the 1990s. He dominated the competition in the pros, and also made a lasting impact on the basketball program at Saint Louis University in his hometown.

THE EARLY YEARS

Anthony Bonner was born on June 8, 1968, and grew up in St. Louis. He played for perennial powerhouse Vashon High School where he led the Wolverines to the state tournament numerous times. He won the honor of Mr. Show Me Basketball in 1986 and was heavily recruited by major college basketball programs across the country during his senior year. Much to the joy of St. Louis basketball fans, the 6′8″ forward decided to stay close to home to play his college basketball at Saint Louis University.

RISE TO FAME

Bonner was an instant force for the Billikens as a freshman. He averaged more than ten points a game during his first season and continued to dominate the "paint" during his sophomore and junior years. During his junior season, he led Saint Louis University to its best record in school history, 27–10.

As he entered his senior year, the city of St. Louis was crazy for SLU hoops. The Arena was packed for every home game, not only with fans but also with NBA scouts. Bonner certainly didn't disappoint. He carried the Billikens to a 21–12 season, led the nation in rebounding, and contributed twenty points per game. His dream of a career in the NBA came true when the Sacramento Kings selected him in the first round in the 1990 NBA Draft.

His first season in the NBA in 1991 was a year of transition as he bulked up in size and became acclimated to the faster pace. The twenty-two-year-old athlete only played in about half the games his first year, but he still managed to put up some good numbers for rebounding and scoring. He stayed in Sacramento for the next two years before the New York Knicks picked him up to complement Patrick Ewing in the paint. The Knicks made it all the way to the NBA Finals in 1994 where they lost to the Houston Rockets in seven games. New York made the playoffs again the following year but fell to the Indiana Pacers in the Eastern Conference Semifinals. He was traded once again the following year, this time to the Orlando Magic. The team again made a playoff run with Bonner on the inside but lost to the Chicago Bulls and Michael Jordan.

After his playing days in the NBA were over, he played in professional leagues in Europe. After Europe, he returned to St. Louis to give back to the community that gave so much to him. There, he sponsored youth basketball camps to help young athletes attain the same level of success he enjoyed.

EXTRA, EXTRA!

He was the twenty-third overall pick in the 1990 NBA Draft.

Bonner is still the career leader in scoring, rebounding, steals, and minutes played for the Billikens.

Ken Boyer

Pro Baseball Player

Ken Boyer was one of the most dominant infielders during the 1950s and 1960s, playing in more than two thousand games, primarily for the St. Louis Cardinals. He played in more than a half-dozen All-Star Games, was named the National League MVP, and even hit a pair of home runs in the 1964 World Series that helped give St. Louis the title.

The Early Years

Kenton Lloyd Boyer was born on May 20, 1931, in Liberty, but he grew up in the small town of Alba. He was born into a large family full of athletes. Two of his brothers also made it to the major leagues and some of his other brothers made it into the minors.

Rise to Fame

Boyer was signed to a minor league contract at an early age. The coaches thought his strong arm made for great pitching. After he showed a remarkable ability as a hitter, he was transitioned into a third baseman. That's where he made his mark on baseball and his place with the St. Louis Cardinals.

Show Me Success

When he was twenty-three years old, Boyer finally broke into the big leagues as a Cardinal. His first year, he played in almost every game and batted .264. In only his second year in the league, he made it to the All-Star Game and played alongside the likes of Stan Musial, Mickey Mantle, and Willie Mays. In that first All-Star Game, he went three for five at the plate, scored a run, and made amazing plays in the field.

He failed to make the All-Star team for a couple of years, but he made it again in 1959 and solidified his place on the team for the next six years.

His amazing 1964 season is one that longtime Cardinal fans still talk about. He was practically flawless at third base and had a good year at the plate as well. He led his team to the World Series against the New York Yankees and his brother Clete Boyer. Ken ultimately proved to be one of the stars of the Fall Classic. In Game 4, he blasted a grand slam to give the Cards a 4–3 win. Then in Game 7, he hit another home run to win the game and the World Series title for the Cardinals.

His final years in Major League Baseball sent Boyer all over the country and even to the American League. Only two years after his World Series heroics, he was traded to the Mets, then two years later to the White Sox, and two years later to the Dodgers. He returned to St. Louis after his playing days were over to manage the club, where he had limited success. He retired from baseball three years later because of illness, and he left the game as one of the most beloved Cardinals of all time.

EXTRA, EXTRA!

He won the Gold Glove Award for five of the first six years it was handed out.

His No. 14 was retired by the Cardinals in 1984.

JOHN BROWN

PRO BASKETBALL PLAYER

John Brown was a small town basketball phenomenon that led his high school team to a record that will never be broken, a perfect 36–0 season. He also helped establish the Missouri Tigers as one of the top teams in college basketball during his playing days; a legacy that continues through today.

THE EARLY YEARS

John Brown was born on December 14, 1951, in Frankfurt, Germany, but grew up in the town of Dixon. His 6′7″ frame was an imposing force in the Frisco League. During his senior year for the Bulldogs, he dominated the competition and averaged 31.5 points per game and led the team all the way to the state championship and a perfect record. He was a dominating player in every facet of the game, and practically every major college in the Midwest wanted him to be a part of their team. Luckily for Missouri basketball fans, he was loyal to his home state and signed with the University of Missouri.

RISE TO FAME

John had limited success his freshman year at Mizzou, but coaches knew a player of his size and ability would be an asset to the team down the road. During his sophomore year, he finally broke into the starting lineup, averaged more than fifteen points a game, and never looked back.

In 1972, John was a junior and one of the best big men in college basketball. He averaged more than 20 points and 11 rebounds per game while leading the Tigers to an appearance in the National Invitation Tournament. He had almost identical numbers his senior year and once again took Mizzou to the NIT. In both of those seasons, he earned the honor of being an All Big 8 Conference First Team selection. He left the University of Missouri as the school's all-time leading scorer, which attracted plenty of attention from NBA coaches. In 1973, the Atlanta Hawks chose him in the first round as the tenth overall pick.

Show Me Success

His first year in the league, he made the NBA All-Rookie team as the Hawks finished second in the Central Division. Brown played a total of seven years in the NBA, most of it with Atlanta. During the final years of his career, he bounced around between Chicago and Utah, before he ended up with the Hawks again in 1980. It was his last year in the NBA, and it turned out to be one of the most successful for the team. Atlanta finished first in the Central Division and made the playoffs against Julius Irving and the Philadelphia 76ers. He finished his NBA career with 3,614 points and 2,126 rebounds. He is still a fixture in the stands at Missouri home games and is still one of the top players to ever emerge from the Show Me State.

Extra, Extra!

Brown scored the first ever basket during an official game at the Hearnes Center in Columbia on November 25, 1972.

The Hearnes Center has been called "The House That John Brown Built."

DAVID CONE

PRO BASEBALL PLAYER

One of the top pitchers in the 1980s, 1990s, and 2000s hails from Kansas City. David Cone not only dominated the competition during his years in Major League Baseball, but he also came along with his own personal cheering section known as "Cone-heads." Cone racked up five World Series rings, a pair of Cy Young Awards, and was also one of only a few pitchers in history to record a perfect game.

THE EARLY YEARS

David Brian Cone was born on January 2, 1963, in Kansas City. He spent his early years in the Kansas City area and graduated from the sports powerhouse Rockhurst High School.

RISE TO FAME

In 1981, Cone's dream of playing in the major leagues took shape. When he was still just a teenager, he was chosen by the Kansas City Royals in the third round of the amateur draft. For the next five years, he perfected his fastball in the minor leagues before finally making it to the major leagues in June of 1986.

SHOW ME SUCCESS

Cone played for the Royals for one season before they traded him to the New York Mets for the 1987 season. His first year in Shea Stadium was frustrating for the up-and-coming pitcher, as he finished with a 5–6 record. But his third year in the league showed that he was a force to be reckoned with, posting a 20–3 record.

Playing in five World Series' between 1992 and 2000, Cone set a postseason standard that few players will ever reach. His first series was with the Toronto Blue Jays where he pitched in two games for the World Champions. His next four World Series Championships came with the New York Yankees in 1996, 1998, 1999, and 2000. In those five years of World Series play, he won five games and never lost.

He finished his career with the New York Mets in 2003 and went down in the history books as one of the greatest pitchers of all time. He completed his major league career with a record of 194 wins and 126 losses.

Extra, Extra!

His contract with the Yankees paid him $12 million for the year 2000 alone.

Cone first retired in 2001 from the Boston Red Sox, but tried to make a comeback two years later with the Mets.

He played in the All-Star Game five times.

Dwight Davis

Tennis Legend

"Really, when you play Davis Cup and you play on a team, it's something different. That's what makes Davis Cup such an unbelievable event."
—*Nikki Pietrangeli*

Most sports fans have likely heard of tennis's annual international team tournament, the Davis Cup. What most fans may not realize is that the Davis Cup is named after a man from St. Louis. Dwight Davis was not only an athlete, but also a lawyer, businessman, and public servant. He left his indelible impression on the state of Missouri, the world of tennis, and society as a whole through his selfless giving.

The Early Years

Dwight Filley Davis was born on July 5, 1879, and grew up in St. Louis. He came from a prominent family where his father attained a considerable amount of wealth from banking and wholesale goods. He graduated from the elite Smith Academy high school in 1895 and then moved on to Harvard, where he excelled as a tennis player. While at Harvard, he teamed up with Holcomb Ward to win the U.S. National Doubles Championship for three straight years. In 1900, he founded the international competition that came to bear his name, the Davis Cup, and he was the captain of the first U.S. team.

Rise to Fame

After graduating from Harvard in 1900, he moved back to St. Louis to attend Washington University School of Law. He graduated in 1903 but never set up legal practice. Instead, he used his education and connections to climb the political ladder, most notably as the city's parks commissioner. At the time, parks were pastoral and less recreational. Davis insisted that the city's parks were for the people, and the grass there to be walked on.

Show Me Success

While serving as parks commissioner, Davis used his position and his passion for tennis to take the game to the masses. In fact, the program that he began was the very first organized effort by any city to build tennis courts for the public. The program was a huge success, which built Davis's reputation as a strong civic leader and a man who could get things done. Most of St. Louis's city parks now have tennis courts. The markee courts are in Forest Park, where the tennis center is named in Davis's honor.

Davis also went on to serve as the secretary of war after World War I until 1929, as the governor general of the Philippines until 1932, and as a major general in the U.S. Army during World War II. Despite his high-profile roles in both city and national government, Davis will forever be known for his contribution to tennis as the namesake of the Davis Cup.

Extra, Extra!

His mother was the daughter of St. Louis mayor Oliver Dwight Filley.

Davis was inducted into the Tennis Hall of Fame in 1956.

Joe Garagiola

Pro Baseball Player and Broadcaster

"Baseball is drama with an endless run and an ever-changing cast."
—Joe Garagiola

Another baseball product from the St. Louis area known as the Hill, Joe Garigiola was one of the kings of baseball in the 1940s and 1950s. He has a World Series ring and numerous other accolades to vouch for his accomplishments. But to many people, he is more famous for his broadcasting career after his playing days were finished, and his famous commercials for Mr. Coffee.

The Early Years

Joseph Henry Garagiola was born on February 12, 1926, in St. Louis and grew up in the St. Louis neighborhood called the Hill. Baseball was the primary pastime for kids in the Italian neighborhood of St. Louis, and Joe proved to be a fierce competitor. He soon had the attention of major league scouts, especially from his hometown team.

Rise to Fame

Garagiola was signed by the St. Louis Cardinals when he was only sixteen years old. The money wasn't much in those days, but playing for the Cardinals in the traveling circuit was still much better than playing in the sandlots where he played with childhood friend Yogi Berra. Garagiola spent the next two years in the minor leagues, then two years serving in World War II. When he returned from the war, he was older, stronger, and more mature. That combination, along with his natural athletic ability, catapulted him into the major leagues in 1946 at twenty years old.

Show Me Success

Garagiola made quite an impact during his first year with St. Louis, catching in seventy-four games as the Cardinals finished the season in first place. They met the Boston Red Sox in the World Series, where the Cardinals won in seven games. He had a great series for the World Champions, playing in five games where he batted .316.

He played a total of five and a half seasons at Sportsman's Park before a shoulder injury forced him to the bench. While recovering, he filled in as an announcer in the broadcasting booth. His playing days weren't over though, and he bounced around to the Pirates, Cubs, and finally the Giants. He retired in 1954 at the age of twenty-eight and returned to St. Louis to broadcast Cardinals games the next year.

Many people say that his second career was even better than his first. He called games for the Cardinals for a few years before heading to New York and the Yankees broadcast booth. He spent nearly three decades behind the microphone, with legions of fans that hung on his every word. He later joined the crew of the *Today* show where he was a fixture on morning television for five years. He was honored for his contributions to baseball and broadcasting in 1991 by being inducted into the Baseball Hall of Fame in Cooperstown, New York.

Extra, Extra!

Garagiola played himself in the movie Catch Me If You Can *in 2002.*

He has written a pair of books, Baseball Is a Funny Game *and* It's Anybody's Ballgame.

His son, Joe Garagiola, Jr., also worked in baseball as general manager of the Arizona Diamondbacks and in baseball operations for Major League Baseball.

TRENT GREEN

PRO FOOTBALL PLAYER

"Trent, I love you and I always will."
—Dick Vermeil *upon retirement*

Trent Green has accomplished the ultimate dream for many Missouri athletes. He has played for both the St. Louis Rams and the Kansas City Chiefs, which made him a star on both sides of the state. Injuries cut short his playing time in St. Louis, but the star quarterback came into his own in Arrowhead Stadium.

THE EARLY YEARS

Trent Green was born on July 9, 1970, in Cedar Rapids, Iowa. and spent many of his early years in the St. Louis area. He attended Vianney High School in Kirkwood where he was an outstanding athlete in both football and basketball. He averaged twenty points per game for his high school basketball team while earning all-conference and all-district honors for three straight years. He was a great basketball player, but football was his real passion and his ticket to college sports.

RISE TO FAME

Green attended college at the University of Indiana, where he was one of the most prolific passers in the history of college football. When he graduated, he was near the top of practically every passing category in the Hoosier record books. He completed his studies at Indiana in 1993 but put his career in business on hold while he pursued a job in professional football. The star athlete was picked by the San Diego Chargers in the eighth round of the draft as the 222 overall pick.

SHOW ME SUCCESS

Trent Green's road to success in pro football got off to a rough start. He was abruptly cut by the Chargers and then cut by the British Columbia Lions of the Canadian Football League soon thereafter. Over the next three years, he saw very

JOHN W. BROWN

little playing time with the Washington Redskins, but he finally got his chance in 1998. He worked his way up to the starting quarterback job for Washington and led the team to a 6–8 record.

In 1999, Green returned to his hometown as he joined the St. Louis Rams. His job as a starter didn't last long after an injury in a preseason game. Even though he was on the bench, he got a Super Bowl ring as the Rams won the championship. He started five games the next year, and played a significant role in propelling the Rams into the playoffs.

In 2000, Green was traded to the Chiefs, where he finally had the breakout year he had always dreamed about. Two years after arriving in Kansas City, Green was named to the Pro Bowl, which established him as one of the all-time great quarterbacks in NFL history. After five years in Kansas City, he was traded to the Miami Dolphins.

Extra, Extra!

*Green appeared on Wheel of Fortune's NFL Week in 2003 and won over thirty thousand dollars for his foundation.

*He was named one of the "Top 100 Good Guys" in sports by The Sporting News in 2003.

MASTEN GREGORY

FORMULA ONE DRIVER

"He was one of my boyhood heroes for three reasons:
*He wore thick glasses.
*He was from Missouri.
*He raced sports cars."
—Mike O'Brien, sportswriter

When most people think of Formula One racing, they probably think about rich European drivers with expensive cars, Italian accents, and sleek appearances. But one of the most famous drivers on the circuit in the 1950s and 1960s was Missouri-born Masten Gregory, with his short body, thick-rimmed glasses, and midwestern drawl. He was a true pioneer in motorsports and was one of the most successful American drivers in Formula One history.

THE EARLY YEARS

Masten Gregory was born on February 29, 1932, in Kansas City. He was born into a wealthy family with a father who was an executive in the insurance industry. His father died when Masten was only three years old, but his inheritance provided the means for the young man to support his passion for fast cars. During his early years, Masten spent his evenings racing the streets of Kansas City in a 1933 Ford Coupe. His interest in racing eventually led to a job in the pit crew for brother-in-law Dale Duncan's race team.

RISE TO FAME

His inheritance allowed him to buy a Mercury-powered Allard, which he drove in his first race in 1952. He didn't finish that race because of engine problems, but he was forever hooked on professional racing.

He continued buying cars to race in events across the country. Before long he was winning with regularity on the minor circuits in both the United States and

Europe. His success led to an invitation to race in the Argentine 1,000 km in 1953, which was the first of many international sportscar races.

Show Me Success

Masten's first Formula One race was on May 19, 1957. In his very first race as a professional driver, he became the first American to score a podium finish in the Formula One World Championship. The "Kansas City Flash," as he was known, was becoming famous on the racing circuit and was soon one of the most successful racers in Formula One.

During his record-setting career, he participated in forty-two Grand Prix races where he won a spot on the podium three times. His success at Le Mans is one of the elements that defined his career as he and a co-driver won the prestigious Le Mans twenty-four-hour race in 1965. He ultimately competed in the Le Mans sixteen times, which was more than any other American in history.

He continued to compete until 1965 when he finished his career with the Italian Grand Prix. After his retirement from racing, Gregory settled in Amsterdam where he worked in the diamond trade. He died in Italy on November 8, 1985, of a heart attack at the early age of fifty-three.

Extra, Extra!

He had very bad eyesight, and was one of very few drivers who wore glasses during races.

Masten was inducted into the Missouri Sports Hall of Fame in 2005.

LARRY HUGHES

PRO BASKETBALL PLAYER

One of the best shooting guards ever to come from the Show Me State, Larry Hughes continues to dominate his position in the NBA. He first came to the attention of the basketball world as a high school All Star in St. Louis and then as one of the best collegiate players in the history of Saint Louis University. He arrived in the NBA as a teenager and continues to prove himself as one of the top guards in the league.

THE EARLY YEARS

Larry Darnell Hughes was born on January 23, 1979, in St. Louis. The 6'5" guard was one of the top college prospects in the country while playing basketball at Christian Brothers College High School, where he led his team to the 1997 Missouri State Championship. He added to his prep school legend by being one of the few Missourians ever chosen to play in the McDonald's All-American High School Game.

RISE TO FAME

Hughes chose to stay close to home to play his college basketball at Saint Louis University. He was a pure scorer from the moment he stepped on the court to play for the Billikens. He set a single-season record for Saint Louis University by scoring 670 points in his one and only year with the team.

Hughes was named the NCAA Freshman of the Year and Honorable Mention All-America by the Associated Press after he averaged nearly twenty-one points per game. That left many fans wondering if he would return for a second season. The lure of the NBA won the battle, as Hughes was selected as the eighth overall pick by the Philadelphia 76ers in the 1998 NBA Draft.

JOHN W. BROWN

Show Me Success

In his very first game in the NBA, he proved to everyone that he belonged in the league. He scored a team-high twenty-one points against Boston en route to a successful rookie season. He finished his first year averaging nearly ten points a game, which ranked him the tenth highest among NBA rookies in 1998–99. He also ranked sixth in rebounds and ninth in steals.

He steadily improved his stats over the next few years, especially after being traded to the Golden State Warriors during his second year in the NBA. He stayed with the Warriors until the 2002 season when he was traded to the Washington Wizards. The Wizards were the center of the basketball universe that year when Michael Jordan returned to the league. The added notoriety helped catapult Hughes into the spotlight and boosted his value when it came time for a new contract. Two years later, he helped the team advance to the second round of the playoffs for the first time in twenty-three years along with fellow Missourian Anthony Peeler. That season he was selected to the NBA All-Defensive First Team.

Hughes was paired with another All Star, Lebron James, when the St. Louisian signed a contract with the Cleveland Cavaliers. It was well publicized that James had personally asked for Hughes to join his team when his contract with Washington was up. One of the reasons for his popularity with other players is unselfish play on the court, making others around him even better.

Extra, Extra!

He won the Conference USA Freshman of the Year Award in 1997–98.

Larry finished sixth in the NBA.com Slam Dunk competition in 2000.

The Cavaliers made him one of the highest paid players in the league, offering him an estimated $10 million a year.

Jamie McMurray

NASCAR Driver

"Anonymity doesn't last long. Once McMurray steps from the car, he's a superstar, armed with $3,000 in trendy shirts, jeans, shoes and coats, a new dye job and a fresh tan."

—Description of Jamie McMurray's appearance at the CMT Awards

One of the hottest young racing stars of today, Jamie McMurray continues a strong tradition of NASCAR heroes hailing from the Show Me State. Much like the Wallace Family and Larry Phillips, McMurray raced all over the state before making it big on the national circuit. He won his first racing title at the age of ten and has continued to rack up titles ever since.

The Early Years

Jamie McMurray was born on June 3, 1976, in Joplin. His early years were spent primarily on racing tracks behind practically anything that had a steering wheel. He raced go-karts when he was only eight and won his first United States Go-Karting title two years later. He racked up a total of four national titles in the next five years and even won the World Go-Karting Championship in 1991.

Rise to Fame

Jamie was already a seasoned veteran on the racetracks when he was old enough to legally drive at age sixteen. He was driving late-model NASCAR racing cars in 1992 all over the Midwest, again racking up wins wherever he raced. Fans of the sport took notice when he won the championship at the I-44 Speedway in Lebanon at age seventeen, defeating fellow Missourian and former NASCAR Winston Racing Series Champion Larry Phillips for the title.

He began his rise to prominence in professional racing in 1999 when he competed in the NASCAR Craftsman Truck Series. By 2001, he was a full-time driver in the Busch Series, which is a training ground for drivers hoping to move up to the big leagues of NASCAR. That year he was named Rookie of the Year on the Busch Series and finished sixteenth in the overall point standings. Less than one year later, he made his name on the major circuit, thanks in part to an injured teammate.

Show Me Success

McMurray was thrust into the spotlight in Winston Cup racing in 2002 when he replaced racer Sterling Marlin, who was forced to sit out because of an injury. He debuted in the EA Sports 500 at Talladega, and recorded his first win in only his second race at the Lowe's Motor Speedway UAW-GM Quality 500. He moved up to full-time status the following year and recorded five finishes in the top five. McMurray finished the year thirteenth in the point standings on the Winston Cup Series. Those accomplishments won him another honor: The Winston Cup Rookie of the Year.

His second full season on the Winston Cup circuit was equally impressive. He had more than twenty top-ten finishes during the 2004 season and finished eleventh in the point standings. That same year, he also won a Craftsman Truck Series race, joining a short list of drivers that have won a race in all three of NASCAR's top touring series.

He had continued success over the next racing seasons, moving from rookie phenom to seasoned veteran winner. In addition to his success on the track, he is also one of NASCAR's most marketable personalities. His movie star good looks make him an in-demand guest at events all over the country as he successfully transitioned his fame from the race track to the A-list of celebrities.

Extra, Extra!

McMurray has appeared in numerous movies, including Talladega Nights: The Ballad of Ricky Bobby.

He was the quickest modern-era driver to win a Winston Cup race.

ANTHONY PEELER

PRO BASKETBALL PLAYER

During the mid-1980s, a basketball phenom from Paseo High School burst onto the scene. This teenager, Anthony Peeler, was such a Missouri celebrity in high school that thousands of basketball fans packed the Hearnes Center in Columbia during the state basketball championships to get a glimpse of him. Much to the delight of Missouri fans, they were also able to watch him star at Mizzou until he made his way into the NBA.

THE EARLY YEARS

Anthony Peeler was born on November 25, 1969, in Kansas City. He rose to prominence in Missouri basketball early in his high school career by becoming the leading scorer in Class 4A during his freshman year. He had a great deal of success over his next three years, leading Paseo High School to the state championship numerous times, where he thrilled the crowds with high scoring performances and amazing dunks. During his senior year, Peeler was named Mr. Show Me Basketball before heading to Columbia to play for the University of Missouri Tigers.

RISE TO FAME

Peeler arrived on the campus in Columbia as one of the most anticipated recruits in Missouri basketball history. His impact on the team was immediate, as he averaged more than ten points a game as a freshman. He continued his dominance as a sophomore and junior, averaging seventeen and nineteen points respectively.

The entire country, and of course NBA scouts, were watching closely as Peeler took the court for his senior year at Mizzou. During his final season in the black and gold, Peeler averaged more than twenty-three points per game. He was named Player of the Year and Male Athlete of the Year in the Big 8 Conference. He also earned the coveted Second-Team All-American honor and was a finalist for the Wooden and Naismith Awards for the top player in college basketball.

Peeler became one of the highest draft picks ever from the Show Me State, as the Los Angeles Lakers picked him in the first round as the fifteenth overall pick in the 1992 NBA Draft. Just like at Mizzou, his first year with the team exceeded expectations. He became the first Lakers rookie in nearly a decade to average double figures in scoring. He played four years in Los Angeles before he was traded to Vancouver. He had a great deal of success with the Grizzlies, averaging twelve points per game with his slash and jam style. He also set a career high for scoring as he poured in forty points against the New Jersey Nets.

Peeler was traded to Minnesota midway through the 1997–98 season and stayed with the team for the next five seasons. He finished his final two years in the NBA with the Sacramento Kings and the Washington Wizards. During his thirteen years in the NBA, he played in the playoffs ten separate years where he averaged seven points per game. Peeler finished his playing career as one of the most prolific scorers in Missouri basketball history at all levels of play.

EXTRA, EXTRA!

He played in a total of fifty-seven playoff games during his NBA career.

His highest yearly salary was in 2003, when he earned $3,350,000.

MIKE SHANNON

PRO BASEBALL PLAYER AND BROADCASTER

"Baseball and radio belong together. It's like they were made for each other."
—*Mike Shannon*

Mike Shannon has been a fixture for the St. Louis Cardinals for nearly half a century, both on the field and in the press box. He first made a name for himself as the right fielder and third baseman for the highly successful Cardinals teams of the 1960s. His second career has seen him behind the microphone for nearly four decades, making him one of the most beloved hometown baseball personalities in Missouri history.

THE EARLY YEARS

Thomas Michael Shannon was born on July 15, 1939, in St. Louis. He was an amazing high school athlete at Christian Brothers College High School where he earned All-State honors in baseball, basketball, and football. He was such an outstanding football player that the high school All-American player accepted a scholarship to play at the University of Missouri–Columbia. His time at Ol' Mizzou was short, as he was soon on his way to the St. Louis Cardinals organization.

RISE TO FAME

Shannon joined the Cardinals in 1958, but he didn't automatically start playing with the big league team. As with most young players, he first had to pay his dues on the road by playing with the minor league teams. He made a few appearances at Sportsman's Park in 1962 and 1963, but most of these years were spent with the farm club.

Mike finally broke into the everyday roster midway through the season in 1964 as an outfielder for St. Louis. It was perfect timing from a career standpoint. The Cardinals had compiled an impressive array of players that year, who led them to the World Series against the Yankees. Shannon impressed everyone during the series by hitting a two-run home run in Game 1 as the Cards went on to win the series in seven games.

He transitioned into playing third base a few years later, where he remained for the rest of his playing days. He again helped lead the Cardinals win the pennant in back-to-back years in 1967–68, and onto the World Series Championship in 1967. He again had a dramatic home run in the 1967 series that catapulted St. Louis over the Detroit Tigers.

In 1970, Mike's playing career was cut short after a doctor diagnosed him with a kidney disease. He stayed with the Cardinals by moving to a job in sales and promotion, then to the broadcast booth in 1972. The rookie color commentator was paired up with broadcasting legend Jack Buck. The two shared the broadcast booth for several decades, acting as the eyes and ears for millions of fans of the St. Louis Cardinals throughout the Midwest. Shannon continues his duties behind the microphone for the Cardinals to this day, more than thirty years after he started. For an entire generation of fans, his voice has been a stable force in these days of transitional players and changing radio stations.

EXTRA, EXTRA!

*Shannon is the only athlete to be named Missouri Prep Player of the Year in basketball and football in the same year.

*In 1999, Shannon was inducted into the Missouri Sports Hall of Fame in recognition of his popularity and performance on the air and, as a player, on the field.

*He won the 1985 Emmy Award in the Midwest for Sports Broadcasting.

Horton Smith

Professional Golfer

Springfield sports enthusiasts know the name of Horton Smith from a golf course named in his honor, but many of those who play the course probably don't realize how important Smith is to the history of the game. He started playing golf in the Ozarks and turned his passion for the game and his skills with a putter into a Hall of Fame career. He forever cemented his legacy when he became the first person to win the Masters Tournament.

The Early Years

Horton Smith was born on May 22, 1908, and grew up in Springfield. It didn't take long for the young man to show an interest in sports. He was already playing golf by the time he was twelve, and he worked as the assistant pro at the Old Springfield Country Club when he was just a teenager. He also played in his first state tournament when he was only sixteen. He was already one of the best golfers in the Midwest by that time and turned pro at an age when most of his peers were still in high school.

Rise to Fame

In 1926, at the age of eighteen, Smith turned professional. In his first pro tournament, he proved that he was a player to watch by winning the Oklahoma Open. At age nineteen, he became the youngest player on the United States Ryder Cup team. Two years later, he had one of the greatest seasons ever for a player on the PGA Tour. At age twenty-one, he won eight tournaments and finished second in six others. That season may have been the best of his career, but his real claim to fame was still to come.

Show Me Success

In 1934, Horton Smith entered a new tournament known as the "Augusta National Invitational," which would later become known as the Masters. He won

JOHN W. BROWN

the very first Masters title, and then won it again two years later in 1936. That means a Missourian owned the Masters crown for two of the tournament's first three years.

Smith also had a great deal of success in other tournaments during his thirty-year pro career. In addition to the Masters, he also won the U.S. Open three times and finished his career with thirty-two professional golf titles. He won the money title in 1929 and again in 1936 thanks in part to his win at Augusta. Amazingly, in his five appearances on Ryder Cup teams, he never lost a single match.

His amazing accomplishments helped him gain entrance into the Pro Golf Hall of Fame in 1958 and the World Golf Hall of Fame in 1990. He is not only a great Missouri golfer but also one of the greatest golfers to ever play the game.

Extra, Extra!

*Smith is recognized by many golf historians as one of the best putters in history.

*Horton Smith Golf Course in Springfield is named in his honor.

*He is believed to be the first pro to use a sand wedge in competition.

Charles "Casey" Stengel

Pro Baseball Player and Manager

"Two-hundred million Americans, and there ain't two good catchers among 'em."

—*Casey Stengel*

Casey Stengel is one of the most famous baseball players and managers in history, hailing from the city where he got his nickname, K.C. By winning five straight pennants in his first five years with the New York Yankees, the Kansas City athlete set the standard by which all other managers will forever be measured. He was immortalized in 1966 when he was enshrined in the Baseball Hall of Fame.

The Early Years

Charles Dillon Stengel was born on July 30, 1890, and grew up in Kansas City. He was a standout athlete at Central High School, where he excelled in basketball, football, and baseball. After high school, he attended the Western Dental College, which is now known as the University of Missouri–Kansas City.

Money was tight for Casey in the early 1900s, so he played baseball on a semipro team to pay for college. His ability on the field began to take precedence over his studies, so college soon took a backseat to baseball. He later told the story that he dropped out of dental school because all the medical equipment was designed for right-handers and he was left-handed. Being left-handed didn't work for being a doctor, but it did work for the diamond!

Rise to Fame

When Charles (now nicknamed Casey in honor of his hometown) was twenty, he signed with a minor league team in Kankakee, Illinois, for about twenty dollars a week. He played in several minor league cities where the team rode in rickety buses through backwoods towns. It was a difficult way to make a meager living, but he was living out a dream. He only played in the minors for a short time before he got a call from the Brooklyn Dodgers in 1912.

Casey Stengel had relative success in the majors, but he was far from a superstar. He played with the Dodgers for five years before being traded to the Pittsburgh Pirates in 1918, the Philadelphia Phillies in 1920, the New York Giants in 1921, and the Boston Braves in 1924. Even though he was known as an average player, he did have some fantastic World Series performances. The 1923 series was the pinnacle of his playing career. He hit two game-winning home runs in two separate games against Babe Ruth and the Yankees.

Stengel made the transition into the managerial ranks only one year after finishing up his last season in Boston. He again spent time in the minors before he got a call from the Brooklyn Dodgers in 1934. Much like his playing career, he had little success in the early years as a manager, but he rose to great success in 1949 when the Bronx Bombers came calling.

Casey's first five years as skipper of the Yankees are still a part of baseball legend. He won ten pennants in his first twelve years as manager, including five in his first five years with New York. He helped guide the Yankees into becoming the most beloved, and most hated, team in professional sports because of their amazing success. He stayed with the Yankees for twelve years and then completed his managerial career with the newly formed New York Mets from 1963 to 1965. One year after he left baseball, he was back in the spotlight by his selection into the Baseball Hall of Fame.

EXTRA, EXTRA!

The Brooklyn Dodgers paid three hundred dollars for Casey to play for them.

Casey's hit in Game 1 of the 1923 World Series was an inside the park home run.

His No. 37 uniform was retired by both the Yankees and the Mets.

Norm Stewart

Basketball Player and Coach

"We're shooting 100 percent; 60 percent from the field and 40 percent from the free-throw line."
—*Norm Stewart*

One of the best-known Missouri sports heroes, Norm Stewart made his impact on the court, on the field, and on the bench. He first made his name as a player at Mizzou, then in the NBA, and to most basketball fans, as the coach for the University of Missouri. His legacy is cemented in the basketball record books by becoming the first person to be both a coach and player selected into the Missouri Basketball Hall of Fame.

The Early Years

Norman E. Stewart was born on January 20, 1935, in Leonard, Missouri. He grew up in northeast Missouri, where he was a star basketball and baseball player for Shelbyville High School.

Rise to Fame

Stewart arrived at the University of Missouri where he wanted to play both sports at the collegiate level. He excelled on the basketball court and earned All-Conference honors. The 6'5" forward was a dominating force in the zone for the Tigers during his tenure as a player scoring 1,112 points in three seasons.

He also made his mark on the baseball field at Mizzou. He pitched a no-hitter during the 1954 season, which helped lead the Tigers to the College World Series Championship. He also led the team in victories over the next two years, becoming one of only a few athletes to earn letters in both baseball and basketball for three consecutive years.

SHOW ME SUCCESS

Stewart was drafted by the St. Louis Hawks in the 1956 NBA Draft but didn't stay in professional basketball very long. He only played in five games, where he averaged about seven minutes a game. The Hawks lost the NBA championship to the Boston Celtics during the season he was there. Later that year, Stewart decided it was time to return to Missouri as an assistant basketball and baseball coach.

Four years after hanging up the sneakers, Stewart took a coaching job at the State College of Iowa. He had a great deal of success in Iowa but was lured back to Ol' Mizzou six years later to become the head coach for the Tigers. He remained in the position for the next thirty-two seasons. He racked up more than 600 wins at Missouri and 731 overall to become one of the winningest coaches in college basketball history.

EXTRA, EXTRA!

*Norm was named the Associated Press and United Press International Men's College Basketball Coach of the Year in 1994.

*His teams won eight Big 8 Conference Championships.

*He was named the Big 8 Coach of the Year five times and National Coach of the Year twice.

STEVE STIPANOVICH

PRO BASKETBALL PLAYER

The big man from DeSmet had Missouri basketball fans flying high during the late 1970s and early 1980s. Steve Stipanovich dominated Missouri high school basketball during the time and brought the state together to root for some of the best college teams ever from the Show Me State during his tenure at Mizzou. His 6'11" frame was a perfect match for the NBA, as he earned his living battling against greats like Kareem Abdul Jabbar.

THE EARLY YEARS

Stephen Samuel Stipanovich was born on November 17, 1960, in St. Louis. He grew up in the St. Louis area and attended the perennial sports powerhouse, DeSmet High School. The near-seven-foot-tall center dominated Missouri basketball during his prep school years, leading DeSmet to a pair of state championships. They also put up a sixty-game winning streak along the way. His inside dominance also got the attention of national basketball writers as he was named a consensus All American.

RISE TO FAME

"Stipo," as he was known, made a big splash on college basketball during his very first year at the University of Missouri–Columbia. He was paired up with guard and fellow Missourian Jon Sundvold as the Tigers compiled one of the best teams in school history. Stipanovich average double figures in scoring all four years at Mizzou, leading the Tigers to four straight Big 8 Conference titles. By the time he graduated, he was the all time leading scorer, the top rebounder, and top shot blocker in school history.

Show Me Success

The 1983 NBA Draft was a tale of two big men. Steve Stipanovich and Ralph Sampson were the two favorites to go No. I, but a coin flip sent Sampson to Houston, and Stipanovich to Indiana. Stipanovich certainly didn't have any first year jitters in professional basketball, averaging more than twelve points and nearly seven rebounds a game while earning a spot on the NBA All-Star Rookie Team.

His success continued for the next four years, averaging more than thirteen points a game as the Pacers dramatically improved. His career, however, came to an abrupt halt in the late 1980s due to a degenerative knee condition. He retired from the NBA in 1989 due to knee problems, but not before leading the Pacers to the playoffs in the 1986–87 season.

Extra, Extra!

Stipo was named the Big 8 Conference Newcomer of the Year in 1980 and the Conference Player of the Year during his senior year.

The UPI and CBS-TV named him the College Basketball Player of the Year in 1983.

Stipo was a great student at Mizzou as well, earning first-team Academic All-American honors.

Jon Sundvold

Pro Basketball Player

The sharp shooter from Blue Springs thrilled basketball fans in Missouri for decades, from high school, to college, and eventually to the NBA. Jon Sundvold faced plenty of speculation that he was too short to play professional basketball, but he proved the critics wrong at every stop. He spent nine years playing against the best players in the world and even set a few records in the process.

The Early Years

Jon Thomas Sundvold was born on July 2, 1961, in Sioux Falls, S.D., but grew up in Blue Springs. He was one of the best point guards to ever play in the state of Missouri, which led to a pair of All-State selections for the 6′2″ guard. He scored more than 2,100 points at Blue Springs High School before he scored a scholarship to play at the University of Missouri–Columbia.

Rise to Fame

Sundvold made the jump to the University of Missouri in 1980, where he became an instant star and fan favorite. As a freshman, he played in almost every game and averaged more than six points a game. During his next three seasons at Mizzou, he continued to increase his production. His senior year at the university was one for the record books, as he averaged nearly twenty points per game, while knocking down 87 percent of his free throw attempts.

His four years at Missouri were some of the best in school history. The team won four consecutive Big 8 Conference Championships during his tenure, which is a mark that can never be broken, only tied. By the time he left Mizzou, he was the third leading scorer in school history and won the honor of being named to the All-Big 8 Team twice and a first-team All American as a senior.

Show Me Success

At the age of twenty-two, Sundvold broke into the NBA and made an instant impact on the league. Seattle drafted him in the first round of the 1983 draft with the sixteenth overall pick. In his first year in the league, he helped lead the Supersonics to the playoffs. He spent only two years with Seattle before he was traded to San Antonio, where he helped the team to the playoffs numerous times during his three years there. He was picked up by the Miami Heat during the 1988 NBA expansion draft. His sharp shooting led to a double-digit scoring average during the Heat's inaugural season, as well as a record for three-point-shooting accuracy. He played for three more seasons with the Heat before retiring and moving back to Columbia to work as an investment advisor.

Extra, Extra!

*Jon led the league in three-point percentage in 1989, hitting more than 50 percent of his long-range shots.

*He played on the 1982 USA Men's World Championship team with fellow Missourian Joe Klein of Slater.

Rick Sutcliffe

Pro Baseball Player

One of the most dominant pitchers in Major League Baseball during the 1980s and 1990s was from right here in the Show Me State. Rick Sutcliffe put together some of the best seasons in National League history, winning both the Cy Young Award and the Pitcher of the Year in two separate seasons.

The Early Years

Rick Sutcliffe was born on June 21, 1956, in Independence. He spent his childhood in the Kansas City area where he was soon one of the biggest names in high school sports. He was a three-sport star at Van Horn High School in Independence, playing baseball, football, and basketball for the Falcons.

Rise to Fame

At the age of seventeen, Rick's career plans were already starting to take shape. He was drafted by the Los Angeles Dodgers in the first round of the 1974 amateur draft as the twenty-first overall pick. He played in the minors for only two years in the Dodgers farm system before finally making a few appearances in the major leagues over the next few years. He was used only sporadically, but it was enough to whet his appetite to succeed.

Show Me Success

Once Rick made his way into the everyday line up for the Dodgers in 1979, it took him very little time to make an impact. He was only twenty-three years old, but his first full season is one of the best ever for a major league rookie. Sutcliffe went on to win seventeen games during that rookie year, which also earned him the honor National League Rookie of the Year.

He was unable to equal the success of his rookie year over the next two years, which led to a trade to Cleveland in 1982, then to the Chicago Cubs in 1984. The trade to Chicago was just the career kick-start he needed, as he put up a record of 16–1 after the trade, ending with twenty wins overall that season. He led to Cubs to the playoffs against San Diego, where he won Game 1 before the Cubs fell in five games. That year he also won the National League Cy Young Award and the Pitcher of the Year Award from *The Sporting News.* He had another award-winning season in 1987 for the Cubs, where he won the Lou Gehrig Memorial Award, the Roberto Clemente Award, and a second National League Pitcher of the Year, and even played in the All-Star Game. Sadly, with his amazing amount of success that year, the Cubs failed to make the playoffs.

Sutcliffe stayed with the Cubs for another seven years, then a pair of seasons with Baltimore, and his final year with the St. Louis Cardinals. He finished his amazing eighteen-year professional career with 171 wins in nearly 400 starts. Rick retired from baseball in 1994 but continued to be involved with the sport. He transitioned from playing on the field to the broadcasting booth. He spent the next few years behind the microphone for the San Diego Padres and can still be heard today nationwide with ESPN Baseball.

Extra, Extra!

Rick hit a home run in Game 1 of the 1984 playoffs. He is one of the only pitchers in history to win a playoff game in which he also hit a home run.

He played in three All-Star Games.

His 1984 contract briefly made him the highest paid pitcher in Major League Baseball.

LOU THESZ

PRO WRESTLER

"We discourage these (gimmick wrestlers). We give 'em a bad time. When we get a chance, we tear their tails off. That's one way of trying to eliminate them—and we do eliminate some of them."

—*Lou Thesz*

Throughout the 1970s, professional wrestling took center stage in Missouri with the hit show, *Wrestling at the Chase*. But before the sport drew large television audiences, another St. Louis native helped put wrestling on the map. Lou Thesz is arguably one of the most accomplished athletes in history, after holding a world title for a total of thirteen years. Before the time of glamorous bad boys in pro wrestling, Lou was the real deal, punishing his opponent and sometimes taking a beating himself.

THE EARLY YEARS

Aloysius Martin Thesz was born in Banat, Michigan, on April 24, 1916, but spent his early years in St. Louis. Lou was an accomplished wrestler in high school but truly fell in love with the sport when his father began taking him to professional wrestling matches. With all of his attention focused on becoming a professional wrestler, he enlisted his father as a coach and learned the ropes of what it takes to make it to the top.

RISE TO FAME

As Lou climbed the ranks, he took on George Tragos as a wrestling coach, who also coached at Mizzou. By the time he was twenty years old, Lou was already getting recognition as a potential star of the sport. His rise to fame was quick because in the early days of wrestling you either made a name for yourself as a winner or you ended up hurt. Thankfully, Lou enjoyed the winning side of most matches and stayed away from most of the injuries that put many of the men out of the sport.

JOHN W. BROWN

SHOW ME SUCCESS

After joining the ranks of professional wrestlers, success came quickly for Thesz. He became the youngest world champion of all time in 1937 at the age of twenty-one. During that match, the 225-pound giant stepped into the ring in St. Louis against a wrestler named Everett Marshall. Lou came out on top, which gave him his first professional win and boosted his drive to perform.

Remarkably, he would wrestle for the next seven, count 'em, seven decades! Beginning in 1937, he held the National Wrestling Alliance title for a total of thirteen years. He held numerous additional titles for the next four decades, including an eight-year reign that started in 1948. That amazing stretch of wins still ranks as the longest world title reign of all time in any sport. His sixth and final title ended in 1967 when he was fifty-one years old. Thesz was immortalized in the wrestling world three years before his death when he was inducted into the International Wrestling Museum and Institute in 1999.

EXTRA, EXTRA!

Thesz broke his kneecap when former NFL player Bronko Nagurski dropped him nine feet onto a concrete floor.

* He was named one of the 100 St. Louis Athletes of the Century."

STAN UTLEY

PRO GOLFER AND INSTRUCTOR

"If anyone gets the short game, it's Utley."
—Travel and Leisure Golf

"Players are flocking to Utley in increasing numbers, and his pupils are winning big."
—PGA Tour Partners

"The hottest instructor in golf."
—Sports Illustrated

Southern Missouri is known for a lot of things, but professional golf isn't one of the things you normally think of, but golfer Stan Utley changed that perception, becoming one of the top PGA Tour veterans and one of the best teachers of the game.

THE EARLY YEARS

Stan Utley was born on January 16, 1962, and grew up in the small town of Thayer, near the Arkansas border in south-central Missouri. He won the 1980 Missouri Junior Championship before taking his skills to the University of Missouri–Columbia. While at Mizzou, he was a three-time All-Big 8 Conference selection. He also achieved the rank of All American twice. He graduated in 1984, and instead of going out and looking for a "day" job, he decided to try his luck in professional golf.

RISE TO FAME

Utley turned pro the same year he graduated from Mizzou, but it took a few years before he joined the PGA Tour. He won a number of tournaments while climbing the incredibly difficult ranks of professional golf, but his career wasn't providing a lot of money yet. His first professional win came in 1985 in Jackson, Missouri. His next was at the 1986 Kansas Open. Utley followed up those early titles with back-to-back victories in the 1988 and 1989 Missouri Open championships.

SHOW ME SUCCESS

Stan joined the PGA Tour by way of a victory at the 1989 Chattanooga Classic thanks to a sponsor's exemption. During the 1990s, he split time between the PGA and Nationwide Tours winning the 1993 Cleveland Open en route to finishing third on the Nationwide Tour money list. Utley finished twelfth on the 1995 Nationwide Tour money list after winning the Louisiana Open and Miami Valley Open by carding rounds of 62 in each of those victories.

Stan set a PGA Tour record that stands today and will likely never be broken. During the 2002 Air Canada Championships, he only putted six times during a nine-hole stretch. The previous record stood for more than fifty years, but Utley's amazing string of holes set a record that most players cannot imagine ever being broken.

Utley continues to be a presence in professional golf, despite rarely playing in events these days. He is widely considered one to the top golf instructors in the country, with people from around the world coming to him for golf lessons. In fact, a large number of touring pros credit him for changing their short game. He may not be racking up wins on tour these days, but he continues to prove that he is still a man to be reckoned with in professional golf.

EXTRA, EXTRA!

Utley hosts the annual "Go for the Gold" skins game in mid-Missouri to benefit Rainbow House charity.

The Wallace Family
(Rusty, Mike, Kenny)

NASCAR Legends

"My teacher would tell me: 'Boy you smell like a shop.' At that time, I realized my life was obsessed with racing."
—*Kenny Wallace*

The names Rusty, Mike, and Kenny mean one thing to a large group of Americans: NASCAR. The Wallace family has been racing cars for generations, starting their climb to fame on the tracks across Missouri. Auto racing is the No. 1 spectator sport in the country, which just happens to be dominated by a family from the Show Me State.

The Early Years

The patriarch of the Wallace family was a man named Russ Wallace, who also happened to be a short track race car driver from Fenton. He dominated races around St. Louis when his three boys were young. The family spent the entire day at the track, often working on the cars their dad would race that night.

In the 1970s, the sons were getting old enough to race the cars themselves. It started with the oldest son, Rusty. Rusty took over where his father left off. From 1974 to 1978, he was one of the most successful drivers in the Midwest, winning more than two hundred races before moving up the ranks of professional racing.

Brother Mike took a different path to NASCAR success by beginning his racing career on dirt tracks. He dominated the dirt track circuit before graduating to asphalt like his older brother.

Kenny started his career working on cars but decided to jump behind the wheel one night at the Illinois Street Stock State Championship. He won his very first race but took his time becoming a full-time driver. He continued working as a crew expert until the late 1980s when he made the transition to full-time driving.

JOHN W. BROWN

SHOW ME SUCCESS

RUSTY

Rusty's rise to fame got a kickstart in 1984 when he teamed up with Cliff Stewart and his Pontiac race car. He was named the Winston Cup Rookie of the Year after finishing fourteenth in points during his inaugural season. He was also the 1989 Winston Cup Series Champion.

He teamed up with Penske Racing in 1991 and continued his track record of success. During the span of 1991–2002, he was a top ten points finisher in ten of those eleven seasons. In twenty-four years of professional racing (through 2004), he has won an astounding thirty-eight races on the Winston and Nextel Cup Series as well as in the Craftsman Truck and Busch Series circuits.

MIKE

Mike first joined the professional ranks of the Busch and Winston Cup Series in 1991. In nine races in Busch Cup, he had one top five finish while also starting two Winston Cup races. He slowly began climbing the ranks of auto racing's elite but found the most success racing in the Craftsman Truck Series.

In his Craftsman career, he has a pair of top ten points finishes for the years 1999 and 2000. Through fourteen years of professional racing (through 2004), he has a total of 8 wins and 110 top 10 race finishes.

KENNY

Kenny debuted on the Winston Cup circuit in 1990 but began racing the Busch Series in 1988. He competed with his brothers on numerous occasions and continues to have a great deal of success on all three circuits, including Busch, Nextel Cup, and Craftsman Truck.

During his first six years in professional racing, he finished in the top ten in total points five of those years. He also finished in second place in just his third year on the circuit. Through seventeen years of professional racing (through 2004), he has a total of 9 career victories and 172 top 10 finishes.

EXTRA, EXTRA!

Russ Wallace worked as a dealership mechanic, newspaper carrier, and co-owner of a vacuum and janitorial supply business in south St. Louis while teaching his sons the ropes of auto racing.

Even their mother, Judy, raced cars on the Powder Puff circuit.

Tom Watson

Pro Golfer

"No other game combines the wonder of nature with the discipline of sport in such carefully planned ways. A great golf course both frees and challenges a golfer's mind."

—*Tom Watson*

Tom Watson is one of the most successful golfers of all time, and he hails from right here in the Show Me State. He has won dozens of PGA tournaments, including several majors. He has dominated the sport for four decades and continues to win tournaments on the Champions Tour today. He has proven himself one of the greatest golfers in history and one of the most famous athletes to call Missouri his home.

The Early Years

Thomas Sturges Watson was born on September 4, 1949, in Kansas City. He won the Kansas City match play championship at the age of fourteen and decided from that time on that he wanted to be a professional golfer. He graduated from Pembroke Hill High School, where he was an outstanding student and athlete. That combination catapulted him to one of the top colleges in the country, both for academics and golf, Stanford University.

Rise to Fame

At Stanford, Watson was good but certainly not a dominating golfer. He graduated from Stanford in 1971 with a degree in psychology but decided to pursue a career in professional golf. He turned pro the same year he graduated, but it took a few years before he was making enough money on the pro tour to earn a living. He was still a young man when he burst onto the scene at the 1974 U.S. Open at Winged Foot. The twenty-five-year-old golfer took a one-stroke lead into the final round, only to shoot a 79 that dropped him to fifth. The frustration and lack of a tournament win early in his career turned out to be a motivator, as he used those disappointments to become a dominating force on the tour.

SHOW ME SUCCESS

Nineteen seventy five turned out to be a turning point in Watson's career. His first win came at the British Open, where he holed a twenty-foot putt to force a playoff, which he later won. Over the next eight years, he won the British Open a total of five times. He built on that success over the next decade, as he was named the PGA Tour Player of the Year six times by the time he was thirty-five years old. He was also the tour's leading money winner five of those years. In addition to the five British Open wins, he racked up three other major titles including two wins at the Masters and the 1982 U.S. Open.

Watson was forever immortalized in the game of golf when he was inducted into the World Golf Hall of Fame in 1988. His impressive total of thirty-nine career PGA Tour victories places him as one of the best of all time. He transitioned into the Champions Tour when he was age eligible, where he has won six tournaments through 2005. He continues to be one of the most successful players on tour, and one of the most popular of all time.

EXTRA, EXTRA!

*In 1999, Tom became one of only five Americans to be inducted as an honorary member of the Royal & Ancient Golf Club of St. Andrews. The other Americans were Arnold Palmer, Jack Nicklaus, President George H. W. Bush, and Gene Sarazen.

*Watson played the final round with Jack Nicklaus during the Golden Bear's last professional tournament.

*His fierce competitiveness, coupled with his innocent looks, earned him the nickname "Huckleberry Dillinger."

FRANK WHITE

PRO BASEBALL PLAYER

"Today, everybody gets along because so many have the same agent. Everybody goes out to dinner with friends on the other team so players don't hate each other as much as players used to."

—Frank White

Frank White is one of the greatest second basemen to ever play Major League Baseball. The Kansas City native won numerous awards, including Gold Gloves, Player of the Year honors, and even playing on the All-Star Team. He was not only a great individual player, but he also helped his hometown team win the famous I-70 series against the St. Louis Cardinals in 1985.

THE EARLY YEARS

Frank White, Jr., was born on September 4, 1950, in Greenville, Mississippi. He grew up in Kansas City playing baseball at a high school that was practically in the shadow of Municipal Stadium. The athletic six-foot baseball star graduated from Lincoln High School in 1968 before heading off to college.

RISE TO FAME

White attended Longview Community College before accepting an invitation to a revolutionary type of baseball school developed by the Kansas City Royals. The Royals Academy was the brainchild of fellow Missourian and owner of the Royals, Ewing Kauffman. It was a school to teach good players how to be better, and White was one of the first to prove the program a success.

SHOW ME SUCCESS

White joined the Kansas City Royals in 1973 at the age of twenty-two. He stayed with the team for his entire career until he retired in 1990, which is very rare for players of today. White became a dominating force only four years after he joined the club. In 1977, he won his first Gold Gloves Award, the first of six in a row.

During that time, he also led the Royals to the American League Championship Series in 1980, when he was also named the league's Most Valuable Player.

The Royals lost the World Series to the Philadelphia Phillies in 1980 and had to wait five more years before making it back to the championship. The Royals made it again in 1985, where they played the St. Louis Cardinals in one of the most heated rivalries in series history. The Royals won the I-70 series in seven games. White played in every game of the postseason for the team, and even hit a big home run in Game 3.

He retired in 1990 after playing in eighteen seasons and more than 2,300 games for Kansas City. In an era when few players stay with a team more than five years, many of White's accomplishments will stand the test of time.

EXTRA, EXTRA!

The Casey Stengel League in Kansas City was renamed the Frank White League in 1985.

He played in four All-Star Games and won eight Gold Glove Awards (which tied a major league record).

White was named Royals Player of the Year twice (1983 and 1986).

In 1977, White played sixty-two consecutive games without an error.

GRANT WISTROM

PRO FOOTBALL PLAYER

"I've always thought Grant played harder than anybody else I've ever played with or played against."
—*NFL player Kyle Vanden Bosch*

Grant Wistrom is one of the biggest forces and best players in pro football of the late 1990s and early 2000s. He is a dominating presence on the field, which gives inspiration to small-town athletes across the state. He graduated from football powerhouse Webb City before making Missouri football fans proud when he became a star with the St. Louis Rams. He forever endeared himself to Missourians when he led the Rams to a Super Bowl title.

THE EARLY YEARS

Grant Wistrom was born on July 3, 1976, and grew up in the southwest corner of the state in Webb City. He was the middle child of three boys, which meant plenty of rough play and impromptu football games around the house growing up. As Grant continued growing, he refined his on-the-field performance and began getting attention from major colleges across the country. He was a first-team All-American selection by several major sports organizations while leading Webb City High School to two state championships. He settled on a college with a great football tradition and a history of elevating players into the NFL.

RISE TO FAME

Grant entered the University of Nebraska with high expectations from everyone surrounding college football. He won a starting role during his sophomore year and made an instant impact on Cornhusker football. Over the next three years he made numerous All-American and All-Conference teams, was named the Big 12 Defensive Player of the Year, and led Nebraska to the National Championship in 1994, 1995, and 1997. It was no wonder that practically every pro team wanted him for their defensive line. His home state team won the battle and drafted him in the first round with the sixth overall pick. He had finally achieved his goal of playing in the NFL, and Missouri football fans were thrilled to see a local boy make it big.

Show Me Success

The Rams were in a rebuilding year during his first year with the team in 1998, so they chose Wistrom to be one of the foundations. He made his presence known the very first year in the NFL as he played in thirteen games and was named the Rams Defensive Rookie of the Year by his teammates and coaches.

The second year of his pro career was one for the history books. Nineteen ninety-nine was a year that Missouri sports fans will remember forever as the St. Louis Rams marched their way to an amazing Super Bowl XXXIV victory. Wistrom was again a major force on defense, starting every game and being selected to the All-Madden team by John Madden. He had now achieved something very few athletes will ever achieve: winning a state title, a college national championship, and an NFL championship.

After an amazing six seasons with the Rams, he became a free agent. Grant expressed his desire to stay in St. Louis, but much to the disappointment of Missouri sports fans, the southwest Missouri all-star signed a contract with the Seahawks and headed to Seattle. After two years in Seattle, he retired from the NFL and moved back to southwest Missouri to work as a football coach at Parkview High School in Springfield.

Extra, Extra!

Grant became a part owner in the Springfield Spirit junior hockey team in Springfield in 2001.

His two brothers also played college football.

His mother wrote a book: Mrs. Wistrom's ABCs: What I Learned Raising Three All-Americans.

His Grant Wistrom Foundation provides a scholarship program for a Webb City High School football player each year.

THE SHOW ME HONOR ROLL

Akers, Thomas: *Eminence* – Astronaut

Allaman, Eric: *Springfield* – Musician

Armstrong, Henry: *St. Louis* – Boxer

Bacharach, Burt: *Kansas City* – Conductor and Composer

Barnhart, C. E.: Baseball Hall of Fame

Basie, William "Count": *Kansas City* – Jazz Musician

Bass, Fontella: *St. Louis* – Singer

Bass, Tom: *Mexico* – Famous Horse Trainer

Beckley, Jake: *Hannibal* – Hall of Fame Baseball Player

Beery, Noah, Sr.: *Kansas City* – Silent Character Actor

Blair, Emily Newell: *Joplin* – Early Female Activist

Blakley, Dwayne: *St. Joseph* – Professional Football Player

Bloodworth-Thomason, Linda: *Poplar Bluff* – Creator of TV shows *Designing Women*

Bluth, Ray: *St. Louis* – Bowler

Boyer, Clete: *Cassville* – Professional Baseball Player

Brown, Molly [Tobin-Brown, Margaret (The Unsinkable Molly Brown)]: *Hannibal* – Activist, Socialite, Titanic survivor

Bryant, Arthur: *Kansas City* – Chef and Barbecuer

Buchanan, Edgar: *Humansville* – TV star of *Petticoat Junction*

Buehrle, Mark: *St. Charles* – Professional Baseball Player

Bumbry, Grace: *St. Louis* – Opera Singer

Burroughs, William: *St. Louis* – Writer

Burton, Jr., Nelson: *St. Louis* – Bowling Broadcaster

Campbell, Charlie: *Forsyth* – Fisher

Carson, Kit: *Franklin* – Frontiersman

Carter, Don: *St. Louis* – Bowler

Chandler, Bill: *St. Louis* – Creator of Big Foot Monster Truck

Chopin, Kate: *St. Louis* – Author of *The Awakening*

Clark, Gene: Musician with "The Byrds"

Clinton, Jerry: *St. Louis* – Race Car Driver, Businessman, Philanthropist

Combs, Loula Long: *Kansas City* – Horsewoman

Convy, Bert: *St. Louis* – Actor and Game Show Host of *Win, Lose or Draw*

Cooper, Chris: *Kansas City* – Actor in *Syriana* and *Me, Myself & Irene*

Copeland, Johnny: *Joplin* – Boxer

Cornelius, Helen: *Hannibal* – Country Music Star

Crede, Joe: *Westphalia* – Professional Baseball Player

Crudup, Jevon: *Raytown* – Professional Basketball Player

Cummings, Robert: *Joplin* – Actor and Host of *The Bob Cummings Show*

Darwell, Jane: *Palmyra* – Academy Award–Winning Actress in *The Grapes of Wrath*

Eagels, Jeanne: *Kansas City* – Actress

East, Jeff: *Kansas City* – Actor—young Clark Kent in *Superman*

Edelman, Brad: *St. Louis* – Professional Football Player

Edwards, Carl: *Columbia* – Professional Race Car Driver

Eikenberry, Jill: *St. Joseph* – Actress in *L.A. Law*

Elliott, Gordon "Wild Bill": *Pattonsburg* – Western Actor

Endicott-Vandersnick, Lori: *Willard* – Olympic Volleyball Player

Ferry, Bob: *St. Louis* – Professional Basketball Player

Foley, Scott: *Clayton* – TV Star

Foppe, John: *St. Louis* – Motivational Speaker

Franciscus, James: *Clayton* – Actor

Frann, Mary: *St. Louis* – Weathercaster and Actress in *The Bob Newhart Show*

Frontiere, Georgia: *St. Louis* – Owner of St. Louis Rams

Garroway, Dave: *St. Louis* – TV Broadcaster and First Host of *Today*

Gilkey, Bernard: *University City* – Professional Baseball Player

Grayson, Kathryn: *St. Louis* – Actress in *Kiss Me Kate* and *Showboat*

Green, Harriet Bland: *St. Louis* – Olympic Athlete

Gregory, Dick: *St. Louis* – Comedian and Activist

Griffin, Eddie: *Kansas City* – Actor and Comedian

Grabeel, Lucas: *Springfield* – Star of *High School Musical*

Grommet, Kristi: *St. Louis* – Contestant on *America's Next Top Model*

Groove, Max: *Kansas City* – Smooth Jazz Musician

Gunn, James: *Kansas City* – Science Fiction Author

Hall, Joyce Clyde: *Kansas City* – Founder of Hallmark Cards

Hamilton, Brutus K.: *Peculiar* – Olympic Athlete and Coach

Henke, Tom: *Kansas City* – Professional Baseball Player

Henning, Paul: *Independence* – Created and produced *Beverly Hillbillies*

Hotchner, A. E.: *St. Louis* – Writer and co-founder of Newman's Own Salad Dressing

Howard, Elston: *St. Louis* – Professional Baseball Player

Howe, Jim: *St. Louis* – Inventor of TUMS

Hubbell, Carl: *Carthage* – Professional Baseball Player

Hughes, Langston: *Joplin* – Writer

Hunter, Julius: *St. Louis* – News Anchor

Huston, John: *Nevada* – Film Director and Producer

Innes, Scott: *Popular Bluff* – Voice of Scooby Doo and D.J.

Jiles, Paulette: *Salem* – Author

Johnson, Jay Kenneth: *Springfield* – Actor in *Days of Our Lives*

Jones, Mike: *Kansas City* – NFL Football Player

Katsulas, Andreas: *St. Louis* – Actor and Musician

Kelly, Emmett: *Houston* – Famous Clown in Clown Hall of Fame

Keough, Ty and Harry: *St. Louis* – Legendary Soccer Players

Koechner, David: *Tipton* – Actor in *Anchorman*

Kohler, Fred: *Kansas City* – Actor

Lay, Kenneth: *Tyrone* – Infamous Business Leader at Enron, Corp.

Lee, David: *St. Louis* – Professional Basketball Player

Lemp, William: *St. Louis* – Brewer

Lumpe, Jerry: *St. Louis* – Professional Baseball Player

Macauley, Ed: *St. Louis* – Professional Basketball Player

Martin, Steve: *Jefferson City* – Professional Football Player

Mason, Marsha: *St. Louis* – Actress and wife of Neil Simon

Maull, Louis B.: *St. Louis* – Creator of Maull's Bar-B-Q Sauce

Maurer, Robert: *St. Louis* – Inventor of Optical Fibers

McBride, Arnold "Bake": *Fulton* – Professional Baseball Player

McBride Family: *St. Louis* – Soccer Players

McClurg, Edie: *Kansas City* – Actress in *Ferris Bueller's Day Off* and Voice Performer on *Clifford the Big Red Dog*

McCord, Charles: *Joplin* – Radio Announcer on *Imus in the Morning*

McDonnell, James S., Jr.: *St. Louis* – Founder of McDonnell Aircraft Corp.

Meek, Larissa: *St. Louis* – Star of *Average Joe: Hawaii* and former Miss Missouri USA

Merrick, David: *St. Louis* – Theatrical Producer

Moore, Derland: *Poplar Bluff* – Professional Football Player

Moorehead, Agnes: *St. Louis* – Actress in *Bewitched*

Moseley, C.J.: *Waynesville* – Professionl Football Player

Muellerleile, Marianne: *St. Louis* – Character Actor

Myers, Lisa: *Joplin* – NBC News Senior Investigative Correspondent

Nelson, Harriett: *Kansas City* – The Star of *Adventures of Ozzie and Harriett*

Newton, Todd: *St. Louis* – TV Host on E!

Novak, Eva: *St. Louis* – Actress

Otto, Gus: *St. Louis* – Professional Football Player

Owen, Mickey: *Nixa* – Professional Baseball Player

Page, Geraldine: *Kirksville* – Academy Award–Winning Actress in *The Trip Bountiful*

Parker, Charlie "Bird": *Kansas City* – Musician

Peters, Mike: *St. Louis* – Cartoonist of *Mother Goose and Grimm*

Phillips, Larry: *Bolivar* – Race Car Driver

Plank, David: *Salem* – Wildlife Artist

Politte, Cliff: *St. Louis* – Professional Baseball Player

Pulitzer, Joseph: *St. Louis* – Businessman and Journalist, Established the Pulitzer Prize

Pyrah, Jason: *Springfield* – Track and Field Athlete

Rand, Sally: *Cross Timbers* – Silent Film Actress Famous for Exotic Fan Dancing

Reedy, William Marion: *St. Louis* – Editor

Rehn, Trista: *St. Louis* – Star of *The Bachelorette*

Richardson, Kyle: *Farmington* – Professional Football Player

Robert McFerrin, Sr.: *St. Louis* – Singer

Rogers, Ginger: *Independence* – Actress and Dancer

Rogers, John: *Hannibal* – Sculptor

Rogers, Steve: Springfield – Professional Baseball Player

Roper, Dean: *Fair Grove* – Race Car Driver

Rush, Kareem: *Kansas City* – Professional Basketball Player

Scantlin, Melana: *Gladstone* – Star of *Average Joe* and *Meet My Folks* and Miss Missouri USA

Schlafly, Phyllis: *St. Louis* – Political activist

Schrader, Kenny: *Fenton* – Race Car Driver

Scott, Martha Ellen: *Jamesport* – Actress in *Ben Hur* and *The Ten Commandments*

Senter, Joe: *Plato* – Writer for *Desperate Housewives*

Sievers, Roy: *St. Louis* – Professional Baseball Player

Smalley, Roy: *Springfield* – Professional Baseball Player

Smiley, Tava: *Independence* – TV Show Host and Actress

Smith, Joseph: *Independence* – Founder of Latter Day Saints Movement

Smith, Willie Mae Ford: *St. Louis* – Gospel Singer

Snidow, Gordon: *Paris* – Artist

Snyder, Bill: *St. Joseph* – College Football Coach

Spinks, Leon: *St. Louis* – Professional Boxer

Spinks, Michael: *St. Louis* – Professional Boxer

Spirtas, Kevin: *St. Louis* – Singer and Actor in *Days of Our Lives*

Stephens, Helen: *Fulton* – Track and Field Athlete

Stover, Russell: *Kansas City* – Founder of Russell Stover Candies

Swarthout, Gladys: *Deepwater* – Singer

Taylor, Jack: *University City* – Founder Enterprise Rent-A-Car

Terry, Clark: *St. Louis* – Musician

Thompson, Kay: *St. Louis* – Actress, Singer, writer of *Eliose*. Godmother of Liza Minelli

Thompson, Virgil: *Kansas City* – Composer

Toya: *St. Louis* – Singer

Traubel, Helen: *St. Louis* – Opera Singer

Trova, Ernest: *St. Louis* – Artist and Sculptor

Turner, Debbye: *Columbia* – Miss America and Broadcaster

Turner, Kathleen: *Springfield* – Actress in *Peggy Sue Got Married* and *Romancing The Stone*

Turner, Tina: *St. Louis* – Singer

Van Dyke, Dick: *West Plains* – Actor from *The Dick Van Dyke Show*

Van Dyke, Leroy: *Sedalia* – Country Singer and Songwriter

Walker, Mort: *Kansas City* – Creator of *Beattle Bailey* Comic Strip

Warren, Steve: Springfield – Professional Football Player

Warrick, Ruth: *St. Louis* – Actress in *All My Children*

Weaver, Earl: *St. Louis* – Professional Baseball Manager

Wehrli, Roger: *New Point* – Hall of Fame Football Player

Wheat, Zach: *Hamilton* – Professional Baseball Player

White, Pearl: *Green Ridge* – Actress

Wickes, Mary: *St. Louis* – Film and TV Actress

Wilkins, Roy: *St. Louis* – Executive Secretary of the NAACP

Williamson, Jay: *St. Louis* – Professional Golfer

Winter, Shelly: *St. Louis* – Actress in *The Poseidon Adventure*

Wyman, Jane: *St. Joseph* – Actress and First Wife of the Future President Ronald Reagan

BIBLIOGRAPHY

Sources used in multiple entries

Corbett, K., *In Her Place: A Guide to St. Louis Women's History* (St. Louis: Missouri Historical Society Press, 1999).

Christensen, L.O., et al., *Dictionary of Missouri Biography* (Columbia: University of Missouri Press, 1999).

Encyclopedia Britannica, 2005–2007. Articles retrieved on various dates from Encyclopedia Britannica Premium Service, www.britannica.com.

Missouri Sports Hall of Fame. Articles retrieved on various dates from www.mosportshalloffame.com.

St. Louis Walk of Fame. Articles retrieved on various dates from www.stlouiswalkoffame.org.

Maltin, L., *Leonard Maltin's Movie Encyclopedia* (New York: Penguin Books, 1994).

Waal, C. and B.O. Korner, *Hardship and Hope: Missouri Women Writing About Their Lives, 1820–1920* (Columbia: University of Missouri Press, 1997).

Wikipedia Encyclopedia, 2005–2007. Articles retrieved on various dates from Wikipedia Online http://en.wikipedia.org/wiki/Main_Page.

Wright, J. A., *Discovering African American St. Louis: A Guide to Historic Sites* (St. Louis: Missouri Historical Society Press, 2002).

Note: Much of this book's material is culled from author-conducted interviews of friends, family, and contemporary entries to this book.

Anderson

Castel, R. *Bloody Bill Anderson: The Short, Savage Life of a Civil War Guerrilla* (Mechanicsburg, Pa.: Stackpole Books, 1998).

Fellman, M. *Inside War: The Guerrilla Conflict in Missouri during the American Civil War* (New York: Oxford University Press, 1990).

Ashcroft

Ashcroft, J., *Columbia Electronic Encyclopedia, Sixth Edition* (New York: Columbia University Press, 2003), www.cc.columbia.edu/cu/cup.

Ashcroft, J., *Britannica Book of the Year, 2003*. Retrieved December 4, 2005, from Encyclopedia Britannica Premium Service.

Baker

Baker, J. and J. Bouillon, *Josephine Baker* (New York: Marlow and Company, 1995).

Lahs-Gonzales, O., *Josephine Baker: Image and Icon* (St. Louis: Reedy Press, 2006).

Wood, E., *The Josephine Baker Story* (United Kingdom: Sanctuary Publishing, 2002).

Barnes

Brown, J., *The Painter of Light* (Springfield, MO: KSPR-TV News Special, 2002).

Bennett

Bennett, R. and G. Ferencz, *The Broadway Sound: The Autobiography and Selected Essays of Robert Russell Bennett* (Rochester, NY: University of Rochester Press, 1999).

Benton

Gruber, J.R., *Thomas Hart Benton and the American South* (Augusta, GA: Morris Museum of Art, 1998).

"Ken Burn's American Stories: Thomas Hart Benton" (Public Broadcasting Service, 1988). Retrieved July 5, 2005, www.pbs.org/kenburns/benton.

Berra

Berra, Y., *The Yogi Book: I Really Didn't Say Everything I Said!* (New York: Workman Publishers, 1998).

Berry

Berry, C. *Chuck Berry: The Autobiography* (New York: Random House, 1989).

Pegg, B., *Brown Eyed Handsome Man: The Life and Hard Times of Chuck Berry* (London: Routledge, 2002).

Bingham

Bloch, M., *George Caleb Bingham: The Evolution of an Artist* (Berkeley: University of California Press, 1969).

Rash, N., *The Painting and Politics of George Caleb Bingham* (New Haven, Conn.: Yale University Press, 1991).

Bloch

Leadership: Henry W. Bloch. (2005) Retrieved July 2, 2005, from H&R Block, www.hrblock.ca/Company/Henry_Bloch_Story.asp.

Bradley

Bradley, B., *Values of the Game* (New York: Artisan, 1991).

Jaspersohn, W., *Senator: A Profile of Bill Bradley in the U.S. Senate* (San Diego: Harcourt Brace Jovanovich, 1992).

Busch

Adolphus Busch: Captain of Industry, 2000. Retrieved August 6, 2005, from American Brewery History, www.beerhistory.com/library.

Budweiser Family, 2003. Retrieved August 6, 2005 from Anheuser Busch Inc., www.anheuser-busch.com/overview.abi.html.

"The Dynasties," *Cigar Aficionado* (March/April 2000).

Caray

Caray, H. *Holy Cow* (New York: Villard Books, 1998).

Carnegie

Kemp, G. and E. Claflin, *Dale Carnegie: The Man Who Influenced Millions* (New York: St. Martin's Press, 1989).

Carver

Carver, G.W., *In His Own Words*, ed. G. Kremer (Columbia: University of Missouri Press, 1991).

McMurry, L., *George Washington Carver: Scientist and Symbol* (New York: Oxford University Press, 1981).

Clemens

Gold, C. *"Hatching Ruin"; or Mark Twain's Road to Bankruptcy* (Columbia: University of Missouri Press, 2003).

Tenney, T., *Mark Twain: A Reference Guide* (Boston: G.K. Hall, 1977).

Cronkite

Cronkite, Kathy. (1981) *On the Edge of the Spotlight: Celebrities' Children Speak Out About Their Lives*. New York: Morrow.

Rottenberg, D., "And That's the Way It Is," *American Journalism Review*, College Park, Maryland, 1994.

Crow

Crow, Sheryl, *Safe and Sound: A Sheryl Crow Website*. Retrieved September 10, 2005, from Sheryl Crow On-line, www.sherylcrowonline.com.

Danforth

Danforth, W., *I Dare You!* (St. Louis: American Youth Foundation, 1988).

Philpott, G., *Daring Venture: The Life of William H. Danforth* (New York: Random House, 1960).

Davis

Evans, R., *The Davis Cup: Celebrating 100 Years of International Tennis* (The International Tennis Federation, 1999).

Davis

Hirschfeld, B., *The Ewings of Dallas* (New York: Bantam, 1980).

Disney

Barrier, M. and B. Thomas, *Disney's Art of Animation: From Mickey Mouse to Beauty and the Beast* (New York: Hyperion, 1999).

Watts, S., *The Magic Kingdom: Walt Disney and the American Way of Life* (Boston: Houghton Mifflin, 1997).

Eads

Miller, H. and Q. Scott, *The Eads Bridge* (St. Louis: Missouri Historical Society Press, 1999).

Eames

Stungo, N., *Charles and Ray Eames* (London: Carlton, 2000).

Eliot

Moody, D., *The Cambridge Companion to T. S. Eliot* (Cambridge: University Press, 1994).

Engelbreit

Engelbreit, Mary. (2004) Retrieved August 29, 2005, from Mary Engelbreit's official web site, www.maryengelbreit.com/AboutMary/InHerOwnWords.htm.

Field

Conrow, R., *Field Days: The Life, Times, & Reputation of Eugene Field* (New York: Charles Scribner's Sons, 1974).

Borland, K. and H. Speicher, *Eugene Field, Young Poet* (Indianapolis: Bobbs-Merrill, 1964).

Froman

Stone, I., *Missouri's First Lady of Song* (Columbia: University of Missouri Press, 2003).

Garagiola

Garagiola, J., *It's Anybody's Ballgame* (New York: Berkley Publishing, 1989).

Gephardt

Cohen, R., "After Gephardt," *National Journal* (June 8, 2002).

Godwin

Woodmansee, L., *Women Astronauts* (Burlington, Canada: Collector's Guide Publishing, 2002).

Grigg

Rodengen, J. (1995) *The Legend of Dr. Pepper/7Up.* Fort Lauderdale: Write Stuff Syndicate.

Guillaume

Guillaume, R. and D. Ritz., *Guillaume: A Life* (Columbia: University of Missouri Press, 2002).

Smith, R., *Who's Who in Comedy* (New York: FOF Publishers, 1992).

Harlow

Parsons, L., *Jean Harlow's Life Story* (New York: Dell Publishing, 1964).

Shulman, I., *Jean Harlow: An Intimate Biography* (U.K.: Warner Books, 1992).

Harrington

Harrington, M., *The Long-Distance Runner: An Autobiography* (New York: Holt, 1988).

Harrington, M., *The Other America: Poverty in the United States* (New York: Macmillan, 1962).

Hearst

Black, W., *The Life and Personality of Phoebe Apperson Hearst* (San Francisco: Printed for W.R. Hearst by J.H. Nash, 1928).

Robinson, J., *The Hearsts: An American Dynasty* (Newark: University of Delaware Press, 1991).

Heinlein

Gifford, J., *Robert A. Heinlein: A Reader's Companion* (Sacramento: Nitrosyncretic Press, 2000).

Patterson, W. *Robert A. Heinlein* (Venice, Calif.: The Heinlein Society, 2004).

Hirschfeld

Shepard, R. and M. Gussow, "Al Hirschfeld, 99, Dies; He Drew Broadway," *The New York Times,* Jan. 21, 2003.

James

Brant, M. (1998) *Jesse James: The Man and The Myth.* New York: Berkeley Publishing Group, 1998).

Dyer, R., *Jesse James and the Civil War* (Columbia: University of Missouri Press, 1994).

Stiles, T., *Jesse James: Last Rebel of the Civil War* (New York: Knopf, 2002).

Johnson

Jordan, L., "Don Johnson: A Star Reborn." *Midwest Today,* 1996.

Joplin

Curtis, S. *Dancing to a Black Man's Tune: A Life of Scott Joplin* (Columbia: University of Missouri Press, 2004).

Kauffman

Morgan, A., *Prescription for Success: The Life and Values of Ewing Marion Kauffman* (Kansas City: Andrews and McMeel, 1995).

Kroenig

Kerr, V. "News 4 Catches Up With the South County Supermodel." *KMOV TV,* Nov. 11, 2004. Retrieved August 18, 2005, from www.kmov.com/localnews/stories/kmov_localnews_041110_supe rmodel.455a41b1.html.

Lambert

Horgan, J., *City of Flight: The History of Aviation in St. Louis* (Gerald, Mo.: Patrice Press, 1965).

Lear

Boesen, V., *They Said It Couldn't Be Done: The Incredible Story of Bill Lear* (Garden City, N.Y.: Doubleday, 1971).

Rashke, R., *Stormy Genius: The Life of Aviation's Maverick Bill Lear* (Boston: Houghton Mifflin, 1985).

Limbaugh

Limbaugh, R., *See, I Told You So* (Atria: New York, 1993).

Seib, P., *Rush Hour: Talk Radio, Politics, and the Rise of Rush Limbaugh* (Summit Publishing Group, 1993).

McBride

Ware, S., *It's One O'clock and Here Is Mary Margaret McBride: A Radio Biography* (New York: New York University Press, 2005).

McFadden

Bennett, J., *Bernarr McFadden: The Father of Physical Culture.* Retrieved September 17, 2005, from Bernarr McFadden Foundation, www.bernarrmacfadden.com.

Muller

Muller, M. and J Calkins, *Dad, Dames, Demons, and a Dwarf: My Trip Down Freedom Road* (New York: Regan Books, 2003).

Pendergast

Larsen, L., and N. Hulston, *Pendergast!* (Columbia: University of Missouri Press, 1997).

Penny

Penny, J., *Fifty Years with the Golden Rule: A Spiritual Autobiography* (New York: Harper and Brothers, 1950).

Pershing

Smith, G., *Until the Last Trumpet Sounds: The Life of General of the Armies John J. Pershing* (New York: Wiley, 1998).

Pitt

Newman, B., *Brad Pitt: A Biography* (New York: Time, 1999).

Rombauer

Mendelson, A., *Stand Facing the Stove: The Story of the Women Who Gave America the Joy of Cooking* (New York: Henry Holt & Co. Publishers, 1996).

Rombauer, I., *Joy of Cooking* (Scribner: Facsimile edition, 1998).

Ross

Scheer, T., *Governor Lady: The Life and Times of Nellie Tayloe Ross* (Columbia: University of Missouri Press, 2001).

Sanford

Foxx, R. and N. Miller, *The Redd Foxx Encyclopedia of Black Humor* (Pasadena: Ritchie Press, 1977).

Travis, D., *The Life and Times of Redd* (Chicago: Urban Research Press, 1999).

Stengel

Berkow, I. and J. Kaplan, *The Gospel According to Casey; Casey Stengel's Inimitable, Instructional, Historical Baseball Book* (New York: St. Martin's Press, 1992).

Stewart

Stewart, T. and K. Abraham, *Payne Stewart* (Nashville: Broadman and Holman Publishers, 2001).

Teasdale

Carpenter, M., *Sara Teasdale: A Biography* (Norfolk, VA: Pentelic Press, 1977).

Drake, W., *Sara Teasdale: Woman and Poet* (San Francisco: Harper & Row Publishers, 1979).

Thesz

Broeg, B., "Old Timers Grapple With Today's Stars," *St. Louis Post-Dispatch*, October 12, 1997.

Truman

Donovan, R., *Conflict and Crisis: The Presidency of Harry S. Truman, 1945–1948* (New York: Norton, 1977).

Ferrell, R.H., *Harry S. Truman: A Life* (Columbia: University of Missouri Press, 1996).

Truman, H. *The Autobiography of Harry S. Truman*, ed. R.H. Ferrell (Columbia: University of Missouri Press, 2002).

Truman, M., *Harry S. Truman* (New York: William Morrow and Company, 1973).

Wagoner
Kingsbury, P. et al., *The Encyclopedia of Country Music: The Ultimate Guide to Music* (New York: Oxford Press, 1998).

Wallace
Covitz, R., "Wallaces Set Pace for Midwest Drivers," *The Kansas City Star*, February 17, 2001.
The Wallaces. (2002, Dec. 21) Retrieved November 11, 2005 from NASCAR official web site: www.nascar.com/2002/kyn/families/02/01/01/wallaces.

Walton
Huey, J., "Builders and Titans: Sam Walton," *Time*, 1998.
Scott, R., and S. Vance, *Wal-Mart: A History of Sam Walton's Retail Phenomenon* (New York: Twayne, 1994).

Wilder
Anderson, W., *Laura Ingalls Wilder Country* (New York: HarperCollins, 1990).
Anderson, W., *Laura Ingalls Wilder: A Biography* (New York: HarperCollins, 1992).
Miller, J. *Becoming Laura Ingalls Wilder: The Woman Behind the Legend* (Columbia: University of Missouri Press, 1998).

Williams
Farrar, R.T., *A Creed for my Profession: Walter Williams, Journalist to the World* (Columbia: University of Missouri Press, 1998).

Williams
Crandell, G., *Tennessee Williams: A Descriptive Bibliography* (Pittsburgh: University of Pittsburgh Press, 1995).

Wilson
Barnett, G., *Lanford Wilson* (Boston: Twayne Publishers, 1987).
Robertson, C., "Lanford Wilson," *American Playwrights Since 1945: A Guide to Scholarship, Criticism, and Performance* (New York: Greenwood, 1989).

Photo Credits

The majority of the photography used in this book came from friends and family of the entrants. Thank you to all who have shared their photographs to enhance this publication. Other sources include: NASA (Godwin, Hubble); Library of Congress (Bradley, Cannary, Carver, James, Pershing, Truman, Twain, Williams); FSN Midwest, David W. Preston (Buck); CBS, John Filo (Mitchell); NBC (Phillips); Saint Louis University (Bonner); and the Saint Louis Zoo (Perkins).